# How to Do Business with the IRS

★

# HOW TO
# DO BUSINESS
# WITH THE

# *IRS*

## THE COMPLETE GUIDE
## FOR TAX PROFESSIONALS

# Randy Bruce Blaustein, Esq.

PRENTICE-HALL, INC.

ENGLEWOOD CLIFFS, N.J.

Prentice-Hall International, Inc., *London*
Prentice-Hall of Australia, Pty. Ltd., *Sydney*
Prentice-Hall Canada Inc., *Toronto*
Prentice-Hall of India Private Ltd., *New Delhi*
Prentice-Hall of Japan, Inc., *Tokyo*
Prentice-Hall of Southeast Asia Pte., Ltd., *Singapore*
Whitehall Books, Ltd., *Wellington, New Zealand*

**Library of Congress Cataloging in Publication Data**

Blaustein, Randy Bruce.
How to do business with the IRS.

Includes index.
1. Tax auditing—United States.
2. United States. Internal Revenue Service.
3. Tax administration and procedure—United States. I. Title.
KF3614.B53          343.7304          82-5319
                    347.3034          AACR2

ISBN 0-13-396168-0 NB21

PRINTED IN THE UNITED STATES OF AMERICA

*To my wife, Gail,*
*without whom I would not be me*

# CONTENTS

1

# ABOUT THE AUTHOR

RANDY BRUCE BLAUSTEIN, a successful New York attorney and former Internal Revenue Agent, has been involved in literally hundreds of matters before the IRS. His success in resolving his client's problems is attributable to his ability to use the tax law creatively and take advantage of every available administrative rule and regulation. Because he knows how the IRS should react and how the IRS actually does react in any number of real-life situations, his clients have the extra edge when they come under IRS scrutiny.

Perhaps the greatest compliment that can be bestowed upon a professional is to have his opinion sought by his colleagues. Randy Bruce Blaustein is the person called on by other attorneys and accountants when they reach a point at which they can no longer confidently handle a particular IRS problem.

Mr. Blaustein is the recipient of the U.S. Department of the Treasury's Certificate of Award and is a member of the American Bar Association Section of Taxation and the New York State Bar Association. He is also a prolific writer, having published numerous articles in national professional and business magazines, and he serves on the editorial advisory boards of the *PC Advisor, Tax Shelter Insider* and *Financial Management Advisor* newsletters.

Mr. Blaustein, who holds the degrees of J.D., M.B.A., B.B.A., is periodically interviewed and quoted by the *New York Times* and has appeared as a guest speaker at seminars and on radio and television programs.

# ACKNOWLEDGMENTS

Special thanks are extended to Edward Mendlowitz, CPA, tax partner at Siegel & Mendlowitz, P.C. He introduced me to the world of writing, encouraged me, and is a professional in every sense of the word.

# A WORD FROM THE AUTHOR

As far as administrative agencies are concerned the Internal Revenue Service is probably more predictable than most. Its internal mechanism can usually be relied on to respond with a reasonable degree of consistency. Its positions in numerous areas of law are promulgated by published regulations and rulings, and there is a comprehensive manual, most portions of which are public record, that permits the practitioner to ascertain the operating procedures of the agency. Because of the structured and well defined organization of the IRS, there is opportunity for the practitioner to utilize the system to the advantage of his client. However, in order to achieve this end he must find out how the system works and how it is likely to react in a given situation.

One way to gain the requisite expertise is of course at the expense of your client. Unfortunately, this can be costly to the client and also potentially embarrassing to you as a professional. In addition, the experience gained would be limited to your own personal exposure. A more comprehensive and practical way to master the art of practicing before the IRS is to use this book as a procedural reference. I have chosen to discuss those problems and questions that invariably arise during the course of an audit and how to resolve them in your client's behalf. In a sense the book suggests answers to questions such as "I wonder what would happen if I told the Agent . . . or if I didn't tell the Agent anything?"

Representing a client before the Internal Revenue Service is and always should be thought of as an adversary proceeding. As such, the practitioner's goal is not only to represent his client's interest so as to minimize civil liability but also to identify the extent of any criminal exposure.

In my experience, which includes literally hundreds of tax examinations, and in discussions I have had with many noted tax authorities, I have found that numerous problems could be avoided if accountants and attorneys who represent their clients before the IRS knew how to respond properly when faced with a precarious situation. Nine times out of ten the IRS needs the taxpayer's cooperation and assistance to make its case against him. This fact of life can and should be used by the practitioner to provide only that information which is absolutely required by law. For example, does the requirement that books and records must be maintained mean that you as the representative are obligated to explain those books and records to a revenue agent who doesn't understand them?

A primary reason for my undertaking this book was that I found that many practitioners with substantial technical expertise lack the fundamental knowledge of how to conduct an audit and how the internal mechanism of the IRS works. Although this may appear to be a contradiction in terms, it is absolutely true. Decisions are constantly required by the practitioner when dealing with the IRS, and some have irreparable consequences for the client if the practitioner does not know how to respond properly, or becomes intimidated by the Service personnel. For instance, would you know when books and records should not be shown to an agent and what to say when he asks you why you won't let him see them?

In various sections of this book, some of which overlap, there are references to the potential constitutional ramifications of an act an agent does or does not perform. Even though there is limited constitutional protection in civil tax examinations, the practitioner must keep in mind that there always exists the real threat of the civil audit evolving into a criminal investigation. This potential problem is compounded by the fact that the client rarely confides his fraudulent activities to his representative until after the fact has been discovered by the agent. With this in mind the practitioner must be aware of potentially self-incriminating information and understand how to protect his client in every legal way possible. This means that an accountant cannot absolve himself of this responsibility by rationalizing that it's up to the client's attorney to take care of legal matters. The fact is that the damage to a client and the subsequent anxiety of undergoing a criminal investigation and indictment may be prevented by a representative who is totally aware of all the potential ramifications and how to control them from the inception of the audit. Accordingly, the practitioner must be able to ascertain when an agent suspects fraud and then know what he should do about it.

Every practitioner will want to minimize the time spent dealing with the IRS. By way of experience and trial and error I have developed numerous techniques and form response letters which can accomplish that. It is possible to circumvent the red tape which exists in almost any IRS matter if the correct approach is taken.

The information in this book should not be considered a substitute for a good technical working knowledge of the tax law. Many of the adversary techniques described will only work effectively after you have impressed the IRS personnel with your technical ability. Accordingly, this book is intended to be a source of answers to procedural and practical questions that will be encountered when practicing before the Internal Revenue Service.

RANDY BRUCE BLAUSTEIN

# HOW TO USE THIS BOOK

The best way to use this book is first to skim through the text. Stop and read those sections which are of particular interest. In giving the book a once-over you can familiarize yourself with the many ideas suggested to help you successfully deal with the IRS.

Chapter and subchapter headings have been written to provide the reader with easy access to those portions of the book which will help resolve an immediate problem. In the beginning of most chapters an outline of what will be covered has been prepared. Use both references to focus in on your problem quickly.

Suppose a revenue agent is questioning various travel and entertainment expenses. Your client has told you that a particular credit card charge the agent wants to know about was incurred when your client paid for the union steward's convention trip to Florida. What do you tell the agent? By skimming through the table of contents you will see that there is a chapter devoted to handling travel and entertainment audits. This would be a good starting point.

Many of the questions and accusations invariably raised by the IRS in the course of an investigation are covered under the appropriate chapter headings. Throughout the book are suggested responses to such questions and accusations. For instance, how should you respond if a special agent asks you if your client reported all of his income? The chapter entitled "Dealing With a Special Agent" would be the place to look for the answer.

Various sample letters are offered throughout the book that are designed to save time when dealing with the IRS. They are provided for you to use as is or adapt to your individual client's situation.

This book offers a novel feature which will be of utmost importance to the practitioner. Real answers are provided for real problems likely to be encountered when dealing with the IRS. Most of the ideas suggested in the text have, at one time or another, been successfully used in practice.

# CHAPTER 1

# The Practitioner's Professional and Legal Responsibilities

A practitioner takes on numerous professional and legal responsibilities when he represents a client before the IRS. Some of these obligations are dictated by the Treasury Regulations governing practice before the IRS while others are set forth by the legal and accounting professions. What happens when the reality of life conflicts with an appropriate published guideline? Worse, what should the practitioner do when confronted with a situation for which there is no authority or guidance? This chapter covers the following areas of interest:

1. Legal responsibility
   • Negligence
   • Unauthorized practice of law
   • Client confidences

2. Practitioner's responsibility to tell the IRS that an error has been made

3. Adversary relationship: Is it you against the IRS?

4. Should you execute IRS documents on behalf of your client?

5. How much should you charge a client to represent him before the IRS?

6. The practitioner's reputation at the IRS

## Legal responsibility

The scope of the practitioner's legal responsibility when dealing with the IRS is considerable. There are duties and responsibilities which are owed to the client, the government, and the practitioner's profession. Sometimes, one or more of these legal obligations may conflict. Unfortunately, there is very little in the way of precedent or other authority the practitioner can rely on for guidance. The practitioner must deal with each situation and take his best shot based on the facts and circumstances. Hopefully, he will make the right decision.

### Can your client sue you for negligence if you fail to represent him properly before the IRS?

The answer, unquestionably, is yes!

The practitioner generally owes it to his client to exercise an appropriate standard of care. This standard is, by and large, very difficult to define. Essentially, the practitioner must act in a manner consistent with those actions which would be taken by another practitioner under similar circumstances.

The following may be held by a court or a jury to constitute negligence:

1) advising your client to agree to an IRS-proposed adjustment even though the IRS is wrong

2) failure to file a tax court petition within ninety days after the mailing of a notice of deficiency

3) failure to file a refund claim within the period allowed for by the statute of limitations

4) failure to prepare a tax return timely or request an extension

### If you are not a lawyer, are you engaging in the unauthorized practice of law by representing a client before the IRS?

After all, in the course of representing a client before the IRS it is generally necessary to research precedent and advise your client accordingly. Don't lawyers do that? Does this constitute the practice of law?

Much has been written about whether dissemination of legal advice by someone other than an attorney in a tax matter constitutes the unauthorized practice of law. Except in cases of abuse, this dilemma is generally confined to a theoretical discussion. As a practical matter nonattorneys do render legal advice with respect to tax laws without any adverse consequences.

*Potential pitfall:* A nonattorney could jeopardize his ability to collect a fee when he renders legal advice with respect to tax matters if a court determines that the practitioner engaged in the unauthorized practice of law.

## Must the practitioner always maintain his client's confidences?

Both the legal and accounting professions have specific rules of conduct which provide that the confidences of a client must not be revealed. The American Bar Association's *Code of Professional Responsibility* provides that "A lawyer should preserve the confidences and secrets of a client." Likewise, the American Institute of Certified Public Accountants' *Ethics Rulings on Responsibilities to Clients* states that "A member shall not disclose any confidential information obtained in the course of a professional engagement except with the consent of the client."

*Conflict:* The IRS Regulations governing the practice of practitioners says you must submit all information which is lawfully requested!

The only justification you may have for not complying with a request for information by the IRS is reasonable grounds and a good faith belief that the requested information is privileged. A confidence is not necessarily a privileged communication.

## What should you do if your client has confessed to you that he did not report all of his income? Must you inform the IRS?

If you are an attorney the answer is probably no since generally it is your duty to reveal a confidence only if your client intends to commit a crime and the requested information is necessary to prevent the crime.

If you are a certified public accountant your client's communication is generally not privileged. Although some states recognize a privilege of confidential communication between an accountant (generally a certified public accountant) and his client, no such privilege is recognized under federal statute. In the course of representing a client before the IRS a practitioner may become privy to information which, if he were compelled to testify, would incriminate his client.

If your client has told you that all of his income was not reported or that he committed some other type of crime the first thing to do is to tell him to stop talking! Explain to him that whatever he tells you is not privileged. The government could make you testify at a trial.

Next, suggest to your client that he retain an attorney. The attorney can then "hire" you to do all the work you would otherwise perform. By working, technically, for the attorney as opposed to working directly for your client a stronger case could be made to prevent you from having to testify against him—if the case ever developed to that point.

*Note:* Attorneys, of course, are not limited in what they can discuss with their clients.

## Practitioner's responsibility to tell the IRS that an error has been made

Suppose in the course of representing your client before the IRS you discover than an error exists on your client's tax return which would result in additional tax if the IRS knew about it. Is it your duty to inform the IRS?

Generally, the answer is no!

The Rules of Practice issued by the Treasury Department provide that where a practitioner knows that his client has not complied with the revenue laws of the United States or has made an error in or omission from any return, document, affidavit, or other paper, the practitioner is required to "advise the client promptly of the fact of such noncompliance, error, or omission." Note that the rule says you only have to notify the client, not the IRS.

The American Institute of Certified Public Accountants has also commented in the area of errors and omissions which the CPA discovers. In *Statements on Responsibilities in Tax Practice,* issued by the AICPA, it is stated that the CPA should request his client's consent to make a disclosure to the IRS of an error or omission. If the client refuses to permit the disclosure then the CPA may have to withdraw from the engagement.

*Be careful:* If you are involved in a tax audit and you are aware of an error or omission, you are not permitted to lie if the IRS asks you a question. When it appears that if you do answer truthfully you will be breaking your client's confidence then just don't say anything. If the IRS really wants the information they can serve you with a summons and then enforce it in court. Being ordered by a court to testify generally relieves you of a breach of a professional rule of conduct.

## Adversary relationship: Is it you against the IRS?

The representation of a client before the IRS puts you in an adversary relationship with the IRS. The practitioner who undertakes the responsibility of representing a client before the IRS must treat the matter quite seriously and appreciate that his role is not that of an errand boy to be used by the IRS employee to gather information. The extent of your cooperation in any IRS matter should be determined by the potential detrimental effect it may have on your client—both from a civil and criminal viewpoint.

Being an adversary does not mean that the practitioner should attempt to mislead or lie to the IRS or otherwise interfere in its investigation. What it does mean is that you should only offer information which is requested and before it is handed over you should evaluate again whether you may withhold it under the law.

The practitioner's goal is not only to get his client through an IRS matter at the lowest possible additional tax assessment but also to resolve the matter as quickly as possible. By maintaining an adversary relationship with the IRS you are more likely to accomplish this goal. (This philosophy contradicts that of the IRS, which advocates that if there is total cooperation the same result will be reached. Unfortunately, this is generally not the case.)

### "A lawyer should represent a client zealously within the bounds of the law"

This statement is taken from the American Bar Association's *Code of Professional Responsibility*. Nonattorneys would be well served to adopt this provision when dealing with the IRS so as to protect the interests of their clients.

## Should you execute IRS documents on behalf of your client?

Form 2848, which is a Power of Attorney, authorizes the practitioner to execute various documents on behalf of his client. The most common forms which will be presented to you by the IRS for your signature will be a waiver of restrictions on assessment or collection of deficiencies, and consents extending the statutory period for assessment or collection of taxes. Should you sign these forms or should you have your client sign them?

It is probably a better idea to have your client execute all IRS documents even though you are technically permitted to do so. The reason? By having your client sign consents and agreements he or she becomes aware of what is going on. This way there can be no misunderstandings between you and your client at a later date.

# How much should you charge a client to represent him before the IRS?

When it comes to fees, certain guidelines have been established:

The IRS:     "No attorney, certified public accountant or enrolled agent shall charge an unconscionable fee for representation of a client in any matter before the Internal Revenue Service."

The AICPA:  No fee for preparing a tax return may be based on a percentage of the tax saved. However, a contingency fee may be charged in a tax matter if such fee is determined on the basis of the results of a judicial proceeding or the findings of a governmental agency.

The ABA:     "A lawyer shall not enter into an agreement for, charge, or collect an illegal or clearly excessive fee." Contingent fees are generally permissable.

### Billing techniques

Since the practitioner never really knows exactly what issues will be raised by the IRS in a given situation a flat fee may not always be appropriate. Base your fee on time. For example, $100 per hour. The hourly rate could be adjusted up or down based on special circumstances which develop.

*Example:* You start an audit with a revenue agent and are able to convince him only to audit one or two items on the tax return. The audit only takes two hours of your time. The fee could be adjusted up since the service rendered was of value (assuming there were other areas of potential exposure on the tax return).

Schedule more than one tax audit a day! If you have to be at an IRS office for an office audit then schedule two or three audits that day. Each audit should take no more than two hours. Substantial time could be saved by not having to run back and forth to the IRS office an extra time or two.

### Receiving part of your fee in advance

In certain types of IRS problems the practitioner should receive part of his fee from the client in advance. In these cases clients generally owe money not only to the IRS, but also to many other people. The following is a list of situations where receiving part of your fee in advance is recommended:

1) collection cases—offers in compromise; 100 percent penalty assessment
2) failure to file—where you have to prepare tax returns for two or more years
3) criminal cases—where your client has been notified that he is the subject of a criminal investigation

## The practitioner's reputation at the IRS

With the exception of very large districts the chances are that the practitioner will have occasion to deal with the same revenue agent at least once every two years—in fact, sometimes more than one client will be audited by the same revenue agent during the same period of time. It is to the practitioner's advantage to maintain a good reputation and a good working relationship with the IRS personnel.

IRS Revenue agents, revenue officers, tax auditors and special agents discuss what they like and don't like about a particular practitioner on a regular basis. It is perfectly all right to establish a reputation as a fighter on behalf of your client. It is not a good idea, on the other hand, to acquire a reputation of being untrustworthy. By and large, most IRS personnel will have a great deal of respect for you if you do everything possible in the best interest of your client, even though such action might make their job more difficult.

# CHAPTER 2

# Requirements for Practice Before the IRS

It is vital for those persons presently practicing before the Internal Revenue Service and persons contemplating such activity to familiarize themselves with the body of rules and regulations to which they are required to adhere. The Treasury Department has codified the rules and regulations of practice before the Internal Revenue Service in a document entitled "Regulations Governing the Practice of Attorneys, Certified Public Accountants, Enrolled Agents and Enrolled Actuaries before the Internal Revenue Service." This publication is also known as Treasury Department Circular No. 230 (Rev. 6–79).

There is a lack of published precedent which might permit the practitioner to discern what type of conduct will be deemed, by the director of practice, to constitute a serious offense warranting the initiation of disciplinary proceedings. Therefore, each person who undertakes the responsibility of representing a client before the Internal Revenue Service will be required to evaluate the facts and circumstances in his own case and determine for himself whether he is actually in violation of any of the rules and regulations. Any tactical suggestion made by the author must, therefore, be evaluated in light of your client's circumstances to determine whether following such suggestion would constitute a violation of the Treasury Department's standards.

The rules and regulations pertaining to practice before the Internal Revenue Service are administered by two different bodies. The commissioner of internal revenue has the authority to recognize those persons who will be permitted to represent others before the various divisions and administrative levels of the Internal Revenue Service. The director of practice, who is appointed by the secretary of the treasury and is not part of the Internal Revenue Service, has the authority to conduct disciplinary proceedings.

This chapter will deal with the qualifications one must possess in order to be permitted to practice before the Internal Revenue Service. In addition, the various ethical standards and sanctions for their violation will be discussed.

## What does practice before the IRS include?

"Practice before the Internal Revenue Service includes all matters connected with the presentation to the IRS or any of its officers or employees relating to a client's rights, privileges, or liabilities under the laws or regulations administered by the Internal Revenue Service."

This definition encompasses the following activities:

1) preparation and filing of documents, correspondence with, and communication to the IRS

2) representation of a client at conferences, hearings, and meetings

## Who may practice?

Generally, practice before the IRS is limited to:

1) *attorneys*—defined as any person who is a member in good standing of the bar of the highest court of any state, possession, territory, commonwealth, or the District of Columbia

2) *certified public accountants*—defined as any person who is duly qualified to practice as a certified public accountant in any state, possession, territory, commonwealth, or the District of Columbia

3) *enrolled agents*—such status is conferred by the commissioner of internal revenue on those persons who pass an examination

## Limited practice

*Enrolled actuaries*—any individual who is enrolled as an actuary by the Joint Board for the Enrollment of Actuaries pursuant to 29 USC 1242 may practice before the Internal Revenue Service upon filing with the Service a written declaration that he is currently qualified as an enrolled actuary and is authorized to represent the particular party on whose behalf he acts. Practice as an enrolled actuary is limited to representation with respect to issues generally in the area of employee plans.

## Limited practice without enrollment

Individuals may appear on their own behalf and may otherwise appear without enrollment, provided they present satisfactory identification, in the following classes of cases:

1) An individual may represent another individual who is his regular full-time employer, may represent a partnership of which he is a member or a regular full-time employee, or may represent without compensation a member of his immediate family.

2) Corporations (including parents, subsidiaries, or affiliated corporations), trusts, estates, associations, or organized groups may be represented by bona fide officers or regular full-time employees.

3) Trusts, receiverships, guardianships, or estates may be represented by their trustees, receivers, guardians, administrators, or executors or their regular full-time employees.

4) Any governmental unit, agency, or authority may be represented by an officer or regular employee in the course of his official duties.

5) Unenrolled persons may participate in rule making as provided by section 4 of the Administrative Procedure Act, 60 Stat. 238 (5 USC 1003).

6) Enrollment is not required for representation outside of the United States before personnel of the Internal Revenue Service.

7) Any individual who is not under disbarment or suspension from practice before the Internal Revenue Service or other practice of his profession by any other authority (in the case of attorneys, certified public accountants, and public accountants) and who signs a return as having prepared it for the taxpayer, or who prepared a return with respect to which the instructions or regulations do not require that it be signed by the person who prepared the return for the taxpayer, may appear without enrollment as the taxpayer's representative, with or without the taxpayer, before revenue agents and examining officers of the examination division in the offices of district directors with respect to the tax liability of the taxpayer for the taxable year or period covered by that return.

The Service has issued Rev. Proc. 68-20 which provides various guidelines for those persons seeking limited practice without enrollment in accordance with provision 7 above. Basically, such individual is held to the same standard as an enrolled agent.

## What does not constitute practicing before the IRS?

A person does not have to be an attorney, certified public accountant, or enrolled agent to:

1) prepare a tax return

2) appear as a witness for another taxpayer

3) furnish information to the IRS if requested to do so by any of its officers or employees

## Witnesses

Any individual who has knowledge of the facts, or who can give information which will assist in establishing the facts, is a proper source of information in determining the tax liability and can be heard in the capacity of a witness whether he is acting at the request of the taxpayer or claims the taxpayer as his client.

A witness cannot:

1) advocate a particular position on issues or controversies arising during a tax examination

2) receive confidential information pertaining to the taxpayer unless the taxpayer expressly authorizes such disclosure.

Rev. Proc. 68-29 offers guidance to Service personnel as to the extent they may accord recognition to witnesses.

## Who may not practice before the IRS?

The following persons may not practice:

1) No officer or employee of the United States in the executive, legislative, or judicial branch of the government, or in any agency of the United States, including the District of Columbia, may practice before the Service. (An exception may be made to allow such a person to represent a member of his immediate family or any other person or estate for which that person serves as a guardian, executor, administrator, trustee, or other personal fiduciary.)

2) No member of Congress or resident commissioner may practice before the Service in connection with any matter for which he directly or indirectly receives, agrees to receive, or seeks any compensation.

3) No officer or employee of any state, or subdivision thereof, whose duties require him to pass upon, investigate, or deal with tax matters of such state or subdivision, may practice before the Service, if such state employment may disclose facts or information applicable to federal tax matters.

## Special appearance

The commissioner, at his discretion, may authorize any person to represent another without enrollment for the purpose of a particular matter.

## How to become an enrolled agent

### Who is eligible?

Any person, other than an attorney or certified public accountant, is eligible if he demonstrates special competence in tax matters by written examination administered by the Internal Revenue Service and if he has not engaged in any conduct which would justify the suspension or disbarment of any practitioner under the provisions of Treasury Department Circular No. 230.

### Examination

An annual examination is given in each district.
Form 2587 must be filed with an examination fee of twenty-five dollars.
The test has four parts:

1) individual, partnership, corporation, fiduciary income taxes
2) individual
3) Schedule C, partnership, and corporation
4) ethics, recordkeeping procedures, and practitioner penalty provisions

### Application for enrollment to practice

After you are notified that you have passed the examination, Form 23 must be filed. This form provides the commissioner with background data with which to judge the applicant's fitness of character to practice.

### Former IRS employees

Those persons who have formerly been employed by the IRS for a minimum of five years may file Form 23 without taking an examination. Such persons will be evaluated on their prior work experience to determine if they possess the requisite level of knowledge to practice. Form 23 must be filed within three years from the date of separation from employment.

### Temporary recognition

Upon receipt of Form 23 the commissioner may in his discretion grant an applicant temporary recognition to allow him to practice. The applicant must make such request to the director, examination division.

### Appeal of denial of application

If the commissioner should deny an application for enrollment he will set forth the reasons therefor. The applicant must file a written appeal within thirty days after receipt of the notice that the application has been denied. This appeal is filed with the director of practice. A decision of the director of practice sustaining the commissioner's determination may be appealed to the secretary of the treasury within thirty days.

### Termination of enrollment

If an enrolled agent should subsequently become eligible to practice as an attorney or as a certified public accountant, the rules require that the enrollment card (which is issued upon acceptance of Form 23) must be returned.

## The special "code of conduct" for IRS practitioners

Although attorneys and certified public accountants are governed by their respective rules of ethics, there exists a list of duties and restrictions which must be adhered to by those persons who are authorized to practice before the Internal Revenue Service. Attorneys should be careful to balance the requirements established by the Treasury Department with the provisions in the Code of Professional Responsibility. In some instances the Treasury Department requires that the attorney conduct himself in a manner which may not be in the best interest of his client. In fact, there could be situations in which the attorney would be technically in violation of an administrative practice regulation at those times in which the attorney seeks to protect his client's Fifth Amendment rights. It is the author's opinion that where such a conflict may exist it would be advisable to notify the director of practice, in writing, that certain actions taken were intended to protect a client's constitutional rights. This notification should be made when it appears to the practitioner that the IRS may be contemplating adverse action against him for violation of a rule of practice.

## Information to be furnished to the Internal Revenue Service

The practitioner is not permitted to neglect or refuse to submit promptly records or information to the IRS upon a proper and lawful request. In addition, the practitioner may not interfere or attempt to interfere with any proper and lawful effort by the IRS to obtain records or information.

Although this rule appears to be quite encompassing there is a provision which authorizes the practitioner to neglect, refuse, and interfere with the attempt by the IRS to obtain records or information if the practitioner believes in good faith and on reasonable grounds that the records or information is privileged or that such request for information is of doubtful legality.

The decision to make records or information available to the IRS must always be made with a view towards the subsequent ramifications it will have for your client. In those cases where information or records will be damaging the practitioner should attempt to develop the appropriate defense so as to avoid compliance with an IRS request. Other chapters will detail the procedures that can be followed to contest a request for information or records.

## Information to be furnished to the director of practice

Each attorney, certified public accountant, and enrolled agent is required to provide the director of practice, upon his request, information he may have concerning the violation of regulations dealing with the duties and restrictions relating to IRS practice. All practitioners are also required to testify in proceedings instituted for disbarment or suspension. Once again the rules permit the practitioner to avoid providing information or testimony if he believes in good faith and on reasonable grounds that such information is privileged or that the director's request for such information is of doubtful legality.

Any practitioner called upon by the director to supply information or testimony should attempt to ascertain whether he is the subject of or could become the subject of a disciplinary proceeding. Counsel should be consulted at this point to ascertain whether any alleged violation of the rules of practice before the IRS may also constitute a criminal violation. An example of such a situation would be where it is alleged that the practitioner offered a false statement in the course of an IRS representation.

## Knowledge of client's omission

Each attorney, certified public accountant or enrolled agent who, having been retained by a client with respect to a matter administered by the Internal Revenue Service, knows that the client has not complied with the revenue laws or has made an error in or omission from any return, document, affidavit, or other paper that the client is required by the revenue laws to execute, shall advise the client promptly of such noncompliance, error or omission.

### Diligence as to accuracy

The practitioner must exercise due diligence with respect to:

1) preparing or assisting in the preparation of, approving, and filing returns, documents, affidavits, and other papers relating to Internal Revenue Service matters

2) determining the correctness of oral or written representations made by him to the Treasury Department

3) determining the correctness of oral or written representations made by him to clients with reference to any matter administrated by the Internal Revenue Service

It appears that a standard of reasonableness would apply to the degree of diligence that must be exercised by the practitioner when dealing with the IRS. Accordingly, if in response to a question raised by Service personnel the practitioner receives an answer from his client, and the practitioner has no reason to believe that such answer is false or misleading, no further investigation would be required on his part. In those situations where the practitioner has doubts about the validity of a client's statement, the practitioner should qualify the information relayed to the Service by stating, "According to my client . . . ."

### Prompt disposition of pending matters

No practitioner may unreasonably delay the prompt disposition of any matter before the Internal Revenue Service.

There is a fine line between an unreasonable delay or blatant procrastination and the exercise of strategy in handling an IRS matter. Other portions of this text will explain how to handle those situations in which it would be beneficial to avoid an immediate resolution of a matter being looked into by the IRS. Notwithstanding any suggestions that are made by the author, it is the responsibility of the practitioner to evaluate the facts and circumstances in his individual case to make sure that he will not be in violation of the above rule.

**Assistance from disbarred or suspended persons and former Internal Revenue Service employees**

No practitioner shall, knowingly and directly or indirectly:

1) employ or accept assistance from any person who is under disbarment or suspension from practice before the Internal Revenue Service

2) accept employment as associate, correspondent, or subagent from, or share fees with, any such person

3) accept assistance from any former government employee where the provisions of section 10.26 of Treasury Department Circular No. 230 ("Practice by Former Government Employees, Their Partners and Their Associates") or any federal law would be violated

**Practice by partners of government employees**

No partner of an officer or employee of the executive branch of the U.S. Government, of any independent agency of the United States, or of the District of Columbia, shall represent anyone in any matter administered by the Internal Revenue Service in which such officer or employee of the government participates or has participated personally and substantially as a government employee or which is the subject of his official responsibility.

**Practice by former government employees, their partners, and their associates**

The rules pertaining to this provision of the rules of conduct can be found in section 10.26 of Treasury Department Circular No. 230.

**Notaries**

No practitioner who is also a notary public is permitted to take acknowledgments, administer oaths, certify papers, or perform any official act in connection with matters in which he is employed as counsel, attorney, or agent, or in which he may be in any way interested before the IRS.

**Fees**

A practitioner shall not charge an unconscionable fee for representation of a client in any matter before the IRS.

The subject of fees is, of course, subjective. Other portions of this book are devoted to how to determine how time-consuming a particular case will be and also how to set a fee structure with respect to IRS matters.

## Conflicting interests

Practitioners may not represent conflicting interests before the Internal Revenue Service, except by express consent of all directly interested parties after full disclosure has been made.

An obvious situation in which a conflict of interest technically could arise is where the practitioner represents both a corporation and its officers. It is the author's opinion that the director of practice is not especially concerned about the same practitioner representing more than one party to an IRS matter unless significant consequences are likely to arise as a result of a conflict of interest.

## Advertising and solicitation

Although the standards for advertising for attorneys and certified public accountants have been liberalized by their respective governing bodies, care must be taken not to violate those provisions issued by the Treasury Department.

Advertising may not contain any false, fraudulent, misleading, deceptive, unduly influencing, coercive or unfair statements or claims. This prohibition includes, but is not limited to:

1) statements pertaining to the quality of services rendered unless subject to factual verification

2) claims of special expertise not authorized by state or federal agencies having jurisdiction over the practitioner

3) statements or suggestions that the ingenuity and/or prior record of a representative, rather than the merit of the matter, are the principal factors likely to determine the result of a matter

A practitioner is also prohibited from making, directly or indirectly, uninvited solicitations of employment in matters related to the Internal Revenue Service. Solicitation includes, but is not limited to:

1) in-person contacts

2) telephone communications

3) personal mailings

any of which when directed to specific circumstances unique to the recipient.

## What type of solicitation is allowed?

The restriction on solicitation does not apply to:

1) seeking new business from an existing or former client in a related matter

2) solicitation by mailings, the contents of which are designed for the general public

3) noncoercive in-person solicitation by those eligible to practice before the IRS while acting as an employee, member, or officer of an exempt organization listed in sections 501(c)(3) or (4) of the Internal Revenue Code

## Permissible advertising

Practitioners may, in a dignified manner, use professional lists, telephone directories, print media, permissible mailings, radio and television to publish or broadcast the following information:

1) the name, address, telephone number, and office hours of the practitioner or firm

2) the names of individuals associated with the firm

3) a factual description of the services offered

4) acceptance of credit cards and other credit information

5) foreign language ability

6) membership in pertinent professional organizations

7) pertinent professional licenses

8) a statement that an individual's or firm's practice is limited to certain areas

9) in the case of an enrolled agent, the phrase, "enrolled to represent taxpayers before the Internal Revenue Service" or "enrolled to practice before the Internal Revenue Service"

10) other facts relevant to the selection of a practitioner in matters related to the IRS which are not prohibited by the rules of conduct

## Fee information

Practitioners are permitted to disseminate the following fee information:

1) fixed fees for specific routine services

2) hourly rates

3) range of fees for particular services

4) a written schedule of fees

5) fee charged for an initial consultation

Practitioners are bound to observe those rates which are published for a reasonable period of time, but no less than thirty days from the last publication of their rates.

### Practice of law

The rules of conduct specifically provide that persons who are not members of the bar are not authorized to practice law. The issue of whether persons who provide tax advice are or are not engaging in the unauthorized practice of law has been debated by bar associations for many years. Nevertheless, practitioners who are not attorneys should determine for themselves, based on the individual facts and circumstances, whether they are rendering legal advice.

## Disciplinary proceedings

The Secretary of the Treasury has the authority to suspend or disbar from practice before the Internal Revenue Service any attorney, certified public accountant or enrolled agent shown to be incompetent, disreputable, or who refuses to comply with the rules and regulations. Persons who have intentionally defrauded or willfully and knowingly deceived, misled or threatened any claimant or prospective claimant by word, circular, letter, or advertisement are also subject to suspension or disbarment.

### What constitutes disreputable conduct?

The following examples are set forth in the regulations as constituting disreputable conduct, but they are not all-encompassing:

1) Conviction of any criminal offense under the revenue laws of the United States, or of any offense involving dishonesty or breach of trust.

2) Giving false or misleading information, or participating in any way in the giving of false or misleading information, to the Department of the Treasury or any officer or employee thereof, or to any tribunal authorized to pass upon federal tax matters, in connection with any matter pending or likely to be pending before them, knowing such information to be false or misleading. Facts or other matters contained in testimony, federal tax re-

turns, financial statements, applications for enrollment, affidavits, declarations, or any other document or statement, written or oral, are included in the term "information."

3) Solicitation of employment as prohibited under the rules and regulations, the use of false or misleading representations with the intent to deceive a client or prospective client in order to procure employment, or intimating that the practitioner is able improperly to obtain special consideration or action from the Internal Revenue Service or an officer or employee thereof.

4) Willfully failing to make a federal tax return in violation of the revenue laws of the United States, or evading, attempting to evade, or participating in any way in evading or attempting to evade any federal tax or payment thereof, knowingly counseling or suggesting to a client or prospective client an illegal plan to evade federal taxes or payment thereof, or concealing assets of himself or another to evade federal taxes or payment thereof.

5) Misappropriation of, or failure properly and promptly to remit, funds received from a client for the purpose of payment of taxes or other obligations due the United States.

6) Directly or indirectly attempting to influence, or offering or agreeing to attempt to influence, the official action of any officer or employee of the Internal Revenue Service by the use of threats, false accusations, duress or coercion, by the offer of any special inducement or promise of advantage, or by the bestowing of any gift, favor or thing of value.

7) Disbarment or suspension from practice as an attorney, certified public accountant, public accountant, or actuary by any duly constituted authority of any state, possession, territory, commonwealth, the District of Columbia, any federal court of record, or any federal agency, body or board.

8) Knowingly aiding and abetting another person to practice before the Internal Revenue Service during a period of suspension, disbarment, or ineligibility of such other person. Maintaining a partnership for the practice of law, accountancy, or other related professional service with a person who is under disbarment from practice before the Service shall be presumed to be a violation of this provision.

9) Contemptuous conduct in connection with practice before the Internal Revenue Service, including the use of abusive language, making false accusations and statements knowing them to be false, or circulating or publishing malicious or libelous matter.

### Violation of the regulations

A practitioner may be disbarred or suspended from practice for the willful violation of any of the rules and regulations.

Because the violation must be willful it appears that a violation which is non-recurring and perhaps even committed unintentionally would not be a basis for disbarment or suspension. Again, the severity of the facts and circumstances would be controlling.

### How are disciplinary proceedings conducted?

Whenever the director of practice has reason to believe that a practitioner has violated any provision of the rules and regulations governing practice before the Internal Revenue Service, the practitioner will normally be afforded the opportunity to admit, explain, justify, or deny the allegations which have been raised against him.

At this point the practitioner has the option of either denying the allegation and requesting a hearing before an administrative judge, or responding to the director of practice. Normally, nothing is lost by responding to the director of practice in an attempt to avoid the institution of a disbarment or suspension proceeding. In fact, it may be possible to enter into one of the following types of stipulations:

1) reprimand, and/or

2) suspension for a period of time

If a stipulation is entered into, the matter is closed without the publicity which would be created in the event of an adverse determination by an administrative judge. Notices of disbarment and suspension are published in the *Internal Revenue Bulletin* when such orders are made by an administrative judge.

The rules pertaining to the procedures involved in a hearing before an administrative law judge are contained in Subpart C of Treasury Department Circular No. 230.

### Who gets in trouble for what?

The Office of the Director of Practice has issued a statistical analysis covering a ten-year period which shows the nature of the offenses it has found practitioners guilty of committing (see accompanying chart). The bulk of the offenses were for unethical solicitation and failure to file personal tax returns.

During fiscal year 1979 only twenty-one administrative proceedings for disbarment or suspension were initiated against practitioners before the Internal Revenue Service. It appears that the director of practice pursues only those cases in which significant violations of the rules exist.

## Power of Attorney

Form 2848 (Power of Attorney) is the practitioner's authorization to deal with the IRS on behalf of his client. IRS employees are quite reluctant even to talk to you if they do not have a properly executed Power of Attorney in their possession. Accordingly, much time can be saved by both preparing the Power of Attorney properly and also implementing an office procedure for getting the Power of Attorney into the hands of the IRS.

A   The taxpayer(s) name, address, and identifying number(s) must be shown.

B   Names(s), address(es), and telephone number(s) of each authorized representative must be shown. More than one authorized representative may be listed on a Power of Attorney.

C   Specific types of tax and specific taxable years or periods must be shown. A single Power of Attorney may cover more than one type of tax and more than one taxable period. "Blanket" Powers of Attorney covering "all types of taxes" and/or "all taxable years" are not permitted.

> For example:
> *Proper Language*:
> "Income Taxes 1974, 1975, and Payroll Taxes 1974, 1975."
>
> *Improper Language*:
> "All tax matters for all tax years."
> "All tax matters—7412, 7512."
> "Income Tax—1974 and subsequent years."

D   The name(s), address(es), and telephone number(s) of the representative(s) who is to receive copies of correspondence must be shown here.

E   A Form 2848 will revoke all previous Powers of Attorney unless the previous representative is identified here.

F   The Power of Attorney must be signed and dated by the taxpayer(s).

G   Each representative shown in Item B above must enter his designation (e.g. attorney, CPA, or enrolled agent), the jurisdiction or enrollment number, signature and date.

# A Properly Completed Power of Attorney

| Form **2848**<br>(Rev. July 1976)<br>Department of the Treasury<br>Internal Revenue Service | **Power of Attorney**<br>(See the separate Instructions for Forms 2848 and 2848-D.) |
|---|---|

**A**

Name, identifying number, and address including ZIP code of taxpayer(s)     (H) 107-56-9987

(W) 398-06-5342

    JOHN & MARY JONES
    10 Briar Lane
    Westfield, New York   10576

hereby appoints (Name, address including ZIP code, and telephone number of appointee(s)) (See Treasury Department Circular No. 230 as amended (31 C.F.R. Part 10), Regulations Governing the Practice of Attorneys, Certified Public Accountants, and Enrolled Agents before the Internal Revenue Service, for persons recognized to practice before the Internal Revenue Service.)

**B**

    SAM BLACK, ESQ.
    Sam Black, P.C.
    155 Main Street
    Jamestown, New York   11675
    (914) 446-9800

as attorney(s)-in-fact to represent the taxpayer(s) before any office of the Internal Revenue Service for the following Internal Revenue tax matters (specify the type(s) of tax and year(s) or period(s) (date of death if estate tax)):

**C**

    Federal Income Tax   1975 and 1976

The attorney(s)-in-fact (or either of them) are authorized, subject to revocation, to receive confidential information and to perform on behalf of the taxpayer(s) the following acts for the above tax matters:

(Strike through any of the following which are not granted.)

    To receive, but not to endorse and collect, checks in payment of any refund of Internal Revenue taxes, penalties, or interest. (See "Refund checks" on page 2 of the separate instructions.)

    To execute waivers (including offers of waivers) of restrictions on assessment or collection of deficiencies in tax and waivers of notice of disallowance of a claim for credit or refund.

    To execute consents extending the statutory period for assessment or collection of taxes.

    To execute closing agreements under section 7121 of the Internal Revenue Code.

    To delegate authority or to substitute another representative.

    Other acts (specify) ........................................................................................................................

Send copies of notices and other written communications addressed to the taxpayer(s) in proceedings involving the above matters to (Name, address including ZIP code, and telephone number):

**D**    and

    SAM BLACK, ESQ.        (914) 446-9800
    Sam Black, P.C.
    155 Main Street
    Jamestown, New York   11675

This power of attorney revokes all earlier powers of attorney and tax information authorizations on file with the same Internal Revenue Service office for the same matters and years or periods covered by this form, except the following:

**E**

........................................................................................................................

(Specify to whom granted, date, and address including ZIP code, or refer to attached copies of earlier powers and authorizations.)

Signature of or for taxpayer(s)

If signed by a corporate officer, partner, or fiduciary on behalf of the taxpayer, I certify that I have the authority to execute this power of attorney on behalf of the taxpayer.

**F**

                                                              July 7, 1981

| (Signature) | (Title, if applicable) | (Date) |
|---|---|---|

                                                             July 7, 1981

| (Signature) | (Title, if applicable) | (Date) |
|---|---|---|

*(The applicable portion of the back page must also be completed.)*         Form **2848** (Rev. 7-76)

If the power of attorney is granted to an attorney, certified public accountant, or enrolled agent, this declaration must be completed.

I declare that I am not currently under suspension or disbarment from practice before the Internal Revenue Service, that I am aware of Treasury Department Circular No. 230 as amended (31 C.F.R. Part 10), Regulations Governing the Practice of Attorneys, Certified Public Accountants, and Enrolled Agents before the Internal Revenue Service, and that:

I am a member in good standing of the bar of the highest court of the jurisdiction indicated below; or
I am duly qualified to practice as a certified public accountant in the jurisdiction indicated below; or
I am enrolled as an agent pursuant to the requirements of Treasury Department Circular No. 230.

| Designation (Attorney, C.P.A., or Agent) | Jurisdiction (State, etc.) or Enrollment Card Number | Signature | Date |
|---|---|---|---|
| ATTORNEY | NEW YORK | *Dan Black* | July 7, 1981 |
|  |  |  |  |
|  |  |  |  |
|  |  |  |  |
|  |  |  |  |
|  |  |  |  |
|  |  |  |  |
|  |  |  |  |
|  |  |  |  |

G

If the power of attorney is granted to a person other than an attorney, certified public accountant, or enrolled agent, it must be witnessed or notarized below. (See Treasury Department Circular No. 230 as amended (31 C.F.R. Part 10), Regulations Governing the Practice of Attorneys, Certified Public Accountants, and Enrolled Agents before the Internal Revenue Service, for persons recognized to practice before the Internal Revenue Service.)

The person(s) signing as or for the taxpayer(s):   (Check and complete one.)

☐ Is/are known to and signed in the presence of the two disinterested witnesses whose signatures appear here:

_____          _____
(Signature of Witness)                                                                 (Date)

_____          _____
(Signature of Witness)                                                                 (Date)

☐ appeared this day before a notary public and acknowledged this power of attorney as a voluntary act and deed.

_____          _____     NOTARIAL SEAL
(Signature of Notary)                                                  (Date)                     (if required)

U.S. GOVERNMENT PRINTING OFFICE : 1976—O-575-286 58-040-1110

OFFICE OF DIRECTOR OF PRACTICE
OFFICE OF THE SECRETARY
DEPARTMENT OF THE TREASURY

NATURE OF ALLEGED OFFENSE OR MISCONDUCT AND TYPE OF DISCIPLINARY ACTION RESULTING

For Attorneys, Certified Public Accountants and Enrolled Agents
for the Period January 1, 1966 through December 31, 1976

| VIOLATION OR OFFENSE | TOTAL CASES | ATTORNEYS | | | CPAS | | | ENROLLED AGENTS | | | |
|---|---|---|---|---|---|---|---|---|---|---|---|
| | | Reprim. | Suspn. | Disb. | Reprim. | Suspn. | Disb. | Reprim. | Suspn. | Disb. | Resign. |
| Unethical Solicitation of Employment in IRS Matters | 190 | 8 | 2 | 1 | 12 | 3 | — | 140 | 13 | — | 11 |
| Failure to File Personal Returns with IRS | 117 | 5 | 31 | 1 | 11 | 43 | 2 | 19 | 5 | — | — |
| Conviction of Bribery or Attempted Bribery of IRS Employee | 66 | — | 12 | 1 | 1 | 46 | 1 | — | 5 | — | — |
| Filing False or Misleading Statements with IRS | 50 | 8 | 7 | 2 | 11 | 12 | — | 3 | 4 | 1 | 2 |
| Other Violations | 34 | 1 | 7 | 3 | 5 | 11 | 2 | 2 | 2 | — | 1 |
| Filing False or Fraudulent Returns for Self | 27 | 1 | 12 | — | 1 | 12 | 1 | — | — | — | — |
| Failure to File Returns for Taxpayers | 21 | 1 | 3 | — | 9 | 4 | — | 4 | — | — | — |

| Filing False or Fraudulent Returns for Taxpayers | 22 | — | 4 | — | — | 10 | — | 1 | 7 | — | — |
|---|---|---|---|---|---|---|---|---|---|---|---|
| Claiming False or Improper Deductions on Taxpayers' Returns | 15 | 3 | — | — | 6 | 4 | — | 1 | 1 | — | — |
| Failure to Comply with IRS Regulations | 13 | 3 | — | — | 5 | — | — | 4 | 1 | — | — |
| Contemptuous Conduct in Practice before IRS | 14 | 3 | 3 | 1 | 6 | — | — | 1 | — | — | — |
| Conviction of Offense Involving Dishonesty | 11 | — | 7 | 1 | — | 1 | — | — | 1 | — | 1 |
| Violation of Conflict of Interest | 6 | — | 1 | — | 2 | — | — | 1 | 1 | — | 1 |
| TOTAL | 586 | 33 | 89 | 10 | 69 | 146 | 6 | 176 | 40 | 1 | 16 |

## Time-saving tips for getting the Power of Attorney back to the IRS

1) Enclose a stamped, self-addressed envelope to your client when mailing him the Power of Attorney to sign. Accompany the Power of Attorney with this short note.

[Date]

Dear [Client's name]:

Enclosed find a Power of Attorney which must be signed by you (and your wife).

Please return the Power of Attorney to me in the enclosed self-addressed envelope.

Sincerely,

Bob Smith, CPA

2) After your client returns the Power of Attorney you should sign and photocopy it. Send the original to the IRS employee you are dealing with along with this covering letter.

[Date]

Re: [Client's name]

Dear [IRS employee]:

Enclosed find a Power of Attorney from the above captioned taxpayer(s).

Sincerely,

Bob Smith, CPA

# CHAPTER 3

# How Tax Returns
# Are Targeted for Audit

At least once a month, and much more often during March and April, I am asked the following question: "What are the chances that I will be audited if I take this deduction?

Unfortunately, the precise criteria used by the IRS to determine if a tax return is worthy of audit are a closely guarded secret. Since no one really knows what triggers the computer to select a tax return for examination, the practitioner can only make an educated guesstimate.

This chapter will discuss:

1. Tax return statistics

2. The process of selecting a tax return for examination

3. What items may "flag" a tax return for audit?

## Tax return statistics

During 1980 the IRS received 143.4 million tax returns and supplemental documents. Of that amount, 99.1 million returns represented individual, fiduciary, partnership and corporation tax returns.

| | |
|---|---|
| Individual | 93.1 |
| Fiduciary | 1.9 |
| Partnership | 1.4 |
| Corporation | 2.7 |
| | 99.1 |

Although 93.1 million individual tax returns were received, 40.4 percent or 37.6 million of these tax returns were 1040As. 1040A tax returns are generally not examined.

# Number of returns filed, by internal revenue regions, districts, states and other areas

| Internal Revenue regions and districts, states and other areas (States represented by single districts indicated in parentheses; total for other states shown at bottom of table) | Total tax returns (1) | Individual income tax (2) | Declaration of estimated tax (3) | Fiduciary (4) | Partnership (5) | Corporation income tax (6) | Estate tax (7) |
|---|---|---|---|---|---|---|---|
| United States, total | 143,445,842 | 93,143,629 | 8,698,811 | 1,876,756 | 1,390,161 | 2,717,606 | 148,228 |
| North-Atlantic Region | 19,573,904 | 12,618,813 | 1,236,888 | 355,996 | 146,953 | 486,097 | 20,128 |
| Albany (See (c) below) | 1,174,334 | 806,443 | 71,818 | 10,056 | 8,645 | 21,284 | 1,236 |
| Augusta (Maine) | 684,171 | 455,084 | 40,283 | 9,637 | 3,752 | 11,600 | 639 |
| Boston (Massachusetts) | 3,728,198 | 2,500,301 | 228,392 | 94,991 | 20,052 | 77,082 | 3,935 |
| Brooklyn (See (c) below) | 4,019,709 | 2,699,651 | 269,860 | 22,799 | 27,507 | 112,637 | 3,643 |
| Buffalo (See (c) below) | 2,648,880 | 1,860,065 | 157,843 | 36,702 | 19,793 | 42,664 | 2,809 |
| Burlington (Vermont) | 332,412 | 206,117 | 21,187 | 4,631 | 2,839 | 7,162 | 269 |
| Hartford (Connecticut) | 2,435,739 | 1,502,658 | 167,979 | 49,210 | 21,075 | 55,582 | 2,639 |
| Manhattan (See (c) below) | 3,356,695 | 1,784,167 | 211,444 | 111,932 | 35,962 | 131,833 | 3,941 |
| Portsmouth (New Hampshire) | 593,555 | 397,910 | 36,532 | 6,305 | 3,808 | 10,648 | 576 |
| Providence (Rhode Island) | 600,211 | 406,417 | 31,550 | 9,733 | 3,520 | 15,605 | 441 |
| Mid-Atlantic Region | 19,222,934 | 12,687,951 | 1,172,207 | 274,472 | 156,872 | 358,727 | 17,343 |
| Baltimore (Maryland & D.C.) | 3,367,260 | 2,212,967 | 198,271 | 41,610 | 27,838 | 56,399 | 3,206 |
| Newark (New Jersey) | 5,167,151 | 3,277,615 | 318,229 | 56,334 | 41,722 | 143,167 | 4,998 |
| Philadelphia (See (e) below) | 4,418,109 | 2,989,813 | 296,728 | 95,782 | 36,927 | 69,113 | 4,058 |
| Pittsburgh (See (e) below) | 2,603,805 | 1,809,046 | 163,077 | 39,546 | 22,623 | 29,305 | 1,871 |
| Richmond (Virginia) | 3,165,203 | 2,149,219 | 173,376 | 30,714 | 25,235 | 51,444 | 2,769 |
| Wilmington (Delaware) | 501,406 | 249,291 | 22,526 | 10,486 | 2,527 | 9,299 | 441 |
| Southeast Region | 20,929,162 | 13,521,863 | 1,205,228 | 196,534 | 165,371 | 396,221 | 19,261 |
| Atlanta (Georgia) | 3,109,453 | 2,071,780 | 136,677 | 25,131 | 22,512 | 54,255 | 1,984 |
| Birmingham (Alabama) | 2,002,981 | 1,359,153 | 90,833 | 16,328 | 14,664 | 30,950 | 1,121 |
| Columbia (South Carolina) | 1,682,940 | 1,147,305 | 83,373 | 10,267 | 12,359 | 27,934 | 1,324 |
| Greensboro (North Carolina) | 3,387,690 | 2,282,777 | 168,558 | 25,437 | 26,418 | 58,641 | 2,484 |
| Jackson (Mississippi) | 1,281,295 | 844,255 | 58,012 | 6,567 | 10,964 | 19,690 | 828 |
| Jacksonville (Florida) | 6,676,370 | 3,964,744 | 545,394 | 92,292 | 51,103 | 167,341 | 9,550 |
| Nashville (Tennessee) | 2,788,433 | 1,851,849 | 122,381 | 20,512 | 27,351 | 37,410 | 1,970 |
| Central Region | 18,330,957 | 12,503,416 | 1,044,707 | 223,105 | 150,813 | 302,834 | 15,664 |
| Cincinnati (See (d) below) | 2,902,076 | 1,934,813 | 162,795 | 36,818 | 22,457 | 42,385 | 2,663 |
| Cleveland (See (d) below) | 3,839,137 | 2,626,349 | 224,538 | 49,417 | 28,674 | 66,277 | 3,483 |
| Detroit (Michigan) | 5,456,931 | 3,757,322 | 297,136 | 67,809 | 48,281 | 92,294 | 3,526 |
| Indianapolis (Indiana) | 3,212,817 | 2,220,494 | 197,472 | 40,176 | 22,149 | 55,358 | 3,707 |
| Louisville (Kentucky) | 1,935,861 | 1,297,138 | 109,852 | 19,163 | 20,253 | 30,596 | 1,570 |
| Parkersburg (West Virginia) | 984,135 | 667,300 | 52,914 | 9,722 | 8,999 | 15,924 | 715 |
| Midwest Region | 19,995,823 | 12,984,580 | 1,307,564 | 331,821 | 198,933 | 376,385 | 31,175 |
| Aberdeen (South Dakota) | 453,884 | 276,640 | 28,127 | 4,500 | 5,746 | 7,557 | 811 |
| Chicago (See (b) below) | 5,498,013 | 3,688,691 | 337,799 | 114,637 | 55,744 | 107,424 | 7,443 |
| Des Moines (Iowa) | 1,936,684 | 1,196,196 | 148,402 | 35,549 | 21,745 | 38,662 | 4,995 |
| Fargo (North Dakota) | 444,762 | 268,266 | 27,554 | 4,758 | 5,421 | 7,682 | 1,088 |
| Milwaukee (Wisconsin) | 3,020,440 | 1,975,350 | 200,584 | 52,413 | 26,071 | 58,119 | 3,620 |
| Omaha (Nebraska) | 1,067,659 | 653,932 | 71,230 | 14,326 | 12,734 | 22,343 | 2,329 |
| St. Louis (Missouri) | 3,052,635 | 1,967,939 | 206,218 | 46,649 | 25,796 | 60,151 | 3,325 |
| St. Paul (Minnesota) | 2,637,425 | 1,716,566 | 151,981 | 31,415 | 26,878 | 50,073 | 3,414 |
| Springfield (See (b) below) | 1,884,321 | 1,241,000 | 135,669 | 27,574 | 18,798 | 24,374 | 4,150 |
| Southwest Region | 18,984,028 | 12,027,633 | 1,031,877 | 188,410 | 221,054 | 340,850 | 17,159 |
| Albuquerque (New Mexico) | 761,706 | 502,968 | 38,457 | 5,959 | 8,298 | 12,355 | 502 |
| Austin (See (f) below) | 5,253,806 | 3,297,362 | 241,282 | 48,943 | 58,041 | 80,470 | 3,781 |
| Cheyenne (Wyoming) | 331,652 | 198,940 | 18,715 | 2,879 | 4,814 | 7,477 | 294 |
| Dallas (See (f) below) | 3,790,554 | 2,363,874 | 210,351 | 46,564 | 55,168 | 65,745 | 3,282 |
| Denver (Colorado) | 1,964,003 | 1,241,727 | 110,660 | 24,972 | 29,346 | 42,060 | 1,809 |
| Little Rock (Arkansas) | 1,240,245 | 800,558 | 71,740 | 9,020 | 12,250 | 21,588 | 982 |
| New Orleans (Louisiana) | 2,281,970 | 1,510,070 | 116,794 | 11,277 | 16,122 | 48,926 | 1,312 |
| Oklahoma City (Oklahoma) | 1,800,520 | 1,141,239 | 110,348 | 17,942 | 21,086 | 34,702 | 2,349 |
| Wichita (Kansas) | 1,559,572 | 970,895 | 113,530 | 20,854 | 15,929 | 27,527 | 2,848 |
| Western Region | 25,717,154 | 16,401,496 | 1,636,415 | 305,489 | 349,284 | 446,437 | 26,609 |
| Anchorage (Alaska) | 275,332 | 175,649 | 7,303 | 1,232 | 5,060 | 5,056 | 145 |
| Boise (Idaho) | 568,289 | 354,255 | 30,805 | 4,498 | 8,264 | 11,011 | 454 |
| Helena (Montana) | 559,389 | 328,987 | 35,040 | 5,207 | 7,773 | 11,523 | 700 |
| Honolulu (Hawaii) | 624,022 | 413,178 | 39,062 | 6,387 | 7,826 | 16,016 | 709 |
| Los Angeles (See (a) below) | 9,215,172 | 6,019,995 | 610,559 | 126,660 | 131,825 | 169,138 | 10,220 |
| Phoenix (Arizona) | 1,615,926 | 1,049,829 | 107,152 | 21,900 | 16,599 | 29,261 | 1,562 |
| Portland (Oregon) | 2,087,671 | 1,210,215 | 115,611 | 20,245 | 25,301 | 34,132 | 1,974 |
| Reno (Nevada) | 548,482 | 362,529 | 25,971 | 6,105 | 6,445 | 11,505 | 332 |
| Salt Lake City (Utah) | 806,691 | 526,841 | 33,182 | 11,609 | 12,869 | 17,261 | 540 |
| San Francisco (See (a) below) | 6,663,917 | 4,218,958 | 464,982 | 73,712 | 91,126 | 94,973 | 8,315 |
| Seattle (Washington) | 2,752,263 | 1,741,060 | 166,748 | 27,934 | 36,196 | 46,561 | 1,958 |
| Office of International Operations | 691,880 | 397,877 | 63,925 | 929 | 881 | 10,055 | 589 |
| Puerto Rico | 279,172 | 79,229 | 15,423 | 87 | 71 | 285 | 38 |
| Other | 412,708 | 318,648 | 48,502 | 842 | 810 | 9,770 | 551 |

### Totals for states not shown above

| | Total tax returns (1) | Individual income tax (2) | Declaration of estimated tax (3) | Fiduciary (4) | Partnership (5) | Corporation income tax (6) | Estate tax (7) |
|---|---|---|---|---|---|---|---|
| (a) California | 15,879,089 | 10,238,953 | 1,075,541 | 200,372 | 222,951 | 264,111 | 18,535 |
| (b) Illinois | 7,382,334 | 4,929,691 | 473,468 | 142,211 | 74,542 | 131,798 | 11,593 |
| (c) New York | 11,199,618 | 7,150,326 | 710,965 | 181,489 | 91,907 | 308,418 | 11,629 |
| (d) Ohio | 6,741,213 | 4,561,162 | 387,333 | 86,235 | 51,131 | 108,662 | 6,146 |
| (e) Pennsylvania | 7,021,914 | 4,798,859 | 459,805 | 135,328 | 59,550 | 98,418 | 5,929 |
| (f) Texas | 9,044,360 | 5,661,236 | 451,633 | 95,507 | 113,209 | 146,215 | 7,063 |

Column Contents:
(2) Includes Forms 1040, 1040A, 1040NR, 1040SS–PR, 1040C and 1042.
(3) Form 1040ES.
(4) Form 1041.
(5) Form 1065.
(6) Includes Forms 1120, 1120 Specials (Sched. PH, 1120L, 1120M), 1120S, 1120–DISC, 1120POL, 1120F and 1120H.
(7) Includes Forms 706 and 706NA.

| Internal Revenue regions and districts, states and other areas (States represented by single districts indicated in parentheses; total for other states shown at bottom of table) | Gift (8) | Employment taxes (9) | Exempt Organization (10) | Employee Plans (11) | ATF Returns (12) | Excise taxes (13) | Supplemental documents (14) |
|---|---|---|---|---|---|---|---|
| United States, total | 215,993 | 26,499,154 | 443,674 | 791,708 | 546,613 | 909,047 | 6,064,462 |
| North-Atlantic Region | 32,560 | 3,733,555 | 46,601 | 85,929 | 66,056 | 85,889 | 658,439 |
| Albany (See (c) below) | 1,728 | 209,067 | | 3,511 | 6,356 | 6,431 | 27,759 |
| Augusta (Maine) | 1,197 | 134,923 | | 1,785 | 3,832 | 6,155 | 15,284 |
| Boston (Massachusetts) | 6,651 | 632,197 | 26,866 | 14,514 | 9,494 | 16,230 | 97,493 |
| Brooklyn (See (c) below) | 3,894 | 716,590 | 9,337 | 13,627 | 8,987 | 10,684 | 120,493 |
| Buffalo (See (c) below) | 4,363 | 425,804 | | 9,970 | 12,809 | 15,219 | 60,839 |
| Burlington (Vermont) | 635 | 74,980 | 1 | 944 | 2,024 | 2,044 | 9,579 |
| Hartford (Connecticut) | 5,631 | 432,498 | 2 | 10,532 | 11,283 | 15,765 | 160,885 |
| Manhattan (See (c) below) | 6,786 | 880,988 | 10,395 | 27,043 | 7,550 | 7,355 | 137,299 |
| Portsmouth (New Hampshire) | 999 | 112,593 | | 1,721 | 2,278 | 4,142 | 16,043 |
| Providence (Rhode Island) | 676 | 113,915 | | 2,282 | 1,443 | 1,864 | 12,765 |
| Mid-Atlantic Region | 27,570 | 3,349,354 | 109,531 | 108,631 | 61,176 | 103,001 | 796,099 |
| Baltimore (Maryland & D.C.) | 6,029 | 563,153 | -2 | 22,181 | 9,756 | 14,327 | 211,525 |
| Newark (New Jersey) | 7,096 | 938,730 | 6,548 | 24,406 | 12,833 | 21,944 | 313,529 |
| Philadelphia (See (e) below) | 5,501 | 749,673 | | 29,360 | 15,127 | 25,816 | 100,211 |
| Pittsburgh (See (e) below) | 2,904 | 429,497 | | 16,997 | 10,923 | 20,592 | 57,424 |
| Richmond (Virginia) | 5,332 | 596,036 | | 13,411 | 11,034 | 18,039 | 88,594 |
| Wilmington (Delaware) | 708 | 72,265 | 102,985 | 2,276 | 1,503 | 2,283 | 24,816 |
| Southeast Region | 29,727 | 4,143,501 | 49,318 | 97,144 | 77,275 | 126,039 | 901,680 |
| Atlanta (Georgia) | 4,704 | 621,430 | 26,621 | 15,313 | 9,724 | 19,031 | 100,291 |
| Birmingham (Alabama) | 2,522 | 404,230 | | 6,699 | 7,578 | 14,737 | 54,166 |
| Columbia (South Carolina) | 2,157 | 334,037 | | 7,490 | 6,704 | 9,529 | 40,461 |
| Greensboro (North Caroline) | 4,959 | 680,238 | | 15,406 | 12,190 | 21,489 | 89,093 |
| Jackson (Mississippi) | 1,386 | 279,576 | | 4,644 | 7,547 | 10,430 | 37,396 |
| Jacksonville (Florida) | 11,049 | 1,313,640 | 22,697 | 36,434 | 23,818 | 31,678 | 406,630 |
| Nashville (Tennessee) | 2,950 | 510,350 | | 11,158 | 9,714 | 19,145 | 173,643 |
| Central Region | 23,770 | 3,063,162 | 56,559 | 119,987 | 76,120 | 123,773 | 627,047 |
| Cincinnati (See (d) below) | 3,841 | 457,358 | 26,939 | 20,018 | 10,279 | 14,787 | 166,923 |
| Cleveland (See (d) below) | 4,982 | 638,896 | 15,005 | 30,135 | 15,432 | 22,345 | 113,604 |
| Detroit (Michigan) | 6,447 | 873,565 | 14,615 | 43,608 | 23,207 | 31,192 | 197,929 |
| Indianapolis (Indiana) | 4,911 | 533,947 | | 15,408 | 12,404 | 30,168 | 76,623 |
| Louisville (Kentucky) | 2,562 | 371,563 | | 7,045 | 9,090 | 16,688 | 50,341 |
| Parkersburg (West Virginia) | 1,027 | 187,833 | | 3,773 | 5,708 | 8,593 | 21,627 |
| Midwest Region | 45,606 | 3,622,208 | 53,005 | 149,702 | 97,338 | 157,256 | 640,250 |
| Aberdeen (South Dakota) | 1,648 | 99,384 | | 2,158 | 3,462 | 5,917 | 17,934 |
| Chicago (See (b) below) | 8,782 | 865,507 | 7,861 | 48,409 | 15,287 | 20,711 | 219,712 |
| Des Moines (Iowa) | 6,551 | 393,574 | | 12,176 | 9,391 | 21,572 | 47,871 |
| Fargo (North Dakota) | 1,976 | 99,041 | | 2,446 | 2,752 | 6,525 | 17,253 |
| Milwaukee (Wisconsin) | 8,376 | 548,157 | | 24,574 | 23,559 | 24,597 | 75,020 |
| Omaha (Nebraska) | 4,443 | 222,387 | | 6,530 | 5,652 | 13,492 | 38,261 |
| St. Louis (Missouri) | 4,854 | 581,035 | 19,618 | 19,395 | 17,477 | 24,178 | 76,000 |
| St. Paul (Minnesota) | 4,743 | 464,444 | 25,526 | 22,779 | 10,833 | 25,495 | 103,278 |
| Springfield (See (b) below) | 4,233 | 348,679 | | 11,235 | 8,925 | 14,763 | 44,921 |
| Southwest Region | 28,316 | 3,727,245 | 55,527 | 82,208 | 86,541 | 151,067 | 1,026,141 |
| Albuquerque (New Mexico) | 857 | 153,068 | | 3,217 | 3,008 | 5,826 | 27,191 |
| Austin (See (f) below) | 6,684 | 931,615 | 28,820 | 20,668 | 25,918 | 30,129 | 480,093 |
| Cheyenne (Wyoming) | 865 | 72,905 | | 1,300 | 2,225 | 4,186 | 17,052 |
| Dallas (See (f) below) | 4,418 | 780,106 | 26,707 | 17,400 | 11,841 | 34,117 | 170,981 |
| Denver (Colorado) | 3,453 | 384,081 | | 12,574 | 7,439 | 12,729 | 93,153 |
| Little Rock (Arkansas) | 2,077 | 258,023 | | 4,211 | 5,745 | 14,511 | 39,540 |
| New Orleans (Louisiana) | 1,995 | 468,536 | | 8,770 | 11,689 | 16,348 | 70,131 |
| Oklahoma City (Oklahoma) | 3,767 | 357,022 | | 7,293 | 10,643 | 16,868 | 77,261 |
| Wichita (Kansas) | 4,200 | 321,889 | | 6,775 | 8,033 | 16,353 | 50,739 |
| Western Region | 28,035 | 4,664,364 | 73,133 | 147,305 | 81,785 | 161,079 | 1,395,423 |
| Anchorage (Alaska) | 252 | 48,797 | | 1,607 | 2,312 | 3,946 | 23,973 |
| Boise (Idaho) | 756 | 119,056 | | 3,084 | 3,408 | 7,147 | 25,551 |
| Helena (Montana) | 2,039 | 122,614 | | 2,477 | 4,654 | 8,706 | 29,669 |
| Honolulu (Hawaii) | 1,714 | 108,760 | | 3,782 | 1,970 | 2,406 | 22,212 |
| Los Angeles (See (a) below) | 6,565 | 1,690,634 | 29,155 | 53,200 | 19,789 | 37,069 | 310,363 |
| Phoenix (Arizona) | 2,024 | 276,777 | | 8,621 | 6,355 | 7,742 | 88,104 |
| Portland (Oregon) | 3,370 | 349,315 | 5 | 14,922 | 7,778 | 16,583 | 288,220 |
| Reno (Nevada) | 546 | 95,958 | | 2,918 | 2,309 | 5,175 | 28,689 |
| Salt Lake City (Utah) | 1,736 | 149,751 | | 5,025 | 2,280 | 6,379 | 39,218 |
| San Francisco (See (a) below) | 6,454 | 1,183,387 | 23,298 | 34,493 | 20,953 | 40,883 | 402,383 |
| Seattle (Washington) | 2,579 | 519,315 | 20,675 | 17,176 | 9,977 | 25,043 | 137,041 |
| Office of International Operations | 409 | 195,765 | | 802 | 322 | 943 | 19,383 |
| Puerto Rico | 48 | 182,525 | | 544 | 306 | 25 | 591 |
| Other | 361 | 13,240 | | 258 | 16 | 918 | 18,792 |

#### Totals for states not shown above

| | Gift (8) | Employment taxes (9) | Exempt Organization (10) | Employee Plans (11) | ATF Returns (12) | Excise taxes (13) | Supplemental documents (14) |
|---|---|---|---|---|---|---|---|
| (a) California | 13,019 | 2,874,021 | 52,453 | 87,693 | 40,742 | 77,952 | 712,746 |
| (b) Illinois | 13,015 | 1,214,186 | 7,861 | 59,644 | 24,212 | 35,480 | 264,633 |
| (c) New York | 16,771 | 2,232,449 | 19,732 | 54,151 | 35,702 | 39,689 | 346,390 |
| (d) Ohio | 8,823 | 1,096,254 | 41,944 | 50,153 | 25,711 | 37,132 | 280,527 |
| (e) Pennsylvania | 8,405 | 1,179,170 | | 46,357 | 26,050 | 46,408 | 157,635 |
| (f) Texas | 11,102 | 1,711,721 | 55,527 | 38,068 | 37,759 | 64,246 | 651,074 |

Column Contents:
(8)  Form 709.
(9)  Includes Forms 940, 940PR, 941, 941PR & SS, 941E, 941M, 942, 942PR, 943, 943PR, CT–1, and CT–2.
(10)  Includes Forms 990, 990PF, 990T, 990C, 5227, and 4720.
(11)  Includes Forms 5500, 5500C, 5500K.
(12)  Includes Forms 7, 8, 11, 4705, 4706, 4707, 4708, Alcohol Excise Tax Returns, and Tobacco Excise Tax Returns.
(13)  Includes Forms 720, 720M, 730, 2290, 11B, 11C, and 4638.
(14)  Includes Forms 1040X, 1120X, 2688, 4868, 7004, Tent. 1120L & M, 7005, 990AR, 4578, 1041A, 2438, 990BL, and 6069.

47

# Returns filed, examination coverage and results (1980)

| | Returns Filed | Returns Examined | | | | |
|---|---|---|---|---|---|---|
| | CY 1979 | Revenue Agents | Tax Auditors | Service Center | Total | Percent Coverage |
| **Individual, total** | **90,727,115** | **292,465** | **1,346,320** | **195,073** | **1,833,858** | **2.02%** |
| NB [1] under $10,000 [2] | 38,538,636 | 26,273 | 372,221 | 39,656 | 438,150 | 1.14 |
| NB $10,000 under $15,000 | 12,631,046 | 15,065 | 192,389 | 48,521 | 255,975 | 2.03 |
| NB $15,000 under $50,000 | 27,270,309 | 57,454 | 580,199 | 87,812 | 725,465 | 2.66 |
| NB $50,000 and over | 1,251,151 | 59,457 | 47,161 | 2,719 | 109,337 | 8.74 |
| B [3] under $10,000 | 3,696,353 | 36,330 | 77,015 | 4,049 | 117,394 | 3.18 |
| B $10,000 under $30,000 | 5,465,678 | 36,408 | 52,447 | 8,876 | 97,731 | 1.79 |
| B $30,000 and over | 1,873,942 | 61,478 | 24,888 | 3,440 | 89,806 | 4.79 |
| **Fiduciary** | **1,820,708** | **9,875** | - | - | **9,875** | **.54** |
| **Partnership** | **1,289,315** | **23,041** | - | - | **23,041** | **1.79** |
| **Corporation, Total** | **2,061,672** | **133,593** | - | - | **133,593** | **6.48** |
| Assets not reported | 125,622 | 5,790 | - | - | 5,790 | 4.61 |
| Under $100,000 [4] | 1,006,189 | 36,520 | - | - | 36,520 | 3.63 |
| $100,000 under $1 Mil | 746,767 | 51,953 | - | - | 51,953 | 6.96 |
| $1 Mil under $10 Mil | 151,663 | 27,636 | - | - | 27,636 | 18.22 |
| $10 Mil under $100 Mil | 26,302 | 7,756 | - | - | 7,756 | 29.49 |
| $100 Mil and over | 5,129 | 3,938 | - | - | 3,938 | 76.78 |
| **Small Business Corp.** | **504,366** | **10,457** | - | - | **10,457** | **2.07** |
| **Domestic International Sales Corp.** | **6,756** | **1,635** | - | - | **1,635** | **24.20** |
| **Estate, total** | **156,392** | **26,808** | **1,606** | - | **28,414** | **18.17** |
| Gross Estate under $300,000 | 119,199 | 9,151 | 1,225 | - | 10,376 | 8.70 |
| Gross Estate $300,000 and over | 37,193 | 17,657 | 381 | - | 18,038 | 48.50 |
| **Gift** | **205,191** | **7,713** | **614** | - | **8,327** | **4.06** |
| Income, Estate and Gift, total | 96,771,515 | 505,587 | 1,348,540 | 195,073 | 2,049,200 | 2.12 |
| **Excise** | **1,065,175** | **68,922** | **10,682** | - | **79,604** | **7.47** |
| **Employment** | **26,429,842** | **40,744** | **9,222** | - | **49,966** | **.19** |
| **Miscellaneous** | - | **418** | **109** | - | **527** | - |
| **Service Center Corrections** | - | - | - | **533,046** | **533,046** | - |

Totals may not add, due to rounding.
[1] Nonbusiness returns.
[2] Adjusted gross income.
[3] Business returns.
[4] Balance sheet assets.

| Recommended Additional Tax and Penalties (In millions of dollars) | | | | Average Tax and Penalty per Return | | | No Change, Percent [5] | | |
|---|---|---|---|---|---|---|---|---|---|
| Revenue Agents | Tax Auditors | Service Centers | Total | Revenue Agents | Tax Auditors | Service Centers | Revenue Agents | Tax Auditors | |
| $1,335 | $602 | $39 | $1,977 | $4,566 | $447 | $199 | 13 | 26 | Individual, total |
| 143 | 109 | 5 | 258 | 5,438 | 294 | 131 | 15 | 30 | NB [1] under $10,000 [2] |
| 46 | 58 | 7 | 112 | 3,086 | 303 | 146 | 18 | 28 | NB $10,000 under $15,000 |
| 120 | 251 | 21 | 392 | 2,087 | 433 | 240 | 13 | 24 | NB $15,000 under $50,000 |
| 365 | 44 | 1 | 411 | 6,146 | 941 | 447 | 12 | 40 | NB $50,000 and over |
| 115 | 69 | 1 | 184 | 3,159 | 889 | 181 | 15 | 22 | B under $10,000 [3] |
| 94 | 42 | 2 | 137 | 2,570 | 792 | 250 | 12 | 20 | B $10,000 under $30,000 |
| 452 | 29 | 1 | 483 | 7,358 | 1,161 | 411 | 12 | 29 | B $30,000 and over |
| 34 | - | - | 34 | 3,429 | - | - | 31 | - | Fiduciary |
| - | - | - | - | - | - | - | 39 | - | Partnership |
| 6,008 | - | - | 6,008 | 44,972 | - | - | 21 | - | Corporation, Total |
| 96 | - | - | 96 | 16,540 | - | - | 22 | - | Assets not reported [4] |
| 61 | - | - | 61 | 1,679 | - | - | 27 | - | Under $100,000 |
| 195 | - | - | 195 | 3,758 | - | - | 23 | - | $100,000 under $1 Mil |
| 378 | - | - | 378 | 13,685 | - | - | 17 | - | $1 Mil under $10 Mil |
| 540 | - | - | 540 | 69,674 | - | - | 10 | - | $10 Mil under $100 Mil |
| 4,737 | - | - | 4,737 | 1,202,893 | - | - | 4 | - | $100 Mil and over |
| 31 | - | - | 31 | 2,963 | - | - | 38 | - | Small Business Corp. |
| 45 | - | - | 45 | 27,531 | - | - | 44 | - | Domestic International Sales Corp. |
| 1,045 | 4 | - | 1,050 | 38,998 | 2,768 | - | 12 | 17 | Estate, total |
| 75 | 3 | - | 79 | 8,247 | 2,827 | - | 15 | 16 | Gross Estate under $300,000 |
| 970 | 1 | - | 971 | 54,935 | 2,578 | - | 10 | 20 | Gross Estate $300,000 and over |
| 89 | 3 | - | 91 | 11,481 | 4,172 | - | 20 | 28 | Gift |
| 8,587 | 609 | 39 | 9,235 | 16,984 | 452 | 199 | 17 | 26 | Income, Estate and Gift, total |
| 99 | 2 | - | 100 | 1,435 | 149 | - | 21 | 14 | Excise |
| 70 | 2 | - | 72 | 1,712 | 191 | - | 29 | 28 | Employment |
| - | - | - | - | 42 | 448 | - | 1 | 26 | Miscellaneous |
| - | - | 123 | 123 | - | - | 230 | - | - | Service Center Corrections |

[5] Service center no-change rate by class is not available. No change resulted in 34 percent of service center examinations.

# Number of returns examined by class of tax and by internal revenue regions, districts and other areas

| Internal Revenue regions, districts and service centers | Total | Individual | Partner-ship | Fiduci-ary | Corpo-ration | Sub-chapter S Corpo-ration | Estate | Gift | Excise | Employ-ment | Exempt Organi-zation | Employee Plans |
|---|---|---|---|---|---|---|---|---|---|---|---|---|
| **Total** | 2,221,955 | 1,833,858 | 23,041 | 9,875 | 133,593 | 12,092 | 28,414 | 8,327 | 79,604 | 49,966 | 23,807 | 19,378 |
| **North-Atlantic** | 334,814 | 274,482 | 2,562 | 1,487 | 20,382 | 2,363 | 5,925 | 1,618 | 11,577 | 7,036 | 4,717 | 2,665 |
| **Mid-Atlantic** | 252,418 | 205,226 | 2,717 | 1,214 | 17,751 | 1,423 | 3,425 | 875 | 7,907 | 5,995 | 2,689 | 3,196 |
| **Southeast** | 343,443 | 288,186 | 2,936 | 1,182 | 19,171 | 1,833 | 3,188 | 1,509 | 14,292 | 7,115 | 2,678 | 1,353 |
| **Central** | 202,953 | 156,407 | 2,292 | 1,148 | 16,205 | 1,382 | 3,505 | 937 | 9,088 | 5,250 | 3,073 | 3,666 |
| **Midwest** | 269,029 | 206,282 | 3,573 | 1,835 | 21,093 | 1,939 | 4,368 | 1,498 | 13,342 | 6,977 | 4,523 | 3,599 |
| **Southwest** | 258,185 | 208,461 | 3,727 | 986 | 15,231 | 1,622 | 2,840 | 895 | 11,560 | 9,329 | 2,594 | 940 |
| **Western** | 544,395 | 481,306 | 5,229 | 2,019 | 23,157 | 1,521 | 4,885 | 915 | 11,750 | 6,121 | 3,533 | 3,959 |
| **International Operations** | 16,718 | 13,508 | 5 | 4 | 603 | 9 | 278 | 80 | 88 | 2,143 | - | - |
| **North-Atlantic Region:** | | | | | | | | | | | | |
| Albany | 12,390 | 9,604 | 173 | 59 | 870 | 103 | 281 | 80 | 551 | 669 | - | - |
| Augusta | 6,720 | 4,503 | 64 | 56 | 660 | 54 | 91 | 30 | 754 | 508 | - | - |
| Boston | 48,151 | 34,902 | 321 | 434 | 4,297 | 263 | 828 | 173 | 2,285 | 1,880 | 2,007 | 761 |
| Brooklyn | 81,470 | 71,544 | 389 | 107 | 3,249 | 647 | 1,226 | 317 | 1,738 | 583 | 993 | 677 |
| Buffalo | 27,220 | 20,852 | 319 | 205 | 2,063 | 153 | 702 | 225 | 1,883 | 818 | - | - |
| Burlington | 4,092 | 3,238 | 69 | 32 | 397 | 56 | 42 | 2 | 128 | 128 | - | - |
| Hartford | 31,100 | 24,237 | 536 | 242 | 2,527 | 381 | 931 | 353 | 1,092 | 801 | - | - |
| Manhattan | 73,262 | 58,244 | 541 | 257 | 5,015 | 634 | 1,601 | 419 | 2,560 | 1,047 | 1,717 | 1,227 |
| Portsmouth | 5,286 | 3,933 | 49 | 26 | 413 | 29 | 89 | 10 | 419 | 318 | - | - |
| Providence | 5,386 | 3,688 | 101 | 69 | 891 | 43 | 134 | 9 | 167 | 284 | - | - |
| Andover Service Center | 14,312 | 14,312 | - | - | - | - | - | - | - | - | - | - |
| Brookhaven Service Center | 25,425 | 25,425 | - | - | - | - | - | - | - | - | - | - |
| **Mid-Atlantic Region:** | | | | | | | | | | | | |
| Baltimore | 51,405 | 40,557 | 642 | 183 | 2,727 | 224 | 610 | 224 | 1,701 | 1,699 | 1,559 | 1,279 |
| Newark | 72,826 | 60,722 | 564 | 162 | 5,292 | 489 | 1,139 | 210 | 1,942 | 813 | 493 | 1,000 |
| Philadelphia | 47,284 | 36,682 | 629 | 563 | 4,145 | 324 | 615 | 149 | 1,290 | 1,333 | 637 | 917 |
| Pittsburgh | 26,112 | 19,720 | 321 | 155 | 2,198 | 122 | 622 | 118 | 1,662 | 1,194 | - | - |
| Richmond | 39,161 | 33,044 | 509 | 105 | 2,679 | 228 | 341 | 128 | 1,248 | 879 | - | - |
| Wilmington | 5,078 | 3,949 | 52 | 46 | 710 | 36 | 98 | 46 | 64 | 77 | - | - |
| Philadelphia Service Center | 10,552 | 10,552 | - | - | - | - | - | - | - | - | - | - |
| **Southeast Region:** | | | | | | | | | | | | |
| Atlanta | 51,468 | 41,298 | 448 | 131 | 3,220 | 276 | 296 | 352 | 2,093 | 1,025 | 1,557 | 772 |
| Birmingham | 30,065 | 25,879 | 264 | 118 | 1,648 | 138 | 222 | 108 | 1,191 | 497 | - | - |
| Columbia | 19,813 | 16,981 | 174 | 58 | 1,044 | 131 | 189 | 66 | 501 | 669 | - | - |
| Greensboro | 41,549 | 32,098 | 526 | 188 | 4,043 | 289 | 406 | 279 | 2,352 | 1,368 | - | - |
| Jackson | 21,886 | 18,473 | 298 | 51 | 949 | 92 | 212 | 135 | 1,095 | 581 | - | - |
| Jacksonville | 96,417 | 76,951 | 690 | 487 | 5,923 | 778 | 1,546 | 433 | 5,811 | 2,096 | 1,121 | 581 |
| Nashville | 32,484 | 26,745 | 536 | 149 | 2,344 | 129 | 317 | 136 | 1,249 | 879 | - | - |
| Atlanta Service Center | 23,524 | 23,524 | - | - | - | - | - | - | - | - | - | - |
| Memphis Service Center | 26,237 | 26,237 | - | - | - | - | - | - | - | - | - | - |
| **Central Region:** | | | | | | | | | | | | |
| Cincinnati | 30,865 | 21,667 | 443 | 258 | 2,764 | 149 | 482 | 131 | 1,482 | 565 | 1,461 | 1,463 |
| Cleveland | 40,215 | 28,425 | 443 | 217 | 3,588 | 171 | 1,115 | 261 | 2,280 | 1,561 | 865 | 1,289 |
| Detroit | 66,061 | 51,563 | 755 | 375 | 5,937 | 369 | 860 | 296 | 2,844 | 1,401 | 747 | 914 |
| Indianapolis | 26,453 | 20,438 | 280 | 145 | 1,773 | 451 | 566 | 86 | 1,967 | 747 | - | - |
| Louisville | 17,563 | 14,201 | 233 | 98 | 1,383 | 192 | 326 | 130 | 411 | 589 | - | - |
| Parkersburg | 7,017 | 5,334 | 138 | 55 | 760 | 50 | 156 | 33 | 104 | 387 | - | - |
| Cincinnati Service Center | 14,779 | 14,779 | - | - | - | - | - | - | - | - | - | - |
| **Midwest Region:** | | | | | | | | | | | | |
| Aberdeen | 5,635 | 4,493 | 83 | 29 | 298 | 36 | 113 | 66 | 262 | 255 | - | - |
| Chicago | 76,984 | 60,937 | 815 | 616 | 5,923 | 525 | 1,064 | 235 | 3,649 | 1,427 | 1,159 | 634 |
| Des Moines | 24,707 | 18,104 | 507 | 188 | 1,805 | 229 | 581 | 257 | 2,177 | 859 | - | - |
| Fargo | 5,729 | 4,969 | 77 | 13 | 274 | 58 | 108 | 31 | 50 | 149 | - | - |
| Milwaukee | 28,561 | 20,978 | 476 | 293 | 3,259 | 225 | 491 | 120 | 2,060 | 659 | - | - |
| Omaha | 14,353 | 10,201 | 268 | 69 | 1,017 | 121 | 367 | 129 | 1,054 | 1,127 | - | - |
| St. Louis | 36,455 | 26,397 | 369 | 217 | 3,166 | 246 | 582 | 194 | 1,492 | 991 | 1,721 | 1,080 |
| St. Paul | 38,475 | 27,455 | 571 | 191 | 3,294 | 339 | 492 | 290 | 1,438 | 877 | 1,643 | 1,885 |
| Springfield | 22,271 | 16,889 | 407 | 219 | 2,057 | 160 | 570 | 176 | 1,160 | 633 | - | - |
| Kansas City Service Center | 15,859 | 15,859 | - | - | - | - | - | - | - | - | - | - |
| **Southwest Region:** | | | | | | | | | | | | |
| Albuquerque | 9,704 | 8,292 | 140 | 41 | 504 | 48 | 57 | 14 | 457 | 151 | - | - |
| Austin | 54,058 | 43,509 | 835 | 194 | 3,248 | 306 | 517 | 124 | 1,707 | 1,627 | 1,484 | 507 |
| Cheyenne | 4,685 | 3,961 | 85 | 6 | 337 | 44 | 50 | 32 | 97 | 73 | - | - |
| Dallas | 51,755 | 39,185 | 1,189 | 251 | 3,671 | 339 | 809 | 254 | 1,898 | 2,616 | 1,110 | 433 |
| Denver | 25,215 | 21,099 | 318 | 137 | 1,624 | 184 | 170 | 75 | 797 | 811 | - | - |
| Little Rock | 15,317 | 12,079 | 217 | 67 | 731 | 123 | 211 | 73 | 1,244 | 572 | - | - |
| New Orleans | 36,614 | 30,874 | 247 | 64 | 2,400 | 248 | 335 | 89 | 1,204 | 1,153 | - | - |
| Oklahoma City | 22,908 | 17,530 | 384 | 125 | 1,378 | 145 | 360 | 114 | 1,919 | 953 | - | - |
| Wichita | 21,101 | 15,104 | 312 | 101 | 1,338 | 185 | 331 | 120 | 2,237 | 1,373 | - | - |
| Austin Service Center | 16,828 | 16,828 | - | - | - | - | - | - | - | - | - | - |
| **Western Region:** | | | | | | | | | | | | |
| Anchorage | 8,317 | 7,221 | 89 | 32 | 393 | 20 | 20 | 8 | 352 | 182 | - | - |
| Boise | 8,634 | 6,668 | 181 | 52 | 549 | 85 | 84 | 26 | 697 | 292 | - | - |
| Helena | 6,658 | 5,090 | 109 | 76 | 450 | 72 | 105 | 33 | 406 | 317 | - | - |
| Honolulu | 10,794 | 9,376 | 157 | 33 | 777 | 53 | 94 | 22 | 170 | 112 | - | - |
| Los Angeles | 232,146 | 209,516 | 1,769 | 251 | 9,196 | 449 | 1,850 | 205 | 3,413 | 1,504 | 1,377 | 2,132 |
| Phoenix | 26,957 | 23,461 | 310 | 143 | 1,698 | 104 | 245 | 90 | 523 | 383 | - | - |
| Portland | 18,593 | 14,450 | 356 | 137 | 1,563 | 158 | 283 | 120 | 851 | 675 | - | - |
| Reno | 13,273 | 11,736 | 72 | 46 | 598 | 45 | 66 | 45 | 512 | 153 | - | - |
| Salt Lake City | 12,259 | 10,627 | 153 | 77 | 508 | 95 | 80 | 26 | 299 | 394 | - | - |
| San Francisco | 123,285 | 107,850 | 1,446 | 505 | 5,181 | 204 | 1,615 | 228 | 2,819 | 1,333 | 994 | 1,110 |
| Seattle | 35,922 | 27,754 | 587 | 183 | 2,244 | 236 | 443 | 112 | 1,708 | 776 | 1,162 | 717 |
| Ogden Service Center | 16,907 | 16,907 | - | - | - | - | - | - | - | - | - | - |
| Fresno Service Center | 30,650 | 30,650 | - | - | - | - | - | - | - | - | - | - |

# Processing Pipeline

Returns are delivered to the Regional Service Centers.

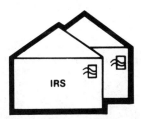

Envelopes are opened and counted.

Returns are sorted by type of return.

Tax returns and accompanying checks are compared.

Returns are edited and coded for computer processing.

Tax return information is placed on magnetic tape for computer processing.

IRS computers check returns for mathematical accuracy.

Tapes are sent to the National Computer Center for Account Posting and Settlement.

Tapes of Refunds are sent to the Treasury Department Disbursing Center for issuance of checks directly to taxpayers.

Once a tax return reaches one of ten IRS Service Centers, it travels through a series of processing steps known as "the pipeline."

While many parts of the pipeline shown here are automated for faster processing and faster refunds, people are involved every step of the way.

Putting these statistics further into perspective, of the 93.1 million individual tax returns filed only 1.8 million were actually examined. This represents about 2 percent of all individual returns filed. Assuming that very few of these 1.8 million individual returns were 1040As, the percentage of individual tax returns examined increases to 3.2 percent.

*Conclusion:* The statistical chance of being audited is quite small.

## The process of selecting a tax return for examination

The first step in the process of selecting a tax return for examination is its initial processing. (See "Processing Pipeline" illustration.)

The IRS computers select tax returns worthy of examination by means of a scoring system known as the Discriminant Income Function (DIF). Each return is assigned a DIF score which measures the probability of error. Accordingly, the higher the chance of error the greater the chance of audit.

Recently, the IRS initiated a new method to group individual returns for examination selection purposes. In addition to the DIF classification the IRS uses a factor called Total Positive Income (TPI). TPI is the sum of all positive income values appearing on a return, with losses treated as zero. The TPI replaces the previously used adjusted gross income (AGI) method of classifying returns. One reason for the change was that tax shelter losses were placing otherwise high income taxpayers into the same category as lower income taxpayers. These high income taxpayers were being "lost" in the classification process under the old system of using adjusted gross income as a selection criterion.

### The human element

In addition to the sophisticated computer selection formula the IRS further classifies tax returns manually. Each district maintains a classification division. Its function, among others, is to screen the tax returns sent by the service center to determine if they are truly worthy of audit. For example, an unusual deduction may be adequately explained by a statement which was included with the tax return. Since the computer does not read statements or notes which accompany the return the explanation was not considered in the first screening process.

*Tip:* Attach notes explaining anything unusual to your client's return. Staple copies of receipts for charitable contributions of noncash donations. It may prevent an audit.

**What else do the classifiers look for?**

According to the Internal Revenue Manual, classifiers are supposed to consider the following aspects of a tax return before deciding that a return selected by the computer is unworthy of audit:

1) Is the income sufficient to support the exemptions claimed?
2) Does the refund appear to be out of line when considering the gross income and exemptions?
3) Is there a possibility that income may be underreported?
4) Could the taxpayer be moonlighting, earning tips, or have other types of income not subject to withholding tax?
5) Is the taxpayer engaged in the type of business or profession normally considered to be more profitable than reflected by the return?
6) Is the taxpayer's yield (net profit) on his investment less than he could have realized by depositing the same amount in a savings account?
7) Is the standard deduction used with high gross and low net income shown on a business schedule?

## What items may "flag" a tax return for audit?

The following is a list of certain deductions which may trigger the computer to select a tax return for an audit. The precise items which are responsible for making the computer think that a particular tax return has a high probability of error is not public record.

1) claiming a deduction for medical insurance and medical expenses without showing insurance reimbursements
2) claiming a deduction for an "unallowable" item, for example, taking a deduction for sales tax paid on a purchase of furniture in addition to the sales tax table deduction
3) claiming a deduction for a charitable contribution of noncash property without attaching a receipt and/or appraisal to the tax return
4) claiming a deduction for a casualty loss
5) claiming large deductions for travel and entertainment expenses
6) claiming substantial amount of interest expense in relationship to the amount of income reported

### Filing an extension may prevent an audit

It can't be proven, but an informal survey conducted by the author revealed that those people who filed tax returns on October 15 (the last day to file if a second extension is granted) were less likely to be selected for a tax audit than those who filed on April 15. A possible explanation is that the computer has already filled its quota for the year by such a late date.

# CHAPTER 4

# How to Handle
# Office Audit Examinations

An office audit examination normally requires that the taxpayer or his representative bring specifically requested books and records to the local IRS office. The scope of the office audit examination is generally limited to two or three areas on the tax return.

The employee who conducts the audit is called a tax auditor. He or she is likely to have a less sophisticated knowledge of the tax law than do revenue agents who conduct field audits. However, tax auditors should not be underestimated, for they gain a particular expertise in those issues which they continually examine. In fact, tax auditors are even reputed to become quite imaginative in their interpretation of the Code (naturally, it is in the government's favor).

Presenting a client's case in an office audit involves evaluating your client's position and then choosing the appropriate strategy which will help to increase your client's odds of emerging from the audit with as little financial harm as possible. This chapter will cover the following areas to aid the practitioner in implementing the proper strategy:

1. **Correspondence examinations**
   - When should you request that an audit be handled through the mail?
   - Which issues won't the IRS handle by correspondence?
   - Getting a correspondence examination even though the IRS has set an appointment for an office interview

2. **On-site examinations**
   - Why an on-site examination may increase your client's odds of getting a better bottom line result

3. **Office interviews**
   - How are audits initiated?
   - Appointments
   - Transferring a case to another office

- Repetitive audits
- Scope of examination
- Examination of a prior year return
- Handling an office audit

---

## Correspondence examinations

The *Internal Revenue Manual* states that correspondence examinations should be used when information concerning questionable items can be readily furnished by mail and the facts and circumstances indicate that the taxpayer can effectively correspond with the Service. Examples of items which can be verified by correspondence are itemized deductions for interest, taxes, contributions, medical and dental expenses, and simple miscellaneous deductions such as union dues and small tools.

It would be advisable for the practitioner to request that an examination be handled by correspondence in those situations in which the client has complete documentation for the questioned items. For example, if $500 worth of contributions were claimed on the tax return then the client should be able to verify $500 with receipts or cancelled checks.

A significant advantage of the correspondence examination is that it saves time. There is no time wasted in traveling to the IRS office or waiting to be interviewed by a tax auditor.

Correspondence examinations may be advantageous if your client has deducted something which constitutes a "gray area" under the law. The tax auditor, reviewing the information you have submitted, will not have the opportunity to ask you any questions. Therefore, if no questions can be asked he or she may not want to bother initiating an additional letter requesting further information. Rather, the auditor may just accept the substantiation provided and close the case.

During the course of an office interview the tax auditor is required to ask whether all federal tax returns which were required to be filed by the taxpayer have, in fact, been filed. In addition, tax auditors are required to ask whether the taxpayer has any bartering income. If there exists any reason why the answer to either of these questions may be detrimental to your client's interests, a correspondence examination would avoid these questions.

From the practitioner's point of view the correspondence examination has two major drawbacks. In those situations where all of the deductions cannot be verified by receipts or where certain expenses are contested by the tax auditor as being unallowable, the practitioner will not have an effective means to persuade the auditor that his client's tax return is correct as filed. In correspondence examinations the tax auditor cannot hear, and so perhaps accept, credible oral testimony or otherwise be favorably influenced by the practitioner's account of why an amount that was deducted on the tax return is really correct even though every dollar cannot be verified with receipts. Arguing a point of law via correspondence with a tax auditor is generally a time-consuming and futile exercise. The tax auditor is usually not sophisticated enough to appreciate the merit of an in-depth analysis of the law or even interested in reading your letter if it is more than two or three paragraphs long. Accordingly, the lack of personal contact could work to the detriment of your client.

A second drawback of the correspondence examination is that it permits the tax auditor to review the substantiation you have submitted at his convenience and refer back to it as many times as he chooses. During the discussion of how to handle an office interview it will be shown that it is normally not to a client's advantage to have the auditor look at a particular bill more than once. The more time he has to study something the greater are the chances that he may find something wrong.

The *Internal Revenue Manual* lists the following types of issues which should not be handled by correspondence but, rather, by an office interview:

1) dependency exemptions unless they clearly meet the criteria for the correspondence method

2) income from tips, pensions, annuities, rents, royalties, and determination of gains such as capital or ordinary income

3) deductions for employees' business expenses

4) deductions for bad debts

5) determination of basis of property

6) complex miscellaneous deductions such as casualty and theft losses requiring determinations of fair market value; education expenses, and fellowships and scholarships

7) salaried employees whose occupations lend themselves to possible outside employment

8) taxpayers whose incomes are low in relation to their financial responsibilities as indicated by entries on the return (number of dependents, interest expense, etc.)

Suppose that your client receives a letter notifying him that an office interview has been scheduled. How can the practitioner have the audit handled by correspondence if such a decision is deemed appropriate? Simple—merely mail the requested information to the IRS. Although it is possible, it is unlikely that they will request an office interview if they have all the requested documentation in their possession. The following letter should be mailed, return receipt requested:

[Date]

Internal Revenue Service
Central Files
120 Church Street
New York, N.Y. 10008

Re: John & Mary Brown
111-22-3456
19__–1040

Gentlemen:

Enclosed find a Power of Attorney.

The above captioned taxpayer has been scheduled for an appointment on March 3. The deductions claimed for contributions and medical expenses were selected for examination (copy of appointment letter enclosed).

In order to save time and expense for both the taxpayer and the government we have made copies of cancelled checks and receipts for all contributions and medical expenses deducted on the taxpayer's 19__ tax return.

Thank you for your attention to this matter.

Sincerely,

Allen Scott, Esq.

## On-site examinations

Subject to supervisory approval, a tax auditor may conduct an examination at the taxpayer's place of business or other location where the books and records pertinent to an examination are located or maintained. Requests by taxpayers or practitioners for an on-site examination will not be granted unless the books and records are too voluminous to be brought into an IRS office or other circumstances exist which clearly indicate that the examination cannot be satisfactorily completed otherwise.

An advantage of having a tax auditor conduct an on-site audit is that you will save time by having the tax auditor come to your office. Additionally, you may have a psychological advantage in that the auditor is not accustomed to conducting examinations outside of his own office; his established routine has been interrupted and the practitioner may be able to capitalize on any apprehension on the tax auditor's part.

## Office interviews

### Initiating the examination

An office interview is usually initiated by an appointment letter (see accompanying example) mailed to the taxpayer informing him that his return is being examined and requesting him to bring certain information and records to an IRS office.

### Appointments

*What should you do if the appointment date is inconvenient?* For various reasons it may be necessary to postpone the appointment date set by the IRS. Generally, two postponements will be granted without any problem. (The number of postponements granted varies between offices—each office has its own policy but one postponement can always be made.)

*How do you request a postponement?* If this is your first request for a postponement all you have to do is call the telephone number on the appointment letter and tell the clerk that you want the audit rescheduled. Sometimes they will ask you why you want the audit postponed. The following are all acceptable reasons:

1) you have another appointment scheduled for that day
2) the client needs time to gather the necessary books and records
3) the audit is for a new client and you need time to review the books and records

Some IRS offices require the practitioner to send in a written request for a postponement if there has been a previous cancellation.

*When should you request a postponement?* Suppose your client informs you that an appointment has been scheduled for a date two weeks from today. Should you cancel the appointment the day you find out about it or should you wait until a day before the appointment to cancel? If you call immediately to reschedule the appointment a new one will be set within two weeks or so of the original date.

**Internal Revenue Service**
District Director

Department of the Treasury

**Date:**

▷

**Tax Year(s):**

**Day and Date of Appointment:**

**Time:**

**Place of Appointment:**

**Room Number:**

**Contact Telephone Number:**

**Appointment Clerk:**

---

    We are examining your Federal income tax return for the above year(s) and find we need additional information to verify your correct tax. We have, therefore, scheduled the above appointment for you.

    If you filed a joint return, either you or your spouse may keep the appointment or you may have an attorney, a certified public accountant, an individual enrolled to practice before the Internal Revenue Service, or a qualified unenrolled individual represent or accompany you. If you are not present, however, your representative must have written authorization to represent you. Form 2848-D, Authorization and Declaration, may be used for this purpose and if your representative does not have copies of this form, they may be obtained from one of our offices. Also, any other individual, even though not qualified to represent you, may accompany you as a witness and assist in establishing the facts in your case.

About the records needed to examine your return—

    We would appreciate your bringing to our office the records you used as a basis for the items checked at the end of this letter so we can discuss them with you.

    The enclosed Information Guides will help you decide what records to bring. It will save you time if you keep together the records related to each item. Please bring this letter also.

    The law requires taxpayers to substantiate all items affecting their tax liabilities when requested to do so. If you do not keep this appointment or do not arrange another, we will have to proceed on the basis of available return information.

About the examination and your appeal rights—

    We realize some taxpayers may be concerned about an examination of their tax returns. We hope we can relieve any concern you may have by briefly explaining why we examine, what our procedures are, and what your appeal rights are if you do not agree with the results.

    We examine returns to verify the correctness of income, exemptions, credits, and deductions. We find that the vast majority of taxpayers are honest and have nothing to fear from an examination of their tax returns. An examination of such a

(over)

Letter 889(DO) (Rev. 8–78)

taxpayer's return does not suggest a suspicion of dishonesty or criminal liability. In many cases, no change is made to the tax liability reported or the taxpayer receives a refund. However, if taxpayers do not substantiate items when requested, we have to act on available return information that may be incomplete. That is why your cooperation is so important.

We will go over your return and records and then explain any proposals to change your tax liability. We want you to understand fully any recommended increase or decrease in your tax, so please don't hesitate to ask questions about anything not clear to you.

If changes are recommended and you agree with them, we will ask you to sign an agreement form. By signing you will indicate your agreement to the amount shown on the form as additional tax you owe, or as a refund due you, and simplify closing your case.

Most people agree with our proposals, and we believe this is because they find our examiners to be fair. But you don't have to agree. If you choose, we can easily arrange for you to have your case given further consideration. You need only tell the examiner you want to discuss the issue informally with a supervisor, and we will do our best to arrange a meeting immediately.

In addition, you may request the Office of Regional Director of Appeals, which is separate from the district office, to consider your case. We will be glad to explain this procedure and also how to appeal outside the Service to the courts.

We will also be glad to furnish you a copy of our Publication 556, Audit of Returns, Appeal Rights, and Claims for Refund, which explains in detail our procedures covering examinations of tax returns and appeal rights. You can get a copy of this publication by writing us for it or by asking for it when you come to our office.

About repetitive examinations—

We try to avoid unnecessary repetitive examinations of the same items, but this occasionally happens. Therefore, if your tax return was examined in either of the 2 previous years for the same items checked on this letter and the examination resulted in no change to your tax liability, please notify the appointment clerk as soon as possible. The examination of your return will then be suspended pending a review of our files to determine whether it should proceed.

About your appointment—

Your appointment is the next step unless, of course, you notify us of a repetitive examination as outlined in the preceding paragraph. If the date or time of the appointment is inconvenient, please call the appointment clerk to arrange a more suitable time. We will consider the appointment confirmed if we do not hear from you at least 7 days before the scheduled date.

If you have any questions, please contact the appointment clerk whose name and telephone number are shown in the heading of this letter.

Thank you for your cooperation.

Sincerely yours,


District Director

Enclosures:
Information Guides
Publication 876, Privacy Act Notice

Letter 889(DO) (Rev. 8–78)

*Please bring the records to support the following items reported on your tax return and its schedules:*

| | | |
|---|---|---|
| ☐ Alimony Payments | ☐ Contributions | ☐ Moving Expenses |
| ☐ Automobile Expenses | ☐ Education Expenses | ☐ Rental Income and Expenses |
| ☐ Bad Debts | ☐ Employee Business Expenses | ☐ Sale or Exchange of Residence |
| ☐ Capital Gains and Losses | ☐ Exemptions | ☐ Sick Pay or Disability Income Exclusion |
| ☐ Casualty Losses | ☐ Interest Expense | ☐ Taxes |
| ☐ Child and Dependent Care Expenses | ☐ Medical and Dental Expenses | ☐ Uniforms, Equipment, and Tools |
| ☐ | ☐ | ☐ |
| ☐ | | |

*Please bring evidence such as accounting ledgers and journals, bank statements, and canceled checks to support the following items shown on Schedule C.*

| | | |
|---|---|---|
| ☐ All Business Expenses | ☐ Insurance | ☐ Taxes |
| ☐ Bad Debts | ☐ Interest | ☐ Travel and Entertainment |
| ☐ Cost of Goods Sold | ☐ Rents | ☐ |
| ☐ Depreciation | ☐ Repairs | ☐ |
| ☐ Gross Receipts | ☐ Salaries and Wages | ☐ |

*Please bring evidence such as accounting ledgers and journals, bank statements, and canceled checks to support the following items shown on Schedule F:*

| | | |
|---|---|---|
| ☐ All Farm Expenses | ☐ Insurance | ☐ Repairs and Maintenance |
| ☐ Depreciation | ☐ Inventories | ☐ Supplies Purchased |
| ☐ Feed and Seed Purchased | ☐ Labor Hired | ☐ Taxes |
| ☐ Fertilizers, Lime | ☐ Machine Hire | ☐ |
| ☐ Gross Receipts | ☐ Other Farm Income | ☐ |

**Letter 889(DO) (Rev. 8–78)**

However, if you wait until the day before the scheduled appointment to cancel it is likely that a new date will not be set for six to eight weeks. The reason for the difference in time is that the IRS will have sent out other appointment letters and will have booked those time slots for their new appointments. If the cancellation is made immediately those new appointment letters will probably not yet have been mailed.

*Should appointments be delayed?* The general rule when dealing with the IRS is that the longer it takes to complete a case the better are the chances that the person you are dealing with will be willing to settle. This general rule is subject to various exceptions which will be explained later in this book.

With this general rule in mind there is no reason why the practitioner should feel compelled to drop all his other work and rush to the IRS office as soon as he discovers that one of his clients is being audited. There is nothing wrong in postponing an appointment if the date set is not convenient.

*The best times to reschedule an appointment.* There are days and times of day to which it may be advantageous to reschedule an appointment. At certain times tax auditors may be more anxious to close a case than at other times and will therefore be more willing to compromise issues. The following is a list of the suggested days and times and the reasons they may be advantageous:

1) *Afternoon before a holiday.* The last thing the tax auditor (or maybe even the practitioner) cares about at that time is the tax audit. Both of you will probably be eager to close the case and start the holiday.

2) *Last week of the month.* Because of production quotas (not dollar quotas) the tax auditor may be anxious to close the case so that it can be submitted and credited to him statistically for that month.

3) *10:30 A.M.* If an appointment is scheduled for 10:30 and you arrive at that time the case will probably not be assigned to a tax auditor until 10:45. This means that the audit will be concluding sometime during lunch hour. If the tax auditor is anxious to go out for lunch he may be willing to settle the case just so that you leave his office and not discuss the adjustments with him anymore.

*When should you not respond to an appointment letter?* Normally, if there is no response to an office audit contact letter the questioned items will be disallowed and a ninety-day letter will be issued. (A ninety-day letter requires that you file a tax court petition within ninety days or else an assessment will be made.)

Occasionally, it may be to a practitioner's advantage not to respond to an office audit appointment letter, and contest any disallowance at a later date. The following are situations where special consideration should be given to not showing up for the audit.

1) *Potential fraud cases.* When the practitioner feels that his client's fraudulent activity may be uncovered if the IRS has an opportunity to question certain areas of the tax return it would be better to suffer an assessment than risk a fraud referral. The fraudulent activity may first be made known to the practitioner at the time of the audit. Practitioners who are not attorneys would be well advised to seek the advice of counsel at this time as no client privilege may exist.

2) *Protecting prior- and subsequent-year returns.* If a taxpayer has deducted an item which is in a gray area the examining tax auditor may try to determine whether the taxpayer has deducted the same expense on a prior-year return which is still open under the statute of limitations or on a subsequently filed return. If such a deduction were taken it would be disallowed also. By not responding to the IRS appointment letter the tax return originally under audit will be summarily adjusted and the case will, for all intents and purposes, be closed. Accordingly, the deductions claimed on the prior or subsequently filed returns will not be uncovered (unless they should be independently selected for audit). If it is determined that the adjustment should be contested the practitioner may always file a tax court petition. This strategy might permit enough time to elapse on previously filed returns to remove them from exposure because of the statute of limitations.

3) *Avoiding questions.* All tax auditors must ask whether all federal tax returns which are required to be filed have, in fact, been filed. If your client has failed to file in a prior year this fact may be uncovered at an audit. A question also asked is whether income from bartering activity was reported on the tax return. These questions would not have to be answered if the practitioner does not appear.

### Transferring a case to another office

Since an office audit requires the practitioner to go to an IRS office to represent his client it is normally in the client's interest to have the examination conducted at a location convenient to the practitioner's office (less travel time will be spent and correspondingly less billing time for the client). In most IRS districts there are numerous satellite offices, called "posts of duties" which contain office audit groups.

What procedure must the practitioner follow if he wants to transfer his client's case to an IRS office from the one to which it was originally assigned?

1)  Call the telephone number on the appointment letter and inform the clerk that the date set for your client's audit should be cancelled. Tell the clerk that you will be requesting that the case be transferred to another office. Don't volunteer any reasons for wanting the case transferred since it is almost never in anybody's interest to volunteer information. If a reason is requested the following reasons, in this order, are acceptable:

    A)  the taxpayer works in the general location of the IRS office to which you want the case transferred

    B)  the books and records are located in the general location of the IRS office to which you want the case transferred

    C)  your firm is representing the taxpayer and the IRS office located near your office would be more suitable as to save expense for the client

Always insist that the transfer request is for the convenience of the taxpayer and not for the representative. For some reason the IRS is averse to accommodating the practitioner.

*Note:* Always obtain the name of the person to whom you are speaking.

2)  The clerk will tell you that a request for a transfer must be made in writing and must be accompanied by a Power of Attorney. Tell the clerk that no action should be taken on the case for about three weeks because that is how long it will take for you to send a Power of Attorney to your client and have it returned.

3)  Mail a Power of Attorney to your client and inform him that it must be signed (by his spouse also if it is a joint return) and returned to your office as soon as possible. It is a good idea to include a stamped, self-addressed envelope with the Power of Attorney to insure that the client takes care of the matter immediately.

4)  After the client sends you back the Power of Attorney the following letter should be written, return receipt requested.

[Date]

Ms. Jones
Internal Revenue Service
Central Files
120 Church Street
New York, N.Y. 10008

Re: John & Mary Brown
111-22-3456
19__–1040

Dear Ms. Jones:

Enclosed find a Power of Attorney.

This letter shall serve to confirm our telephone conversation in which I requested that the above captioned taxpayer's appointment originally scheduled for June 1 at 9:30 be cancelled.

It is requested that the taxpayer's audit be transferred to the Bronx office as both the taxpayer works in the Bronx and the taxpayer's records are located there. Changing the location of the audit will be for the convenience of the taxpayer, enabling him to attend any meetings, should it become necessary.

Thank you for your attention to this request.

Sincerely,

Allen Scott, Esq.

If the request to transfer the case is approved the IRS will mail you a form informing you that the case has been transferred. In about four to six weeks the new office will either call you to set a new appointment date or send you another appointment letter.

In the event that the request should be denied the practitioner should ascertain who denied the request and for what reasons. On occasion, the IRS office to which you want the case transferred may have a backlog of work and will not accept transferred cases. This real reason is rarely given as the reason for the denial of the request.

If you are unable to convince the clerk to change his or her mind about the refusal to change the place of the examination ask to speak to his or her supervisor.

That person will be the manager of central files. Central files is the division that coordinates office audit appointments and maintains a control of office audit cases. The next person in the chain of command will probably be the branch chief.

In the event that you are still unsuccessful after speaking to all these people it is best to give up your protest. However, it is still possible to accomplish your initial goal of not having to spend time traveling to an inconvenient IRS location. Simply send a letter to the appointment clerk with photocopies of the documentation required to substantiate the items which were checked off on the appointment letter. This course of action may not be practical where voluminous records must be copied or where a personal meeting would be in your client's benefit. (For instance, where the records are incomplete and you will have to provide an explanation for missing amounts.)

The following letter should be mailed, return receipt requested.

[Date]

Ms. Jones
Internal Revenue Service
Central Files
120 Church Street
New York, N.Y. 10008

Re: John & Mary Brown
111-22-3456
19___-1040

Dear Ms. Jones:

The above captioned taxpayer has an appointment scheduled for June 9 at 9:30.

Enclosed find photocopies of the documentation needed to substantiate the items selected for examination on the appointment letter (a copy of which is enclosed).

It is requested that the tax auditor assigned to this case call me if there are any questions.

Thank you for your attention to this matter.

Sincerely,

Allen Scott, Esq.

## Repetitive audits

The *Internal Revenue Manual* provides that a taxpayer shall not be subjected to needless and repetitive examinations.

*What constitutes a repetitive audit?*

1) The rule applies only to individual tax returns (1040s).

2) The same issue(s) must have been examined in either of the two preceding years and that audit must have resulted in no change or a small tax change (deficiency or overassessment).

3) Tax returns selected for examination under TCMP (Taxpayer's Compliance Measurement Program) do not qualify.

4) If both of the tax returns for the two preceding years were examined for the issue(s) in question and examination of one resulted in a small tax change and the other required a substantive adjustment, the current-year examination will be continued.

*How is the repetitive audit procedure initiated?* The practitioner must inform the examining tax auditor that his or her client's situation qualifies under the repetitive audit guidelines in the *Manual*. The tax auditor must then conclude the interview. (Do not show the tax auditor any records for the current year.) The tax auditor will then ask you for the following documents:

1) a copy of the appointment letter from the prior year indicating which items were selected for audit

2) a copy of the no-change letter or audit adjustment

3) a copy of the prior year's tax return

Normally, these items can be given to the tax auditor although your client's rights will not be jeopardized if you tell the tax auditor that you don't have the documents and that he should requisition them from the Service Center files.

*Note:* If the prior year's file is requested from the Service Center then the tax auditor has a chance to see other areas which were examined and/or commented upon which would otherwise not come to his attention. Therefore, unless compelling reasons exist it is usually advantageous to give the tax auditor the requested information.

The *Manual* provisions in the area of repetitive audits are quite limited. As such, there may be situations in which you feel that an audit is unwarranted because of a previous examination but there exists no specific *Manual* provision which can be used to convince the tax auditor.

1) Suppose a prior year's audit (within two years) covered contributions, medical, and business expenses in which there was an adjustment made only to contributions. If in the current year the IRS wants to verify the same three categories the practitioner should argue that only contributions are subject to examination again since that was the area in which a previous change was made. It is important not to let the tax auditor or his group manager intimidate you if they respond that "The *Manual* doesn't provide for this situation so we will audit all the items again." You can argue that the spirit of the repetitive audit provision will be violated if your client has to produce the same documentation again for items which were previously accepted. If you are not successful with this argument then you should request a meeting with the branch chief and then the chief of the examination division. Finally, it may be appropriate to request technical advice from the national office (see Chapter 12).

2) Similarly, if the prior-year audit covered three items and the current year audit covers the same three items (which were accepted the last time the return was examined) plus an additional issue, the practitioner should request that the audit be limited to the new issue.

## Scope of examination

When a tax return is selected for office audit the examination is normally limited to two or three items. The majority of returns have already been "classified." This means that a senior tax auditor has previously screened the tax return and has selected those categories of deductions in which he feels a potential disallowance may exist because the amount appears large or unusual. Unless significant reasons exist the tax auditor assigned a return will limit his examination to the items previously selected for him to review. Where the tax auditor seeks to raise a new issue, approval must be secured from his group manager. If a tax auditor surprises you with questions about a new issue your response should be that you are , prepared to discuss only the issues indicated on the appointment letter. Furthermore, you should insist that if the tax auditor wants to raise a new issue you want to have a conference with his group manager. (Your reasons may include harassment, that the issue was examined and accepted on a prior-year audit, the issue is immaterial, etc.)

Regardless of the scope of an office audit interview the tax auditor must ascertain whether the taxpayer has filed all federal tax returns required to have been filed. What should you say when the tax auditor asks you if your client has filed all returns and (1) you really don't know, or (2) you know all returns have not been filed?

If you don't know you should say "I really don't know—I'll ask him [the client] about it." If you know all returns have not been filed merely respond "I'll ask him about it." Under no circumstances should the practitioner ever lie. However, since failure to file a tax return is a crime, the practitioner should not voluntarily disclose information which may be used by the government, at a later proceeding, as evidence against the taxpayer. Ninety-nine out of 100 times an answer such as "I'll ask him about it" will be acceptable and will be interpreted by the tax auditor as meaning that the taxpayer *did* file all required tax returns. If the question should ever be raised by the tax auditor again at a later occasion you should repeat that you'll ask your client about it. At this point an attorney should be consulted as to whether the answer to such a question could prove incriminating to your client.

## Examination of a prior-year tax return

Tax auditors may request that a taxpayer bring copies of returns from prior years to the office audit interview; however, the extension of an examination to a prior year will not be made unless a sound basis exists for doing so and only with supervisory approval.

Unless special reasons exist to do so it is normally not to your client's advantage voluntarily to show a tax auditor a return which is still open under the statute of limitations. If a return has been requested and you do not want to show it to the tax auditor merely say "I forgot it." The tax auditor then has two choices. He can forget the matter (which is usually the case) or he can requisition the return in question from the Service Center. The requisition process is quite time-consuming and will prevent the tax auditor from closing the case until it is received. Additionally, prior-year returns must be separately listed for internal statistical purposes which requires the tax auditor to fill out a special report each month. If the tax auditor is just curious, the chances are that he won't do anything. If he really suspects something he'll get the return anyway—so why make it any easier for him?

(Remember, if there is a problem then the longer it takes to complete the case the better are the chances of an amicable settlement.)

## Handling an office audit

*Step #1: The client's telephone call.* Generally, your client will call you with the news that he or she has just received an appointment letter from the IRS and that he's quite upset. After assuring the client that he has nothing to worry about since he has retained you, the following information should be requested:

1) date the appointment is scheduled
2) the time the appointment is scheduled
3) at what IRS office the audit will take place
4) the appointment clerk's telephone number
5) the year(s) under audit
6) the items requested for audit
7) the appointment letter itself

*Step #2: Changing the appointment date or the location of the audit.* If the date of the appointment or the office location is inconvenient then the practitioner should request a change by calling the appointment clerk. (See those sections of this chapter dealing with appointments and transferring a case to another office.)

*Step #3: Preparing for the audit.* The following documentation should be gathered and reviewed prior to the appointment date:

1) Obtain a Power of Attorney from your client. The Power of Attorney should be mailed with a stamped, self-addressed envelope to assure that your client will return it promptly. If the tax return under audit is a joint return then instruct your client that the spouse must also sign the Power of Attorney.

2) Tell the client that he or she must either bring in or mail in all their records pertaining to the issues selected for examination.

3) Review all documentation to determine what is missing and what should be done about it. For instance, can missing bills be obtained by writing to someone, do certain invoices need further explanation, etc.

In travel and entertainment audits, a letter from the client's employer is usually required to show that the business expenses which are being deducted were required to be incurred as a condition of employment and that no reimbursement was received. The following is an example of an effective letter which covers those situations in which there was reimbursement for some expenses and those cases where no reimbursement was received:

A.B.C. COMPANY, INC.

[Date]

IRS
New York, N.Y.

Gentlemen:

During 19__, Mr. Jones was employed by our company in the capacity of [name position, e.g. sales manager]. As a condition of his employment he was required to incur expenses for business travel and entertainment for which he received no reimbursement.

Sincerely,

A.B.C. Company, Inc.
Jim Smith, President

4) Schedule all receipts and cancelled checks so that the amount of verification you have ties into the amount claimed on the tax return. What happens if you don't have all the receipts which are needed? Prepare a schedule with all you have and list the balance as "Other". For example:

SCHEDULE OF CONTRIBUTIONS

| | |
|---|---|
| St. Mary's Church | $350.00 |
| YMCA | 25.00 |
| Red Cross | 150.00 |
| Other | 115.00 |
| | $640.00 |

A separate schedule should be prepared for each issue requested. If appropriate, this schedule can be handed to the tax auditor. The preparation of the schedule not only makes it easier for you during the audit but it also tends to lend credibility to the deduction taken since the tax auditor will be able to see immediately how the number deducted on the tax return was arrived at.

5) If important information is missing it is advisable to call the client and inform him or her that they must try to furnish you with the missing details. If necessary, the client should be asked to come to your office so that you may interview him.

6) See Appendix II for the suggested details a taxpayer should bring to an audit for different issues.

*Step #4: The day of the appointment.*

1) Get to the IRS early—first come is usually first served. The IRS usually schedules more appointments for a given time than they have staff to handle because they know that some people will not respond to the appointment letter.

2) Hand the receptionist your client's appointment letter and then sit down until your name is called.

*Step #5: Meeting the tax auditor.*

1) Your name will eventually be called and you will be escorted to the tax auditor's desk.

2) If the tax auditor you are assigned to happens to be someone you had on a previous occasion and can't work with because he is unreasonable, demand that the case be assigned to another person. Do not even sit down. If there should be any problem in fulfilling your request ask to speak to the group manager and then to the branch chief. (Since office audits are usually conducted in an open office setting, with partitions for limited privacy, it may be advantageous to speak *very loud* if the person to whom you are making the request should take a negative position. The IRS hates a taxpayer or his representative to start a commotion.)

3) If you do not know the person you are assigned to either personally or by reputation then no request should be made to change the auditor. Introduce yourself to the tax auditor and hand him or her the Power of Attorney.

4) At this point you should not say anything unless you are asked a question. Don't volunteer to show the auditor any documentation before it is requested or otherwise volunteer any information. (If you want to talk about the weather, last night's ball game, etc. it is okay as long as the subject does not concern your client.)

*Tactic:* Instead of being friendly, sometimes it is effective if you just stare at the tax auditor and do not speak until spoken to. This will normally make the tax auditor somewhat nervous—no matter how experienced he or she may be. If you create a tense atmosphere it is possible that the auditor will not want to spend more time than is absolutely necessary to review documentation and will be anxious for you to leave.

*Step #6: During the audit.*

1) If a question is asked and you are unsure why the question was asked or what the tax auditor will do once he or she receives an answer, you must proceed very cautiously. In order to protect your client's interest it is imperative that you know what is going on at all times. If a question is puzzling simply ask "Why do you want to know that?" Most times the tax auditor will tell you why. Then you can respond accordingly. However, if the tax auditor says "I just want to know," or "I don't have to tell you the reason," simply respond that his or her question is an improper one and that if he or she won't tell you why the question was asked then you'll have to find out the answer (don't say "I won't tell you the answer"). This type of response is effective since it puts the issue to bed, at least temporarily. Also, the tax auditor may never ask the question again.

2) The practitioner must not be afraid that his attempt to intimidate an auditor will hurt his client's position. More damage can be done by being overly cooperative. Of course, in most situations it will be in your client's best interest to cooperate and maintain a cordial relationship with the tax auditor. However, it must always be remembered that practice before the IRS is adversarial in nature and as such the client's interest must come first. If you can disrupt the tax auditor to the point where he becomes emotionally upset, to the point that it interferes with the performance of his work, issues which may have otherwise been raised may not be raised.

3) During the course of the audit numerous questions will be raised by the tax auditor. How the practitioner answers these questions may make the difference between your client having to pay the IRS money or not having to pay. It cannot be emphasized too much that the general rule is never to

volunteer information. With this in mind the practitioner should listen carefully to each question asked and answer only what is asked. Tax auditors, like most persons, do not usually ask all-encompassing questions. Therefore, it is possible to answer most questions with just a few words. Make sure that all answers given do not contain information or new facts. If the tax auditor does not ask the right questions to elicit the information he needs to resolve the case in the government's favor, then the practitioner should not offer any assistance. Answers which are ambiguous can often work to the advantage of your client. Many times a tax auditor may give your client the benefit of the doubt or not even raise an issue if you haven't given him the ammunition he needs in the form of the answer he was seeking.

It must be stressed that under no circumstances should the practitioner ever offer false or misleading information in response to a tax auditor's question.

4) When presenting the tax auditor with bills, receipts or other documentation the practitioner should hand the auditor one document at a time. After he has reviewed each item you should take it back, put it away and then show him another document. By proceeding in this fashion the tax auditor does not have the opportunity to refer back to any specific piece of documentation unless he specifically asks for it again. The likelihood that he will remember similar dates or amounts (if these items should present a problem to the client) will be reduced.

A distracting tactic that can be used to create anxiety is for the practitioner to say "I already showed you that receipt—why do you want to look at it again?" if he is asked to produce something for a second time. This tactic should be used only in those situations in which the requested piece of documentation is harmless. If there is some problem with it you won't want to draw extra attention to the bill or receipt.

*Step #7: Discussing proposed adjustments.* It is normally to your advantage to try to have the tax auditor tell you what, if any, adjustments he is thinking of after he has reviewed each area on his list. You will then have the opportunity to challenge him before he goes on to other areas. The purpose of raising the challenge is to lock him into a position so that it will be difficult for him to change his mind at a later point. For example, if he agrees that a particular disallowance will be $500, you know that if you then tell him that you forgot to deduct a $1,000 expense when the return was prepared, he will not be able to tell you his $500 adjustment should really be $1,500.

There is also a strategic reason for discussing each proposed adjustment as it is developed. The practitioner can spend substantial time arguing about an irrelevant adjustment and thereby reduce the amount of time the tax auditor can spend on other items he will be reviewing.

The practitioner should keep in mind that the goal of the tax auditor is to close the case. No prizes are given out for assessment of large deficiencies against taxpayers. The auditor will be evaluated on the basis of the issues developed and the time spent to develop and resolve those issues. Therefore, everything you do as a representative for your client should be geared toward closing the case on favorable terms. Since closing the case is the one end that both you and the tax auditor are seeking you should constantly remind him of that fact if it appears that more time than necessary is being spent on the case. (A "normal" office audit should last no more than two or three hours.)

If the tax auditor should propose an adjustment and you are unable to convince him of the merits of your argument, then you say "If it is necessary for me to further prove my point then I will bring my client back with me next time." Most tax auditors do not relish sitting through a session with an irate taxpayer as he tries to prove his story. This may be the added incentive the tax auditor needs to compromise one or more issues.

Tax auditors will make "deals." Although no official IRS publication will admit to it, this is a fact that every practitioner with any degree of IRS experience will confirm. The term "deal" does not indicate anything illegal or improper. It means a compromise on an issue. For instance, the tax auditor may raise three issues knowing that one of those issues is very weak (the taxpayer could not prove a charitable deduction but he could get a receipt if he was willing to spend three hours writing letters). The tax auditor knows that a receipt could be obtained but raises the issue anyway so as to provide himself with leverage on a stronger issue. It is not appropriate to say "What kind of deal can we work out?" Rather, the practitioner should approach the proposed adjustments by offering explanations (no matter how feeble) as to why certain issues he wants traded should be allowed. The tax auditor will normally be sophisticated enough to know what you are suggesting. For example, you might say "I'm quite sure that my client would agree to issue number one but would fight you on issue number two," or "I agree that issue number one is correct but my client could ultimately win at least fifty percent of issue number two."

If a tax auditor is absolutely wrong about an issue and refuses to change his or her mind then you may request that his or her group manager be called into the discussion. Requesting that a group manager intervene should only be done where there is exposure in no other area of the examination. For instance, if the tax auditor allowed other items which are "borderline" you may be running the risk of having the group manager review those areas as well.

Try to come into the audit with some item that was not deducted on the tax return because of an oversight on the preparer's part (make sure that it can be fully verified). Bring up this item after you listen to the tax auditor's explanation of the proposed adjustments. If you bring it up in the beginning of the examination, the tax auditor will always come up with something extra so as to negate its effectiveness in reducing the proposed deficiency. Don't push for a refund. Rather, use this item as leverage for a no-change outcome.

If the tax auditor says "I'll have to audit other items on the tax return since that area (where extra credit is requested) wasn't examined, then respond by saying "I don't care what you want to audit—you can look at every item on the tax return for all I care!" Normally, the tax auditor will not expand the audit. But if he or she trys to, don't show any more records and immediately request a conference with the group manager.

*Step #8: Taking your client to the audit.* A client should attend an IRS audit only as a last resort to prevent the tax auditor from going ahead with a disallowance of a deduction. Even at this time the practitioner must weigh the consequences of having the client exposed to the tax auditor. Generally, the client's appearance is effective only where the practitioner feels that he has lost credibility with the tax auditor. For example, the auditor may refuse to believe the practitioner's account that certain expenditures made by his client were for business purposes. The client's personal appearance and intimate knowledge of the situation the tax auditor is questioning may restore the credibility needed for the deduction to be allowed.

Before bringing your client to the IRS office he should be thoroughly briefed as to the questions he will be asked and how he should respond. Instruct your client to answer only those questions which are asked and not to volunteer any information.

If the tax auditor should ask a question which you do not want your client to answer just interrupt your client by saying "That is an improper question. I don't think that is any business of the IRS." (Whether it is or not is really irrelevant.)

# CHAPTER 5

# Job Pressures Faced by Revenue Agents: How to Use Them to Your Client's Advantage

Perhaps the greatest pressure faced by the revenue agent is time. Although the IRS is somewhat flexible regarding the number of hours an agent should charge to a case, management does use various guidelines to measure efficiency. This chapter will give the practitioner the ability to determine what these pressures are and how to capitalize on them.

1. Does the revenue agent have a quota?

2. How much time should an agent be charging to a case?

3. How to make an agent charge more time to your client's case than he should

4. Keeping a case activity record

## Does the revenue agent have a quota?

Contrary to what may be generally believed, revenue agents are subject to absolutely no quota with respect to tax dollars they are expected to assess. IRS management is not impressed by an agent who is able to come up with large tax deficiencies.

### Quota for closed cases

There is a quota, so to speak, on the number of cases that the revenue agent is expected to start, examine, and close. Although no actual number of cases is ever mandated, the revenue agent is guided by his own level of experience, the difficulty of issues, and general office policies. If the number of cases in his inventory is too high or if his cases have been open for too long a period, management makes it quite clear that he is not performing at the expected level. Accordingly, pressure is applied by management for the revenue agent to close those cases, whether or not every last dollar of tax has been assessed.

The pressure to close cases is started by the national office as they monitor, through regional offices, the compliance of each district with the annual "audit plan." For example, if the audit plan for the year calls for the examination of 10,000 corporation returns with gross receipts in the range of $10,000–50,000 and it is midyear then the number of cases closed is expected to be at the 5,000 level. If not, then pressure is applied down the chain of command to make sure that the audit plan will be met.

*Inside info:* Group managers are rewarded in proportion to their group's performance, which is measured by their production of closed cases. In fact, the group manager's most important function is to move cases.

### Using this knowledge to your client's advantage

If you have had one meeting with the agent, but for a variety of reasons the next appointment was not scheduled until nine months later, there is a very good chance that the agent is more anxious to close the case than you are!

It is generally in your client's interest if an audit takes a longer time to be completed than a shorter time. The longer the agent has to carry the case in his inventory the greater are the chances that he will be pressured, by his boss, to close the case.

*Tip:* Try to place at least two or three months between appointments! Don't call an agent to check on the status of the case. If he doesn't call you, don't call him to remind him that he hasn't seen you for a few months.

## How much time should an agent be charging to a case?

The following list represents general guidelines which group managers normally apply to their agents. Of course, if a case should be unusually complicated then the time needed to develop and close the case would be greater than the norm.

*Individual tax returns:*

| | |
|---|---|
| No business income | 4-8 hours |
| Schedule C | 8-16 hours |

*Corporation tax returns:*

| | |
|---|---|
| $5 million in assets or less | 16-24 hours |
| Over $5 million in assets | 32+ hours |

*Note:* Eight hours constitutes one day, which includes travel time.

## Keeping a case activity record

Always write down the appointment dates and the approximate amount of time the agent actually spent working on your client's case. This will give you a running total of the amount of time charged to the case (exclusive of time charged at the office) and the amount of time the agent actually spent on audit work.

Use this record as a guide to determine at what point the agent will start being pressured by his group manager to close the case.

# CHAPTER 6

# Deciding Where the Audit
# Should Take Place

The practitioner's ability to control where the audit will be conducted is one of the "little" things which may have an effect on how the client fares. Although there are exceptions where an agent's appreciation of your client's operation may be necessary, by and large it will be better if your client and his business remain nonentities to the agent. This chapter suggests ways to insure that the examination is conducted in the practitioner's office.

1. The importance of conducting the audit in your office

2. How to have the examination in your office

## The importance of conducting the audit in your office

It cannot be emphasized enough—the audit must take place in your office. That does not mean that you should object if the revenue agent wants to see your client's place of business. However, the physical checking of records must be done in your office.

**Why is it so important?**

If the agent conducts the audit at your office he cannot:

1) wander around your client's place of business talking to employees

2) overhear employees talk about various business matters which may provide leads for tax issues

3) observe little things—like pictures in your client's office of him in his airplane, boat, or Rolls-Royce

4) notice that certain employees on the payroll are never in the office, or that employees on the payroll (like your client's wife) who are in the office, do not know where anything is located.

If the revenue agent is at your client's place of business he is likely to ask to see more records (invoices, bills, etc.) since he can walk over to the bookkeeper and ask for them. Even if you tell the agent not to talk to the bookkeeper he will ask you constantly to get more records for him.

### Fairness to your client

If you are present at your client's place of business you will have to bill him for a full day's worth of your time. In fact, there may be times when you do not have to be involved with the agent at all. If the examination was at your office you would be able to generate chargable time to other clients. This is an important fact which must be brought to the agent's attention—and especially important for smaller-scale practitioners who must be very time-conscious.

### Keeping the client away from the agent

You can generally tell the agent that "I'm not letting you talk to my client," and that will be the end of the discussion. However, clients almost always want to talk to the agent, if only to satisfy curiosity, or in an effort to ingratiate themselves. The client may want to tell the agent that business is terrible or any one of a hundred other things, hoping the agent will not propose a large assessment. In fact, the agent is not really interested in your client's problems. The agent is more anxious to ask your client questions to which you haven't provided satisfactory answers. If the client is readily available and likes to talk to the agent (most agents will be *very* friendly and low key with the client), your client will say things which are not in his interest.

## How to have the examination in your office

Even though the *Internal Revenue Manual* requires the agent to conduct the audit at the taxpayer's place of business whenever possible (there is even an Internal Revenue Code section—7605—which states that the time and place of the examination shall be determined by the IRS), the practitioner may still have the examination conducted at his own office.

When you speak to the agent to set up an appointment tell him (don't ask) that you will meet him at your office. If he resists and tells you that he must conduct the audit at your client's office, give all the legitimate reasons why it would not be convenient:

1)  no spare desk space
2)  no privacy (you don't want customers and employees to know the IRS is auditing your client)
3)  accounting records (but not the bills or invoices) are already located in your office

If this doesn't convince him then say: "I will be happy to give you a personal tour of the taxpayer's place of business anytime you want. One office (or factory) is the same as another. Since I don't mind letting you see my client's place of business whenever you want, where the actual audit takes place shouldn't matter."

**What about an agent who still insists on having the audit at your client's place of business?**

Tell the agent that you will write him a letter formally requesting that the examination be conducted at your office for any of the legitimate reasons which may exist.

If, after writing a letter and speaking to the agent's group manager about the situation, you still cannot change their minds, then there is not much you can do about it—short of refusing to turn over any records and going through a summons enforcement proceeding.

# CHAPTER 7

# What You Should Know Before You Meet the Agent

The practitioner may have to make numerous decisions before he ever meets with the revenue agent. Knowing the potential traps that may exist and how to take care of them may mean the difference between success and failure when the time to meet the revenue agent actually arrives. This chapter will cover the following areas:

1. What every client should be told when he has been notified of an audit

2. How much does the IRS know about your client?

3. Determining your client's potential exposure before the audit starts and what to do about it

4. What to do if your client's records are missing or lost

5. What to find out from a client who has started the audit himself and then brings you in on the case

6. What happens if you ignore the letter sent by the revenue agent requesting that you call him to make an appointment?

7. Pros and cons of constantly postponing appointments

8. When does a tax return become "old" and therefore unlikely to be examined?

9. When can a revenue agent "survey" a case without examining it?

10. Repetitive audits: what the rules are and how to deal with them

11. How to put an audit into suspense

12. The only reasons which can be used to avoid a "TCMP" audit

13. When to start devoting time to technical research

## What every client should be told
## when he has been notified of an audit

All people are understandably nervous and upset when they hear that they have been selected by the IRS for an audit. As your client's representative, you have an obligation to try to alleviate some of his/her fears by assuring your client that you are competent to deal with any matter that the IRS agent may raise.

### What to say to your client when he asks,
### "Why are they auditing me?"

Simply say: "Generally, people they pick to audit are chosen by a formula. Nobody knows what the formula is. Don't worry about anything. That's why you are paying me—I'll worry."

By reassuring your client you will enable him to better deal with and provide answers to the inevitable questions which will be asked by the revenue agent during the course of the audit. A client who becomes too nervous and upset by the audit experience cannot be relied upon to assist in his own defense.

### "Don't ever speak to the agent!"

Instruct your client that if he should be called by the revenue agent he is to only say, "Please call Mr. Jones, my accountant, who is handling the audit. His phone number is _____."

Inform your client that even the most casual question the revenue agent may ask may have implications. If he doesn't talk to the revenue agent other than to say "Call my accountant," he cannot get himself into trouble.

### "Don't discuss the audit!"

Tell your client not to tell employees, neighbors, or business associates that he is being audited. The fewer the people who know that the IRS is looking into his financial affairs the better. An unhappy employee or customer could be the one who decides to inform the IRS concerning "what they should really be looking for." Even if the information they may supply to the IRS is completely untrue it will cause the agent to spend countless extra hours of time and bring untold aggravation.

## How much does the IRS know about your client?

Most of the time the only thing the revenue agent knows about your client before he starts the audit is what can be ascertained from the tax return. For example, the revenue agent will be able to tell what kind of neighborhood your client lives in, his occupation, and the amount of his disposable income. Generally, what you tell the revenue agent or what you show him, is what he knows.

One situation in which the revenue agent may have some background information is when your client has been audited within the past few years. The agent may be able to obtain a copy of the audit file from a previous year. But that is only if a prior file was maintained (normally they are not unless there was an unusual adjustment made) and if the revenue agent has requested the file from storage. Again, most agents do not request prior-year files because of the additional amount of paper work involved.

### How to tell if the agent has an "informant's allegation"?

One way to find out is to ask: "Are you here to confirm an informant's allegation?" If the revenue agent says no, then you can generally believe him. He will not say yes. Rather, he will say he can't tell you, which means yes.

Since you may not want to ask the question the minute after the revenue agent walks into your office, you should be aware of clues which indicate he may suspect something.

*What kind of clues?* If the revenue agent asks a question about something you have told him nothing about then you can safely suspect he has been given an informant's allegation to check out. For example, if the revenue agent asks whether your client runs a business from his home and your client is an executive employed by a firm uninvolved in business of that kind, then you know that he has reason to suspect something.

If you determine that an allegation has been made then do the following:

1) Write down all the questions the revenue agent has. This will give you an outline of what he is trying to get at.

2) Tell the agent you will get back to him after discussing the matter with your client.

3) Don't give any answers to any questions and do not allow the agent to proceed with the audit. (Now is the time to consider preserving your cli-

ent's Fifth Amendment right not to incriminate himself if it appears that he may have committed a tax crime.)

## Determining your client's potential exposure before the audit starts— and what to do about it

The first and obvious thing to do to determine your client's potential exposure is to review his tax return. If you prepared it then you will probably have a good idea of any "gray areas" which exist or in which you may have taken an aggressive position.

Now is the time to refresh your memory as to the facts and circumstances of what you have done and to rehearse the answers to the questions the revenue agent is likely to ask.

If you have not prepared the tax return, then determining the areas of exposure may not be so easy. Start by reviewing the tax return. Then, ask your client if he recalls any conversations with his former accountant with respect to aggressive tax planning.

Now that you are aware of the areas in which the revenue agent may want to develop his case—what do you do about it?

If the issue involves an area of the tax law which is somewhat complex, your chances of being able to keep the agent from fully developing it are enhanced. Your goal will be to make it as difficult as possible for the revenue agent to piece together the transactions which make up the area of exposure.

*Important:* The rules are that you can't lie to or mislead the agent. However, you do not have an obligation to help the revenue agent build his case against your client.

1) Only answer questions which are actually asked.

2) Do not volunteer information.

For example: Let's say that all the revenue agents in the country read this book and they figure out a way to get you to reveal your client's position by saying to you "Tell me *everything* about the XYZ transaction your client consummated." You merely answer, "Sure, what do you want to know about the XYZ transaction?"

### How to do your own preaudit

Revenue agents are supposed to prepare a preaudit plan before they start the audit. Generally, it is a rough outline of those areas they will examine. Typically, the two areas which are always included are gross receipts and travel and entertainment. If there should be any problem in any area of your client's return then you should know about it before the agent tells *you* about the problem.

*Confirm gross receipts.* Suppose your client has a cash business and when it was time to prepare his tax return he said to you "My gross receipts were $52,500." He did not show you any records at that time. It would now be in your client's interest for you to analyze all his bank records to determine if the figure he gave you was accurate. Since the revenue agent will request bank deposit information you do not want to be in the position of having to hand it over to him and then having him tell you that there were more deposits than there was income reported.

*Review cancelled checks.* Review all cancelled checks and endorsements to ascertain whether they will identify any irregularities. If so, can they be adequately explained? If not, will you be providing the agent with the information he needs to develop a fraud case?

If there is a problem, *now* is the time to think about protecting your client's Fifth Amendment privilege against self-incrimination.

*Review travel and entertainment substantiation.* Take a few minutes to determine the general condition of the documentation available to substantiate travel and entertainment expenditures. If copies of receipts from credit card companies or hotels or airlines have to be obtained then you should tell your client to make the necessary calls to get this information.

## What to do if your client's records are missing or lost

Occasions will arise when you will be retained by a client to represent him in a tax audit and the client has had four or five different accountants since the time that his tax return was prepared. As a result, records have been shifted around and now that you are trying to assemble them for the revenue agent some are inevitably lost or missing.

What do you do now? Tell the revenue agent before the audit starts that some of the records are lost. Explain to him what is missing *before* the audit starts. This way, he will not suspect that you are intentionally holding back records from him.

*True story:* I had to represent a client who had retained no less than five different accounting firms from the time his tax return was prepared until the time of the audit. As a result, there were only six month's worth of books and records. The second half of the year just disappeared.

I met with the revenue agent and showed him the books of original entry for the first six months of the year and explained the circumstances. After a few minutes of disbelief the revenue agent worked out a fair audit plan. He would test check the amounts in the records we had. If he found any adjustments (to T & E –type accounts only) he would set up a ratio as follows:

$$\frac{\text{Disallowed T \& E in six-month period}}{\text{Total T \& E in six-month period}}$$

This fraction would then be applied against the total amount of T & E deducted on the return. That would be the agreed-upon adjustment.

### How to handle a nasty agent

Suppose the agent tells you to reconstruct the records if some are missing—how do you respond? Tell the revenue agent, "Here are all the bank statements and cancelled checks—you recreate the record!" or "Even if I were to try to reconstruct the records, I would never be able to tie into the numbers on the tax return. It would be a waste of time."

In the event that the revenue agent is still not satisfied that a test check of the available records would be sufficient, speak to his group manager. The group manager wants to see the cases in his group closed. If you tactfully explain that the time it will take the revenue agent to reconstruct the records would be exorbitant and that you have a fair solution, he will more than likely be amenable.

### Do not reconstruct the records yourself—the revenue agent won't succeed in disallowing anything!

If the revenue agent threatens that he will disallow all items not completely documented—don't worry! First, the review staff, which will check the case before it goes to the appellate division, will probably send it back to the revenue agent because it is not fully developed. If the case should get past the review staff then the appellate conferee will probably send it back for the same reason.

You are bound to be able to convince somebody at the IRS that under the circumstances it would not be equitable to require the taxpayer to reconstruct half a year's worth of records.

Other suggestions you can make to the agent:

1)  Audit the previous or subsequent year instead.

2)  If there was a prior-year audit see what items were adjusted. Limit the audit in the year that records are missing to these items only.

## What to find out from a client who has started the audit himself and then brings you in on the case

Where the client or another practitioner has already started the audit, you enter the case at somewhat of a disadvantage. Essentially, the revenue agent will know more than you do at this point about many things and also may have identified one or more problem areas. That is probably the reason that you have been called in—the client may have started the audit himself and has gotten himself into trouble or else his representative was unable to settle an important issue with the revenue agent.

The first thing to do is to acquaint yourself with the issues, from your client's point of view and from that of the revenue agent.

Set up an appointment with the revenue agent to review *his* work papers. Explain to him that you have just been retained and would like to review the case with him so that the case may be resolved. At your meeting ask him the following questions:

"What are the issues? Why do you think you are right? Why is the taxpayer wrong? What facts do you have to support your position?"

Do not ask all the questions at once! Try to develop a relationship where the revenue agent feels that you have entered the case to make his job easier. That is, you will convince your client that the revenue agent is right so he can close the case. All the agent has to do is show you that he is right and how he arrived at that conclusion. Do not argue with the revenue agent or challenge anything he says at this point. Just let him do the talking. Take notes.

After you have ascertained the information the revenue agent has in his possession then you should speak to your client or your client's former representative to determine what information they have already supplied. You probably don't want to contradict anything the previous representative said *unless* doing so enables you to develop a new angle.

## What happens if you ignore the letter sent by the revenue agent requesting that you call him to make an appointment?

*Caution:* Procrastination is a violation of the Rules of Practice which could result in a practitioner's suspension from practice before the Internal Revenue Service. In practice, it is not so terrible if you do not reply to the agent's letter. If he wants to make an appointment that badly he will call you or your client.

### What is the benefit of not responding promptly?

The principal advantage is that the case gets "older". The older the case the less likely it is that the revenue agent, once he eventually starts the case, will pursue all the areas he may have otherwise looked into. Why? The statute of limitations is closer to expiring. Waivers to extend the statute of limitations have to be secured. Reports have to be filed every month explaining why the agent has an "old" year case in his inventory. More reports have to be filed! It becomes a pain in the neck for a revenue agent to hold onto old cases.

*Better chance that the return will merely be surveyed:* If the revenue agent has never spoken to you or your client he may survey the case and not even audit the return. (This is not entirely correct since the case has technically been started after the appointment letter is mailed—but it is done anyway.)

## Pros and cons of constantly postponing appointments

**Pros:**

1) The case gets older.
2) The revenue agent is less likely to go into all areas of the tax return.

3) The agent may be pressured by his group manager to close the case even though it is not fully developed.

4) Time, generally, works to your advantage—the agent could retire or quit or be reassigned.

Cons:

1) Delay may constitute a violation of the Rules of Conduct.

2) A subsequent-year return will have to be filed if the audit is not completed by its due date.

3) It may be necessary to extend the period of the statute of limitations.

4) It creates hard feelings and may reduce your credibility.

## When does a tax return become "old" and therefore unlikely to be examined?

The IRS official policy states that tax returns will be examined and disposed of within twenty-six months for individuals and twenty-seven months for corporations after the due date of the return or the date filed, whichever is later.

Returns filed late, called "delinquent returns" are considered as being filed with returns for the current year. The late-filed returns are classified and screened under the same procedures as current-year returns.

However, classifiers are reluctant to put "old year" returns into the audit cycle because they know what a headache they cause for the revenue agents. (Statute of limitation waivers must be secured, reports must be prepared, etc.)

*Tip:* Filing a return on an extension may reduce the chances of it being audited! The IRS will never admit to it but just ask yourself and other practitioners which clients are being audited. Most probably did not file extensions.

## When can the revenue agent "survey" a case without examining it?

The *Internal Revenue Manual* provides that "Examiners should be encouraged to carefully study cases assigned to them before starting their examinations. If such study convinces the examiner that an examination is not warranted, he/she may survey the assigned return."

Technically, after the case is started (after the agent has notified the taxpayer of an audit) an actual examination would have to take place before the case could be closed.

*Idea:* Some agents may agree to "forget" that they ever notified the taxpayer if you can convince them that auditing the tax return would be a waste of time and that the audit would result in no change anyway. For example, if the tax return the agent has shows a loss and the subsequent and prior years also have losses— impress upon the agent that even if he came up with an adjustment, no tax would be due because of the availability of carrybacks and carryovers of losses. Or explain to the agent that, not only will no tax be produced, but the circumstances indicate that the audit will take forever to complete because:

1) The records have been lost because of a move.
2) The accountant who prepared the tax return has died and nobody knows exactly what he did when he was working on the account.

## Repetitive audits: what the rules are and how to deal with them

See Chapter 4, "How to Handle Office Audit Examinations."

## How to put an audit into suspense

Practitioners may want their client's case to be put into suspense pending the outcome of a final IRS determination on a particular issue.

Note that, normally, the agent should take the initiative in putting the case into suspense, but many agents are not aware of the current issues which are in suspense.

The national office publishes the *Audit Suspense Digest* which identifies the principal issues in suspense and summarizes significant development of those issues.

The *Internal Revenue Manual* contains a descriptive list of those issues presently in suspense.

## The only reasons which can be used to avoid a "TCMP" audit

A TCMP (Taxpayer's Compliance Measurement Program) audit is a line-by-line examination of the entire tax return which is done for the purposes of gathering data for use by the IRS in determining the best methods of selecting tax returns for audit and to evaluate the level of voluntary compliance in various regions of the country. These audits last a long time since every item has to be examined by the agent.

The *Internal Revenue Manual* provides that "All TCMP returns must be examined. There are no correspondence audits or surveys before or after assignment."

The *only* reasons that can be used to avoid a TCMP audit, according to the *Manual*, are:

1) The taxpayer cannot be located.
2) The taxpayer is too ill, has become incompetent, or has died, and the guardian or executor cannot be contacted.
3) The taxpayer is outside the United States and unavailable for an interview audit.

## When to start devoting time to technical research

It rarely pays even to begin getting involved in technical research before the revenue agent lets you know that he intends to develop a particular issue. The obvious reason is that a considerable amount of time may be spent on building an unnecessary defense—the revenue agent may not spot the issue! Or, he may spot the issue, but you may be able to convince him that his position has no merit.

**Should you provide the revenue agent with your research?**

This is a tricky question. If you give him the fruits of your efforts then he may do one of two things:

1) He may use the research to help him close the case upholding your client's position, as you have justified it.
2) He may use the research to help him develop his own position and tear apart your own.

# CHAPTER 8

# Showing the Agent
# Your Client's Records

Your client's records are, after all, the basis for whatever problem your client will ultimately face with the IRS. The practitioner must appreciate the importance of making sure that he is fully aware of what records the agent is being shown. Revenue agents use records as building blocks to determine the true substance of a transaction. That is precisely why only the information actually requested should be handed over. Generally, it will not be in your client's best interest to volunteer information during an audit.

A very serious ramification of showing the agent your client's records is that, if fraud should exist, any privilege your client would otherwise be able to claim at a later date will be effectively waived. Approach each tax examination as a potential fraud problem since you, as the practitioner, rarely if ever are privy to the fact that your client may have commited a crime.

This chapter will cover the following areas:

1. Reviewing documentation before it is submitted to the agent: What should you do if you find nondeductible items?

2. When the agent requests "the books and records," what should he be shown?

3. Why you should never let the agent examine the cancelled checks

4. Which records should you not permit an agent to photocopy or copy by longhand?

## Reviewing documentation before it is submitted to the agent: what should you do if you find nondeductible items?

After the agent has reviewed your client's various journals and ledgers he will usually ask to see a test-check selection of the original invoices, bills, contracts, etc. which were reflected in the books and records. Before you hand over the requested information, you should be looking for:

1) altered documents
2) personal expenses
3) nondeductible expenses
4) items which could lead into other areas (expenses paid for other entities)

If you find any of the above items while reviewing your client's papers, should you just hand over everything, say nothing and hope that the revenue agent overlooks the problem items? Or, should you just not show him those bills or invoices which are not deductible?

Generally, the way to approach such a situation is not to show the agent any of the records for nondeductible items. Why? If in the course of his examination the agent is shown nondeductible expenses it will give him a sense of how far short of voluntary compliance your client falls. Accordingly, if he sees too many problems he may decide to expand the scope of his audit.

What should you say when the agent asks: "Where are the missing records?" Tell him that you will have to get them for him at a later date. If you never come up with the records the agent will probably do one of two things. Either he will disallow in full everything he has not seen or else he will try to reach a compromise with you on how much of the unsubstantiated expenses to disallow.

### Another school of thought

Some practitioners feel that allowing the agent to "find" certain adjustments in the way of nondeductible items will give him a sense of accomplishment and the agent will not be reluctant to close the case. There is some merit to this theory, but it is dangerous. You never know at what point the agent will stop looking at the records. One thing could lead to another—and often does.

*Conclusion:* Evaluate your client's situation. Are most of the expenses nondeductible? If so, then you cannot very well not show the agent any records. It will just not make sense. However, if there are gray issues that you wish the agent would not develop, then make it easier for the agent to spot those expenses which are not deductible in an effort to satisfy him sufficiently to close the case.

## When the agent requests "the books and records," what should he be shown?

The agent can only look at one record at a time. Therefore, there is ordinarily no reason to furnish him with every single business record maintained by your client at the first meeting. A good reason not to furnish all the records is that the more records the agent has, the freer he is to browse through them and spot potential adjustments.

### "Here are the records—help yourself"

Bob Smith, a practitioner, met the agent at his client's place of business (his first mistake) but was in a hurry to make another meeting located downtown. Instead of carefully reviewing all records before he gave them to the agent he just showed the agent how the filing system worked. The agent had a field day looking through all the paid bills and as a result came up with adjustments for items which were expensed on the books which Bob didn't even know about!

### For starters

At your first meeting with the agent have available the following records:

1) general ledger
2) cash receipts journal
3) cash disbursements journal
4) trial balance
5) adjusting journal entries

"Have available" does not mean "hand over" as soon as the agent walks into your office. Let him ask you for what he wants. If he doesn't ask to see the year-end adjusting journal entries then don't volunteer them.

*Pointer:* If possible, record year-end journal entries only in the general ledger so that the agent doesn't need your work papers to tie numbers into the tax return.

It is easier to spot adjustments if all the adjusting entries are laid out for him on one work paper.

### No prior or subsequent year records

Make sure that all pages in the general ledger and journals from prior and subsequent years are removed. The agent is examining only one year (at least to start with) and there is no reason why you should provide him with the information contained in any other years.

### Paid bills

At some point during the audit the agent will ask to see bills, invoices and receipts. *Do not ever hand an agent a paid bill file!* If your client files bills alphabetically, then remove those bills from each file that the agent wants to review. If bills are filed by vendor then repeat the same process of removing those invoices which are requested.

An agent can have a great time if you let him rummage through the paid bill files. Not only will he select those items which were on his test check list but he will look at everything he can in order to identify potential adjustments.

### Work papers

There exists much controversy over whether the IRS is entitled to review the accountant's internal work papers. Here are some positions you can maintain if you do not want to show the agent your work papers:

1) "The work papers are mine and not part of my client's books and records."

2) "The work papers are used to analyze management and operational functions—they have nothing to do with taxes."

3) "I'll think about it."

You may want to volunteer your work papers if you are confident that no tax issue could be developed from them. For example, during the course of your certified audit or review and compilation you may have examined a particular account and confirmed that all charges were correct.

### Inventory records

The IRS makes a big deal about requiring agents to confirm the accuracy of the taxpayer's ending inventory. As a practical matter most small and medium-sized businesses and even some larger companies lack the resources to maintain perfectly accurate inventory records. Again as a practical matter the practitioner is generally provided with the ending inventory figure by his client who determined the dollar value of the inventory by "looking around the place and adding everything up."

How do you respond to the agent when he asks to see the inventory records—and there really aren't any? Tell him: "There aren't any formal records maintained by my client."

*What can the agent do?* Technically, the agent can recommend that an "inadequate records notice" be issued. This would have the effect of putting the taxpayer on notice of his legal obligation to maintain adequate books and records. In the event an adjustment should be found in a subsequent period the negligence or civil fraud penalty may be applicable.

Practically speaking, nothing happens. The agents know what is going on and generally overlook the issue, for to prove that the inventory was really higher than reflected on the books would be extremely time-consuming. (Even if the agent had the time to spend, most lack the cost accounting knowledge to do the job right anyway.)

If the agent should persist, just tell him that "Even if you were able to come up with an adjustment it would only create a 'rollover adjustment' since next year's opening inventory would be higher than we have reported."

## Why you should never let the agent examine the cancelled checks

The revenue agent may say "Let me see the cancelled checks." Your response should be "Sure, which ones do you want to see?"

If you can help it, avoid showing the agent all the cancelled checks for the following reasons:

1) He can identify expenses he initially did not test check. He has, in a sense, a second chance to spot adjustments.

2) A review of the cancelled checks provides the agent with a profile of your client with respect to spending habits and patterns. For example, the agent will be able to determine the extent of your client's cash availability by examining cash which was not deposited and checks (or lack of checks) made payable to "cash."

3) There is always the possibility that endorsements on checks will provide the leads the agent needs to uncover bank accounts, brokerage accounts, etc. which you did not know existed (and into which unreported income may be funneled by your client).

## Which records should you not permit an agent to photocopy or copy by longhand?

If an agent starts to photocopy or transcribe certain records you should immediately suspect that the agent may have uncovered fraud. Why? The agent knows that once he makes a fraud referral he will generally be unable to look at these records again. (The Fifth Amendment is generally asserted by a taxpayer in a criminal investigation which precludes the IRS from obtaining his records, which may be incriminating.) Accordingly, he wants to get down as much information as possible.

**Which records should you be concerned about?**

1) all gross receipts records
   A) sales invoices/journal
   B) account receivable cards/journal
   C) cash receipts journal
   D) bank deposit information including deposit slips
   E) shipping records
2) cancelled checks

If you notice that the agent is transcribing records onto his work papers or has asked your permission to photocopy records, ask him "Why are you doing that?"

At that point—no matter what he says—it would be advisable to terminate the audit for the day. Tell the agent that you will get back to him to set up another appointment.

Now, carefully examine your client's records in an effort to determine what the agent has located. This step is crucial, for if there is a problem you certainly do not want to hear about it from a special agent.

*Caution!* The tedious transcribing of records is generally the first step toward a criminal investigation. If you can limit the agent's access to information at this point, the odds of your client being able to defend himself successfully are increased.

# CHAPTER 9

# Getting Through a Tax Examination Without the Agent Seeing the Books

The less time the agent spends reviewing your client's books and records the more likely it is that the number of issues that will be raised will be reduced. Looking through the books, even on a casual basis, affords the agent the opportunity to notice items that may appear unusual. This normally leads to questions and eventually to the development of an issue.

Using your rapport with the agent, you may be able to avoid actually having to show him your client's books. Here is how it's done.

1) On the first appointment with the agent have available your work papers which show the trial balance and adjusting entries so that the agent will be able to tie those amounts he wants to confirm into the tax return.

2) Tell the agent that he should select those accounts which he wants to test check.

3) Tell the agent that you will get him a copy of the general ledger account for those items which he has selected and that you will also analyze the entire account for him so that he can select various items, of his choosing, for a test check.

**Will an agent really agree to this?**

More times than not the agent will go along with such a suggestion because you have, in fact, done the time-consuming part of his job. You have analyzed the account completely and have tied it into the tax return for him.

The obvious advantage to this tactic is that you have prevented the agent from looking through the cash disbursements and/or purchases book to identify certain charges which he may determine are not deductible. If payments were made to related entities these payments would go unnoticed and the likelihood of him questioning the existence of a related entity may be reduced.

### This idea could backfire

There is, of course, a disadvantage to this suggestion. The primary disadvantage is that you have cut the amount of time that the agent will work on the case by at least 75 percent. Accordingly, he may feel that he now has the time to pursue other items. Therefore, before undertaking the task of analyzing the accounts which were selected for testing, the practitioner should reach an informal agreement with the agent to the effect that the items he has selected constitute the only items he will be looking into and that will be the end of the audit, notwithstanding something unusual. Depending upon the expertise of the agent, your helping him may bring to his attention an expenditure which he may otherwise have missed. For instance, an inexperienced agent, who may not be able to understand the books and records without your assistance, will have the advantage of having the adjustments given to him on a silver platter.

### Don't be too anxious to suggest to the agent that he shouldn't look at *any* books

My suggestion, although it may be implemented during the audit of the initial year selected for examination, normally will only be acceptable to an agent for an examination of a subsequent-year return. This is because the agent normally wants to get a feel for the types of records which are available and the manner in which the books are maintained.

The practitioner has another advantage when he does the agent's work for him. That is, he will be able to determine his area of exposure and perhaps steer the agent away from it. For example, if during the course of the analysis the practitioner spots an item which could be characterized as a constructive dividend he would have the opportunity to question his client about this item and develop a response to the agent's anticipated challenge. I have found that, if an explanation of a questionable T & E item is forthcoming immediately and is also authoritative, the likelihood of the explanation being accepted is increased. For some reason agents tend more readily to accept a logical explanation for a T & E item at the time they raise their question than to accept the answer at a later meeting.

The practitioner must make sure that his analysis is complete and that it ties in exactly to the books and to the tax return. Doing a complete and accurate job has the psychological effect of building credibility for both you and your client. Although credibility won't win an issue in which your client is obviously wrong, it can go a long way toward making the agent lean in your client's direction when the issue is gray.

## Suggestion: "I'll do a test check"

It may sometimes be to your client's advantage to suggest to the agent that, not only will you do a complete analysis of the account that he has selected, but that you will also select for test check (subject to his approval) three or four large expenditures during the year or during the test-check period he chooses. By doing the test check before it is shown to the agent you will be able to preselect for him those items which you want him to see. Accordingly, if you tell the agent you'll select three or four large items it will be at your discretion to select the three or four you want him to see. It is most unlikely that the agent will ask to see other items.

## Limiting an audit of a subsequently filed tax return

In those situations where a subsequently filed tax return is picked up by the agent for examination the above described test-check analysis can be a great time-saving device. You should try to insist that the areas examined on the subsequent year's return be limited to recurring items. That is, the agent should only test check those accounts which have resulted in an adjustment in the first year. Other areas which are unique to the tax return will also be looked into. However, these unique items are often limited and the agent will often be willing to go along with your analysis because he has already developed a sense of where the adjustments will be found. (A tip for preparing tax returns: instruct the client's bookkeeper to charge certain T & E items to differently captioned travel and entertainment accounts each year so that in the case of an audit the same items won't be found in the identically titled accounts. The agent may assume that the items do not exist in the next year. Do not mislabel any account or charge an amount which is obviously wrong to the account. Just change one or two account captions. Selling expense could become promotional expense in the next year.)

# CHAPTER 10

# Cooperation During an Audit

When it comes to conducting a tax examination there is cooperation and there is cooperation. The practitioner should be careful about cooperating to such an extent that it may prejudice his client's interest. As a general rule a relationship of mutual respect should be developed between you and the agent.

It is possible to cooperate with the agent but still maintain control of what the agent sees and when he sees it. This chapter offers practical suggestions in the following areas:

1. The importance of establishing and maintaining credibility: What to do if you lose it

2. Should you ever volunteer information?

3. Why you should always say you will cooperate—even if you won't

4. Consequences of lying to the IRS

5. How to "direct" the audit

6. What happens if you tell the agent you won't give him something he has requested?

7. How available should you make yourself to answer the agent's questions?

8. When is it advisable to have your client meet with the agent?

9. How to control the interview between your client and an agent

## The importance of establishing and maintaining credibility: what to do if you lose it

Revenue agents do not check and verify everything you tell them—unless they sense they can't believe you.

If you can establish a high level of credibility, the amount of time that the agent will spend on the examination will be reduced. For example, if you have answered a few questions accurately and the agent finds no contradictory information in the books and records then it is safe to assume that all future answers you give will go unchallenged and be accepted.

The worst thing to do is to give an answer to a question you really do not know the answer to. Just say, "I don't know, I'll find out for you." This type of response is even preferable to "I really don't know but I think. . . ." The agent may find you are wrong and forget you said "I think. . . ." The bottom line is that no answer is better than the wrong answer.

### You want the agent on your side

Part of the game that practitioners play when dealing with the IRS is getting the agent on their side. Many issues are not black and white but gray. By instilling a sense of confidence in the agent you might be able to create the small edge you need to convince him that your position in a given issue is correct.

### Lost your credibility? How to re-establish it

Probably, the only way to re-establish your credibility is to have your client or his employees (bookkeeper, controller, etc.) verify what you have told an agent about a particular matter. An agent is more inclined to believe your client about certain things (involving, for example, "intent" on travel and entertainment questions) than you—even though both of you give identical answers. Revenue agents have a somewhat inherent distrust of practitioners (until you prove trustworthy), whereas they feel that the client is too scared about the whole audit to say something which may not be true, and the client's employees have nothing to gain by lying.

## Should you ever volunteer information?

As a general rule, the answer is *no*.

Even if you think what you are offering is harmless and irrelevant it may turn out to have some relevance at a later point in the examination. It's very simple: your client has nothing to gain by your volunteering information that the agent hasn't asked for.

Some people just have an urge to talk. If that's you then talk about anything you want except your client and his business.

The right way to answer a question

Answering a question is an art. Only answer the question you were asked. An agent who asks good questions knows what he is doing. When you meet an agent who asks precise and accurate questions you know you have to be very careful about how you answer. Your responses must be precise, accurate and short. An inexperienced agent can sometimes be identified by his lack of ability to ask enough questions or ask the right kind of questions. The practitioner has no obligation to provide the right answer to a poorly phrased question. Take advantage of an inarticulate agent by answering only what is asked—and no more!

## Why you should always say you will cooperate—even if you won't

*Reason #1:* The Rules of Practice require that the practitioner cooperate during the course of an examination. Therefore, it doesn't serve any purpose to wave a red flag in front of an agent by telling him you will not cooperate with his requests for information.

*Reason #2:* If you try to give the agent a hard time (at least if you tell him outright you intend to make his life harder) he can do some nasty things himself, like:

1) issue a summons requiring that you produce all your client's books and records at *his* office

2) make third-party contacts which will embarrass your client and possibly hurt his business

3) initiate a referral to the director of practice which could lead to your suspension to practice before the IRS

## Consequences of lying to the IRS

The worst consequence of lying is that you can be convicted for violating 18 USC 1001 which provides for a $10,000 fine and/or five years in jail.

### Remember

If you are asked a question that you just cannot answer truthfully then:

1) Don't answer the question—sit there and smile.

2) Answer the agent's question with a question of your own. For example:
R/A: Did your client report all his income?
PRACTITIONER: Do you think he hasn't?

3) Say, "I'll get back to you at a later date with an answer."

*Caution:* You must always weigh the risk of offering potentially incriminating information about your client to the IRS against a potential charge that you are interfering with the administration of the Internal Revenue laws, which is a crime (Code section 7212). If in doubt it may be best to obtain the opinion of counsel.

## How to "direct" the audit

Revenue agents are instructed to conduct the audit themselves and not let the practitioner assume that role. However, with practice and a bit of psychological intimidation it is possible for you to dictate what will be shown to the agent and when he will see it.

**How it is done**

Start off by saying "Here is the general ledger. Let me know whether you have any questions." (Don't say, "What records do you want to see?")

Obviously, he can only go so far with the general ledger. Eventually he will ask to see the cash disbursements book. At that point you may say "What account do you want to review? I'll analyze it for you." If he accepts, then you have limited his inspection of charges made during the year to those he specifically wants to test check. Suppose the revenue agent has selected the accounts he wants to review and you have analyzed them for him. What next? He may ask for invoices and bills. You say: "I can't give you all those bills—it will take forever. I'll pick out three or four of the largest ones—and that's it!"

The revenue agent will either acquiesce or tell you that if you don't show him everything he wants he will disallow the unsubstantiated portion. If he gives in, you win. If he says no, then you can always give him what he wants.

**Discussing adjustments**

Always try to get the revenue agent to talk during the audit about an item he proposes to disallow. (Most like to wait until the end to avoid confrontations.) If the agent should tell you that he plans to disallow a certain expense, no matter how small, then argue. Continue either to justify the deduction as allowable or challenge the agent's basis for making the adjustment. Don't stop! Talk about it all day! Why?

1) If the agent sees that you become visibly upset at the thought of him making an adjustment, he won't propose too many more. (Sounds strange? Just try it and see what happens.)

2) It is extremely annoying and distracting for the practitioner to harp on one item for hours. Most agents will be thinking about the end of the day rather than the work they are supposed to be doing.

## What happens if you tell the agent you won't give him something he has requested?

For starters, don't ever say you won't give the agent something he has asked for. That sort of remark only serves to put the agent in a fighting mood—you want to keep him as lethargic as possible!

The agent will act differently depending upon what he fails to get to see. For instance, if he asks for a copy of a particular contract or to review the corporate minutes there really is not too much he can do if you don't show it to him. On the other hand, if he asks to see receipts or other types of substantiation and they are not forthcoming, he can disallow the deduction claimed.

### Ultimate weapon

With his group manager's approval a summons can be issued. As a general rule summons are not issued unless the agent can convince his boss that the "need to know" about the information he wants is very important.

## How available should you make yourself to answer the agent's questions?

*Remember!* Time is the best leverage you have to insure that your client fares as well as possible in an audit. Therefore, the manner in which you answer questions can determine how much actual audit time the agent will be able to squeeze into the day.

### Answer questions once during the day

Tell the agent to write down all his questions and that you will try to answer them. Don't permit the agent to interrupt you constantly with one question after another. Answer all his questions at the end of the day.

*Why is this important?* If an agent cannot understand how a particular number was arrived at he may spend two hours trying to figure it out himself. If you showed him it would take no more than five minutes. Almost two hours could be wasted this way—or better yet, it may prove too difficult and the agent will just skip the matter altogether.

### Your responsibility—how far does it extend?

The practitioner has an obligation to make the books and records available. But do you have to explain them to an agent who doesn't understand them?

If an agent walks into your office and doesn't know what he is doing, you do not have an obligation to teach him accounting (he was supposed to know this before he was hired). True, this is a hard-nosed approach which shouldn't be used in every case. Sometimes you may want to explain just enough so that the agent doesn't become so frustrated that he asks that someone else be assigned to the case to assist him.

## When is it advisable to have your client meet with the agent?

More harm than good generally comes from allowing a client to be interviewed by a revenue agent. Any request for an interview should be discouraged or absolutely refused. The chances of a summons proceeding to compel testimony from your client are extremely remote.

There is only one situation in which your client should meet with the agent— that is when your own credibility has been diminished or lost. Sometimes the only way to get the agent to believe something you have told him about a given situation is to have him hear it from your client's own mouth.

Unless there is another good reason do not ever permit an agent to talk with your client. Why?

1) The agent may ask "trick questions."
2) Your client may volunteer information which was not asked for.
3) Your client may lie.
4) Your client may contradict something you have already told the agent.

## How to control an interview between your client and an agent

### Establish the ground rules

Tell the agent that you will let him talk to your client, but only about issue $X$.

Tell him not to ask any other questions because you are not going to permit him to answer any other questions.

### Brief your client

Explain to your client what questions the agent will ask him then rehearse the answers. Tell your client not to lie! If he can't answer truthfully, he should say absolutely nothing, or say "My accountant will give you that answer."

*Note:* There is no law that says you cannot discuss the answers you intend to give to the agent's questions. If the agent should ask your client whether he discussed the questions with anyone, your client should say "Yes, with my accountant—he told me to tell the truth."

### Control the interview

Keep small talk to a minimum. The objective is to get your client in and out of the meeting as soon as possible. You want the agent to accept the answers but you don't want to have your client there any longer than is necessary.

If the agent should get out of hand by insisting on certain answers, just end the meeting. Tell your client to walk out of the room.

# CHAPTER 11

# How to Deal with Problems
# with an Agent

Inevitably, certain problems will arise during the course of an audit. Your adeptness at handling such touchy situations could mean the difference between your client emerging as a winner or a loser. Of course, all the possible problems that could come up during the audit could not possibly be anticipated. However, there are typical situations which may arise and these are addressed:

1.  When and when not to be low key with an IRS agent

2.  Pros and cons of intimidating the agent

3.  When to request an informal conference with the agent's group manager

4.  How and when to request that a new agent be assigned to a case

5.  How to deal with an agent who refuses to honor your Power of Attorney and contacts your client directly

6.  What to do about an agent who is spending too much time on a case

7.  When should you throw an agent out of your office?

8.  Techniques for handling an audit with a brand new agent

9.  Coping during an on-the-job visitation by a group manager

## When and when not to be
## low key with an IRS agent

When dealing with an agent or, for that matter, any IRS employee, it is always advisable to treat him or her courteously as long as such treatment is reciprocal. Essentially, as long as the agent does not become demanding or threatening it will be to your client's best interest to try to develop a good rapport. The cliché about catching more flies with honey is applicable when dealing with the IRS. Although a nasty agent ultimately may not cost your client more in tax dollars, he or she can put you through a time-wasting appeal which will cost your client money.

## Become friends

When meeting with an agent for the first time make every effort to make the agent your friend! Sit down and talk about him. (Everyone likes to talk about themselves.) Then tell him about yourself and your firm. Always address the agent by his first name.

### Typical conversation when meeting with the agent

"Hi! I'm Jim Jones [not Mr. Jones]. Which office are you from? Oh, I know some people from that office. Do you know Bill Smith? I just had a case with him. What a nice guy! How long have you been with the Service? How do you like it? Are you getting many interesting cases? Are you married? Any children? Where do you live?"

This type of conversation should last at least a half an hour. Don't discuss your client or the audit—there will be plenty of time for that later. By making the agent your friend at the beginning the audit will usually progress more smoothly. You give yourself an absolute psychological edge. The agent will naturally be reluctant to make life too difficult for you if he considers you a friend.

Some agents, by virtue of their own personalities, may approach the audit as if it were a sporting event. Since there can be only one winner, they want to be it. If you see that the agent you are dealing with is clearly vindictive, don't put up with him. At this point take your cue from the agent. If he revels in giving you a hard time, give him a hard time back.

## True story

An agent I was dealing with had decided that whatever I said he would challenge and make me prove. Certain of his questions had no tax consequence—it didn't matter what the answer was. Every time he would ask a question I would respond by saying "Why do you want to know that?" After he struggled with a response, I said "Your answer is not good enough. Until you come up with a good reason for your question you are not getting an answer." This drove the agent crazy! Finally, he began to act like a human being after he saw that he couldn't push me around.

## Don't worry

Bob Smith, a practitioner, was always concerned that an agent would seek revenge against his client if he did or said something to upset the agent. (In fact, he was hurting his client by being too passive.) What Bob did not realize was that nothing would happen if he spoke up once in a while when the agent proposed to do something outrageous. The worst the agent could do would be to disallow a deduction. Bob could always file an appeal and win with hardly any effort.

If you are dealing with an agent who upsets you then upset him back. Hit back hard enough so that the agent is unable to handle the case rationally any longer. He generally will not take the steps to develop the issues properly because he will be acting out of anger and frustration.

## Pros and cons of intimidating the agent

It is hard to say whether an attempt to intimidate an agent verbally will work to the advantage of your client. Generally, much depends upon the personality of the agent and the level of his experience. An old-timer who has been around for a while will probably not be too concerned about what you say to him or how he perceives you feel about him. On the other hand, a younger and more inexperienced agent can be devastated by an intimidating remark, almost to the point of packing up his attaché case, running out of your office and closing the case with a "No Change" designation just so he does not have to talk to you again.

*Pros:*

1) The agent may back down from an unreasonable position.

2) He may become too upset and nervous to develop other issues.

*Cons:*

1) The agent may become defensive and try to get even with you.

**Tactic: how you can intimidate an agent**

Ask or say any of the following:

1) What is the name and telephone number of your group manager? branch chief? I want to call him and let him know that you don't know what you are doing!

2) Did you ever study accounting in school?

3) Why do you want to know that? (in response to every question)

4) Get out of my office! (last resort)

## When to request an informal conference with the agent's group manager

Generally, a conference with the group manager should only be considered if the agent:

1) is unreasonable in his conduct of the audit (for example, he calls up your client to ask him a question even though you have supplied the agent with a valid Power of Attorney)

2) proposes an issue which is absolutely without merit

A telephone call to the group manager will usually be enough to slow down an overaggressive agent. The IRS expects its agents to follow its own rules about procedure. In light of Watergate and the Privacy Act the IRS top brass frowns on aggressive behavior that circumvents established policy.

When it comes to discussing tax issues you should only get the group manager involved if the agent proposes an issue which is clearly wrong and will not listen to your reason.

*Typical case:* Revenue Agent Jones decides that he wants to be creative—at the expense of your client. He tells you that the office building owned by your client is not subject to an allowance for depreciation. Why? Because it is appreciating in value—not depreciating!

Group managers have been away from the technical side of the job for many years and normally will not be able to appreciate the position you are advocating on behalf of your client. The group manager's function is primarily administrative. His job is to move cases out of his group and not necessarily be concerned that the issues raised by the agent are 100 percent correct. In order not to embarrass himself the group manager will usually side with the agent—it is easier for him that way.

On the other hand, if you should get a group manager who has a certain degree of experience with your issue you may be asking for trouble. A conference could open the door for more questions and additional adverse tax ramifications.

*Look out!* Some Districts require that the Group Manager hold a conference with the practitioner if a case will be closed unagreed. Generally, it is not a good idea to have a meeting. Chances are that the agent will be sustained and that the meeting will only provide the agent with additional information to enhance his position.

## How and when to request that a new agent be assigned to a case

If a personality conflict arises between you and the agent it may be advisable to request that a new agent be assigned to the case. Weigh the advantages of having an inexperienced agent whom you can't stand against getting someone else with more experience. However, if an opposite set of circumstances exist—you have an intolerable "old-timer," then try to get rid of him as soon as possible.

Start by calling the group manager and asking him to intervene. Explain that you just cannot deal with the agent who was assigned to the case and that there must be someone else in the group who can handle this case.

If you are not successful at the group manager level then a series of letters should be written to the following people (in this order):

Chief, Examination Branch
Chief, Examination Division
District Director

### Sample letter

[Date]

John Jones
Chief, Examination Branch
Internal Revenue Service
120 Church Street
New York, N.Y. 10008

Re: Michael Smith

Dear Mr. Jones:

The above captioned client's tax return is currently being examined by Revenue Agent Roberts of Group 1206.

After having one appointment with Revenue Agent Roberts it became apparent that a conflict of personalities developed and that it would be impossible for either of us to expeditiously resolve this examination. Accordingly, it is requested that my client's case be transferred to another agent.

I have been a practitioner for many years and rarely find that I cannot deal, at least to some degree, in a professional manner with the agents that I meet. Revenue

Agent Roberts refuses to meet me halfway and as such I refuse to deal with him on this case any longer.

Thank you for your prompt consideration of this letter.

Sincerely,

Sam Stone, CPA

*Remember:* No matter how unpleasant your meetings with an agent are, consider whether the present agent is failing to identify and develop potential issues before you request someone else. Do not be overly concerned that the agent is setting up frivolous issues which you will ultimately settle and/or win anyway. This reason, alone, is not good enough to justify requesting another agent. You may be suffering now, but your client will be better off in the long run.

## How to deal with an agent who refuses to honor your Power of Attorney and contacts your client directly

After obtaining approval from the chief, examination division, an agent is permitted to bypass a practitioner's Power of Attorney if he can show that the practitioner is procrastinating or is generally uncooperative.

If this should happen then you should be concerned about two things. First, you have been characterized as a troublemaker and there is a possibility that a referral will be made to the director of practice to review your conduct to determine if it has violated any of the Rules of Practice. Second, your client will be notified that from now on the agent expects to deal with the client directly.

**What should you do?**

1) Respond to any communication you may receive from the examination division which is accusatory. Set forth your position in writing so as to "create a record" in the event that the matter is pursued.

2) Notify your client that when he is contacted by the revenue agent he should not discuss the case but merely set up an appointment. At the scheduled appointment you are permitted to be present and generally resume your role as your client's representative. The revenue agent may

challenge you by stating that since you no longer hold a valid Power of Attorney that the IRS recognizes, he will not discuss adjustments with you. Respond by telling him that you have no intention of discussing adjustments and that you are present at your client's request to assist in the presentation of information.

Generally, after the storm blows over, business as usual can be conducted with the revenue agent. If severe problems should develop a second time it may be in your client's best interest to resign from the case.

## What to do about an agent who is spending too much time on a case

There will be times when an agent just cannot bring himself to close a case. For any number of reasons he will be unable to make a decision. At some point, hopefully before your billable time gets to a point at which you know you will not be able to collect, make the revenue agent give you a list of all his proposed adjustments and end the case.

*A good example:* A revenue agent I was working with decided that he would disallow a particular issue. After at least two meetings about this issue he wouldn't change his mind, but he still insisted on asking more questions about the issue. I told him that I didn't want to waste any more time on this issue since he wasn't going to allow it anyway—so I wouldn't answer any more questions about it. He had no choice but to close the case.

**What can you do to make the agent close the case?**

Speak to the agent's group manager. Ask the group manager to define the "scope of the examination." Nothing is more frustrating than having an agent go from one issue to another, without ever really finding a significant adjustment, merely because he doesn't know when to quit.

In the course of your meeting with the group manager explain what the agent has already examined and what you think were his findings. If the agent sits in on the meeting, try to get him to commit himself as to whether what you are saying is correct. Also, point out that the number of hours charged to the case is already excessive, and as a result, your client is being forced to pay a considerable amount of money for your time.

*This always works:* Make it a point to say "It is just not fair and we are not putting up with this any more!"

In lieu of speaking to his group manager, just confront the agent with a hard-line position. Tell him in a firm and authoritative manner that "You are spending much too much time on this case and I'm not showing you any more books and records. The audit is over! Disallow whatever you want!" If the agent responds by threatening to serve a summons, tell him that you will challenge the summons, in court if necessary, since the matter is getting out of hand.

*Don't worry:* If the agent is just wasting time and spinning his wheels his group manager will never approve a summons.

## When should you throw an agent out of your office?

All IRS employees have a responsibility to act fairly and with a certain degree of common sense. In the event you encounter an employee who lacks these characteristics then do the following:

1) Call his group manager and complain about his conduct
2) Throw him out!

As a rule you will find that special agents and revenue officers, as opposed to revenue agents, are more likely candidates for ejection from your office since they have a tendency to come on stronger and abuse their authority. In fact, you may even find that their group managers condone their behavior!

*A special agent story:* I had occasion to represent a client in a criminal investigation where the special agent acted as obnoxiously as possible whenever he had the opportunity. After his latest indiscretion I called his group manager to register a complaint and, to my dismay, his group manager would not speak to me. I simply left a message that I would call the division chief and ask him if it was now IRS policy for group managers to refuse to speak to practitioners. (He called me back right away and things got better.)

### Revenue officers who get carried away

When a revenue officer showed up, unannounced, at my client's office, my client called me and asked the revenue officer to get on the telephone and talk to me. The revenue officer apparently did not like something I said—and hung up on me! I called my client back and told him to tell the revenue officer that if he did not leave the premises in five seconds he might call the police department and register a trespassing complaint. (I don't know whether a trespassing complaint would really stick but it would cause the revenue officer to account for his behavior. You can be sure everyone from the district director down would want to know why the taxpayer wanted him arrested.)

## Techniques for handling an audit with a brand new agent

An audit conducted by a recently hired and trained agent can either be a blessing or a curse. A blessing because he or she does not know the ropes yet, will be easily confused by books, records, and documentation, and will be inclined to accept your rationale in justifying a particular issue. A potential curse because he or she is fresh from training and may remember something which was recently taught and accept it as gospel. Nothing you say, at this point, will matter. But generally, audits with new agents are blessings!

One technique that may work is actually to help the new agent get through the case. For example, show him how to set up his work papers, how to do a test check and how to move from one issue to another. By being helpful you are minimizing the potential hazard of having the agent stumble across something you would rather not have him or her look into.

*Tip:* Make sure that when you help the agent with a test check you suggest which items should be checked!

Another useful technique is to supply the agent with your research material (which supports your position) if he or she has already identified and somewhat developed the issue. The agent lacks the skill, at this point, to do tax research to any significant degree. If you supply the agent with something "official" (precedent) it spares the agent from having to spend hours trying to research the issue himself.

## Coping during an on-the-job visitation by a group manager

Group managers are required to conduct field visitations to enable them to evaluate the performance of their employees. Basically, the group manager will accompany the agent for a few hours in the morning or the afternoon to observe how the agent asks questions, prepares work papers and develops issues.

Group managers usually lack technical expertise since their job is primarily administrative in nature. They rarely admit that they forgot much of what they used to know when they themselves were in the field. As a result the group manager may try to come up with novel issues to compensate for his lack of knowledge and impress his subordinate. It is then up to the revenue agent to develop the issue.

How do you defend against this happening? You have to do everything possible to keep the conversation from being focused on the audit. Talk to the group manager about the weather, his kids, your kids—anything. Hopefully, time will pass and the group manager will only make a cursory review of what the agent is doing.

## Summary

Since dealings with the IRS are chock full of potential problems it is incumbent upon the practitioner always to be able to respond quickly and effectively. Try to maintain control of any situation in which you are involved. Put the IRS agent on the defensive whenever possible.

Everything you say which relates to your client may have some impact. Unfortunately, sometimes you don't always know what a later investigation of the records will show or what the IRS already knows about your client. That is why it is a good idea to handle any problem situation by saying as little as possible and asking questions rather than providing answers. (That is exactly how to put the agent on the defensive.)

Don't permit stumbling blocks to turn themselves into large problems. It is generally better to resolve problems, as they occur, in favor of your client.

# CHAPTER 12

# Handling Problems During the Audit

This chapter discusses how to handle certain common problems which arise during the course of a tax audit:

1.  How to resolve unclear technical and procedural matters in your client's favor; requesting technical advice

2.  Limiting the scope of an audit

3.  What to say when an agent wants to look at a subsequently filed tax return

4.  What to do if the agent discovers that your client has altered receipts or documentation

5.  How to respond if an agent asks you a question you don't want to answer

## How to resolve unclear technical or procedural matters in your client's favor

Situations may arise when you feel that the agent is taking a position inconsistent with what you know or think to be established IRS policy. Local IRS offices often develop their own unofficial policy with respect to certain issues. For example, one IRS office may disallow a business deduction for the purchase of a daily newspaper by a professional whereas another office may allow the same deduction. Which office is right?

In other cases, you might just have a novel issue. Under these circumstances you may want to request the national office rule on a specific matter. Here is how you do it.

### Request technical advice

Tell the agent that you want him to make a request for technical advice on the grounds that a lack of uniformity exists as to the disposition of the issue, or that the issue is so unusual or complex as to warrant consideration by the national office. Submit your request in writing to the agent setting forth the facts, law and argument with respect to the issue and the reasons for requesting national office advice.

After reviewing your request for technical advice the agent will inform you that either a request will be made or that his office will deny the request for technical advice.

If your request is accepted you will be furnished with a copy of the statement of pertinent facts and the question or questions that the district IRS office will submit to the national office. If you do not agree with the district office presentation of the issue you may take exception. If you and the district office cannot reach an agreement both their statement and yours will be forwarded to the national office.

If after considering your request, the agent is of the opinion that the circumstances and facts do not warrant referral of the case to the national office, he will so advise you.

### Revenue agents don't like to request technical advice!

Why? Because it hampers their ability to close the case. (They would sooner have you disagree with their proposed adjustment and go to the appellate division.)

What the *Manual* says:

1) "When there is doubt as to whether or not a case should be submitted for technical advice, such doubt should be resolved in favor of requesting technical advice."

2) "Subjective factors such as concern that requesting technical advice may unduly delay closing the case should *not* influence judgment on the need to request technical advice. The benefits of the technical advice program transcend merely resolving issues in particular cases. Responses to technical advice frequently result in publication of Revenue Rulings and Revenue Procedures which set forth Service position, thereby promoting uniformity in the treatment of tax issues and permitting more expeditious disposition of cases on a nationwide basis."

**How to appeal if the revenue agent will not request technical advice**

You may appeal the decision of the revenue agent not to request technical advice by submitting to him, within ten calendar days after being advised of the decision, a statement of facts, law and agreements with respect to the issue and the reasons why you believe the matter should be referred to the national office for advice. If a longer period is necessary, an extension must be justified by you in writing and approved by the chief, examination division.

Your appeal will be reviewed by the chief, examination division. If he denies your request then you have fifteen days to notify him that you disagree and still want technical advice from the national office. At this point all data will be submitted to the national office for their review of the denial. After review in the national office, the district office will be notified whether the proposed denial is approved or disapproved.

*No adverse action can be taken.* While the proposed denial is being reviewed in the national office, the revenue agent must suspend action on the issue (unless the delay would prejudice the government's interest) until he is notified of the national office decision.

## Limiting the scope of an audit

The practitioner should make every effort to persuade the revenue agent to limit the scope of his audit. That is, pressure him to identify those items he wants to review and make him stick to it. (He can always change his mind but usually he will not as long as the items he has selected prove satisfactory.)

If the agent wants to see new items then tell him, "We agreed that you would limit your audit if everything was all right—why are you changing your mind now? It's not fair!"

### Related returns

Suppose the agent wants to examine a related return and you don't want him to. What do you do?

Explain that the return he thinks is related, is not (at least "technically" not related according to the Internal Revenue Code rules of attribution).

If the related return is indeed related but you still don't want him to see it, tell the agent to "get the return yourself." Maybe he will and maybe he won't. Unless he is very curious about the tax return he probably will not bother. It is a time-consuming process for an agent to requisition a tax return.

### Prior years

If an agent wants to review a prior year's return in which the statute of limitations has expired, tell him "Since you can't make any adjustments because the statute of limitations has expired, there is no reason to look at the return." (The exception to this is when you have to prove carryover items—capital loss, NOLs, contributions, etc.)

### Schedule "G"

Technically, an adjustment of income can be made in a base year, even if no tax can be collected, for purposes of reducing the benefits of income-averaging.

### Subsequent years

Do not file a subsequent year's tax return while an audit is in process. File an extension. If the return is ready to be filed and is filed the agent will normally include that newly filed tax return as part of his audit.

### When should you file a subsequent-year return?

If the agent you are working with is willing to agree merely to review the return only and deem it unworthy of audit.

## What to say when an agent wants to look at a subsequently filed return

If for any reason you are reluctant to furnish the agent with a copy of a subsequently filed tax return, there are a few alternatives which can reduce the chances of having it audited.

1)  Don't give the agent a copy of the return while he is at your office. Tell him that you will mail it to him. In the event he has any questions it would necessitate another appointment (which, of course, can't be made for at least another six weeks). If the agent has already charged too much time to the case he might decide to forget the whole thing. Or, he might get assigned to a detail for a month or two and be anxious to close the case now.

2)  Insist that the agent furnish you with a formal written request for an audit and insist that a report be furnished if it is not audited. Many agents look

at tax returns, ask some questions and then don't issue a report. This means that the IRS could select the same tax return for an audit at a later date. (Note: The agent is not supposed to ask questions unless he actually audits the return!)

3) You can always say no and tell the agent to requisition the tax return from the service center if he wants to look at it. This could take months!

## What to do if the agent discovers that your client has altered receipts or documentation

Although you should carefully review all documents before submitting them to the agent, sometimes your client may have altered a document without your knowledge. If the agent shows you that an alteration or forgery is apparent, what should you do?

First, ask the agent to let you see the altered document. Tell him that you will have to find out what the matter is all about and that you will get back to him.

After looking at the document, put it away (in your file or briefcase) and do not give it back. If the agent has already made a copy of it try to get the copy back.

### Gray area

The document constitutes a piece of evidence which could be used against your client in a criminal case. Query: If you take this evidence are you protecting your client's privilege against self-incrimination or are you obstructing justice by withholding evidence?

## How to respond if an agent asks you a question you don't want to answer

*Rule # 1: Don't ever lie to or mislead anyone at the IRS!* Supplying false information is a crime. Although it may be tempting to tell a "white" lie now and then (and you may think everyone else does it)—don't!

If you are confronted by a question which you do not want to answer there are a few ways you can respond without lying or giving misleading action.

1) Answer by saying, "Why do you want to know that?" If the agent tells you why then respond by saying, "That's not a good enough reason!"

2) Answer by saying, "I'll get back to you with an answer." (*Tip:* If you continue to say "I'll get back to you with an answer" to every other question which is asked, the agent will never remember everything he originally asked.)

3) Say, "I don't want to answer that question." (Risky, since the agent will then want to know why not?)

4) Laugh and smirk—nobody likes to think they asked a stupid question.

5) Sit there and don't say anything—and stare. Depending upon the experience of the agent that response alone could make him never want to talk to you again.

*Caution:* You must always weigh the risk of offering potentially incriminating information about your client to the IRS against a potential charge that you are interfering with the administration of the Internal Revenue laws, which is a crime (Code section 7212). If in doubt it may be best to obtain the opinion of counsel.

# CHAPTER 13

# Handling T & E Audits

Almost every tax audit includes an investigation of travel and entertainment expenses. Revenue agents know that this area always produces some type of adjustment. As such, you can count on the agent to delve into the T & E accounts even if he skips over some or all of the other potential issues on the tax return.

This chapter focuses on some of the things the practitioner can do to help minimize the amount of the travel and entertainment deductions an agent may attempt to disallow. Specifically, the following topics will be covered:

1. Why you *want* an experienced agent to examine a travel and entertainment issue

2. Preparing for a T & E audit

3. How you can decide which items are examined

4. When is it better to have an item disallowed than to show the agent the documentation

## Why you *want* an experienced agent to examine a travel and entertainment issue

Since travel and entertainment will be audited in almost every audit it is to your client's advantage if the examination is conducted by an experienced agent. If the agent has been with the Service for a few years he already has a feeling for the "degree of tolerance" the practitioner will have with respect to swallowing a proposed adjustment. Accordingly, it is unlikely that an experienced agent will attempt to propose a disallowance which is substantial (as long as the expenses can be documented with any degree of reasonableness).

Most experienced agents also find it boring to examine travel and entertainment expenses because it is an unrewarding exercise. By and large they come across the same type of expenses and the same kinds of reasons to justify the expenses at every audit. They also know that even if they were to make large adjustments in this area it would undoubtedly be the first issue compromised on appeal.

### Handling a T & E audit with some experienced agents

After the agent has made a cursory review of the expenses, but before supplying him with back-up bills and records, just say, "Let's agree on an amount to disallow and not waste any more time. I know you'll probably find something—disallow five percent of the total expenses claimed."

This approach is surprisingly successful. You and the agent both know that there may be some nondeductible expenses but neither of you really want to go through the time-consuming process of identifying which expenses they are, especially if a large number of expenses have been deducted.

Revenue Agent Smith is examining your client, Amusement Sales Corp., which employs twenty-five salesmen. The travel and entertainment expense deducted on the tax return exceeds $125,000. However, most of the expenses were incurred by nonstockholder employees, who were required to submit expense reports before they are reimbursed. Revenue Agent Smith, who has many years of experience, knows that it would be unproductive to spend much time in this area. The chances of him agreeing to your proposed amount of adjustment are quite good.

### Inexperienced agents

A recently hired agent or an agent who still has not learned how to close a case could be a nightmare when it comes to travel and entertainment expenses. They will ask for numerous receipts and then systematically examine each and every expenditure trying to find a required element of substantiation that is missing.

*A real-life nightmare:* An inexperienced agent I was dealing with decided that all of my client's expense records were no good! Why? Because his secretary had recorded (from his diary) the name of the person entertained and the business relationship on the back of the "hard copy" of the American Express voucher when it was returned with a bill. The rationale offered by this agent was that since the recording on the charge card receipt was not made at the time the expense was incurred, it should not be allowed. Needless to say, a meeting with the agent's group manager straightened out the agent's strained interpretation of the provisions of Section 274 of the Code.

# Preparing for a T & E audit

You can generally expect an agent to test check various expenses charged to T & E accounts. Three-quarters of a successful battle in a T & E issue is properly assembling and presenting the necessary data to the agent. It would be a good idea to read the regulations under Internal Revenue Code section 274 so that you know what kinds of documentation are required for a particular type of expense.

## Lost or unavailable records

Situations will arise where your client will not be able to fully substantiate the expenses which have been deducted on the tax return. However, the regulations do provide that, under certain circumstances, a deduction will be allowed even if the required records are lost or were not available at the time the expense was incurred.

U.S. Treasury Reg. 1.274–5(c)(4) provides that:

"If a taxpayer establishes that by reason of the inherent nature of the situation in which an expenditure was made—

(i)   he was unable to obtain evidence with respect to an element of expenditure which conforms fully to the 'adequate records' requirement,

(ii)  he is unable to obtain evidence with respect to such element which conforms fully to the 'other sufficient evidence' requirements, and

(iii) he has presented other evidence, with respect to such element, which possesses the highest degree of probative value possible under the circumstances,

such other evidence shall be considered to satisfy the substantiation requirements of section 274(d).

## Home entertainment

One of my clients did a fair amount of business-related entertaining in her home. However, she failed to keep all of the receipts for money which she spent when preparing for her expensive dinner parties. I told her to provide me with a copy of each guest list (indicating the company each person was from and what she discussed) and the complete menu (indicating the approximate amount spent for each item served and also the names of the stores where everything was purchased). She also provided me with pictures which were taken at the dinner parties and also copies of extra invitations.

At the same time that I told the agent that we did not have all of the receipts I presented him with an entire package of documentation proving that dinner parties were, in fact, held, the business relationship of the guests invited, and relevant business conversation and the approximate cost of all food and liquor purchased. The agent allowed every dollar deducted!

This is a good example of how to prepare for an audit where source records just do not exist.

## Gifts

Problem: Your client kept no record of whom he gave Christmas presents to. He only has a receipt from a department store indicating that he purchased fifty leather wallets shortly before Christmas time.

What do you do? First, have your client reconstruct a list of those persons he gave presents. Even if he only remembers twenty names it will still lend credibility to the fact that the gifts were purchased for business associates. Also, ask your client if he saved any thank-you notes which were received. Then, at the audit, tell the agent that your client could not possibly use fifty wallets himself—even if he gave one wallet each to his wife and two children.

Always make some effort to present the revenue agent with some type of written proof—even if it is weak proof. If the agent sees nothing it is difficult for him to rationalize allowing the deduction. However, if he sees some form of documentation he may be more inclined to make concessions.

## Hotels

The regulations require production of a receipt for a hotel expense but your client never keeps his hotel bill (and also pays with cash). What can you do?

1) Establish that on a particular day your client was really in the city where he claims to have been. Telephone calls made collect and charged to a business or home number, gasoline charge receipts in or near that city, toll receipts, etc. are all useful in establishing that your client was away from home.

2) Ask your client to provide you with the name of the hotel he stayed at and the approximate daily rate. Also, ask your client to provide you with a list of those customers he met with (to further establish that he was away from home and must have stayed somewhere).

3) As a last resort, contact the hotel and ask for a copy of the bill. Smaller hotels will generally be unable or unwilling to provide you with a copy of the bill since it is an incredible job to locate their copy.

### No records at all for cash expenses

Your client informs you that he spends money for business entertainment but never gets a receipt or makes a diary entry at or near the time of the expense.

An effective solution: Tell your client to reconstruct (from existing records *only* —like an appointment schedule maintained by his secretary or his wife's personal calendar/diary) the names and places and amounts spent for business entertainment. Make sure to inform the agent that the list of expenses was reconstructed in this fashion.

Technically, this method does not meet the requirements of the regulations to the letter of the law. Most agents will overlook that fact, at least to some extent, if you can prove what you are claiming with some degree of reasonableness.

*Remember:* Always make an effort to give the revenue agent what he needs in the form of substantiation. Even if what you have is not perfect, try to assemble an impressive package of documentation to make it easier for the agent to allow at least the majority of the deductions claimed.

### Review documentation before giving it to the agent!

Look at each receipt *before* you give it to the agent. Is it complete? Does it identify the person entertained, the business purpose, etc.? If not, then on a separate piece of paper have your client fill in the missing information for each expenditure. Don't alter the existing documentation!

If the agent should spot a problem all you have to do is tell him that you have reviewed the expenses with your client and that you have an answer. Generally, this approach resolves the matter in your client's favor without further discussion.

## How you can decide which items are examined

One of the practitioner's objectives in handling a T & E audit is to limit the number of items the agent will review. The fewer expenses the agent examines the smaller the chances that a significant adjustment will be proposed.

The approach taken by most agents is to perform a test check of the travel and entertainment accounts. Based on the results of the test check a projection is computed to arrive at the proposed disallowance. (Note: Some districts don't permit projections but actually want the agents to identify specific items.)

### Control the test check

Have the agent pick two or three months from which he will conduct a test check. Then, tell him that you will provide him with substantiation for all the "large" amounts. This way you have the opportunity to pick and choose those items *you* feel are significant. The worst that can happen is that the agent will ask to see something additional. However, the odds are that unless you have omitted a significant item no further questions will be asked.

*Added benefit:* If you do the work the agent does not get the opportunity to rummage through all of the expenses.

## When is it better to have an item disallowed than to show the agent the documentation?

Sometimes strategy dictates that it is more advantageous to your client to permit an agent to disallow an expense than to try to substantiate it. The expense may be of a nature that could lead to the discovery of other items which may constitute "gray" areas.

*What boat?* Suppose an agent asks to look at the back-up for a check paid to a gasoline company. The bill from the gasoline company indicates that it was for fifty gallons of fuel which was purchased at a marina. Your client entertains on his boat—but the agent does not know there is a boat. It may be better to just accept a disallowance of the particular expense rather than raise in the agent's mind the question of all the expenses associated with the boat.

Not showing the agent a particular bill is not always so easy. He generally has a right to look at all books and records and you are not allowed to lie or mislead the agent by saying you lost the bill.

If you don't want to show the agent something, it is best to say "Just disallow the expense!" More often than not the agent will not pursue the matter any further. He will be happy to get an adjustment.

# CHAPTER 14

# How to Successfully Challenge Constructive Dividend Issues Based Upon Disallowed T & E Expenses

Travel and entertainment expenses are areas which revenue agents almost always review and in which, to some extent, they will inevitably propose adjustments. When corporations are being audited, disallowed travel and entertainment expenses can also be attributed to their shareholders as a constructive dividend. The tax effect of a constructive dividend can be confiscatory in those instances where both the corporation and the shareholder are in the top brackets.

Rarely will a client be able to substantiate every travel and entertainment expenditure in accordance with the letter of the law. Therefore, the practitioner is continually placed in the position of helping his corporate client avoid a disallowance of travel and entertainment expenses and also preventing the assessment of a double tax on the shareholders because of the constructive dividend problem.

This chapter will be of special importance to those practitioners representing closely held corporations where the number of shareholders is relatively limited. These clients tend to be most vulnerable to disallowance of travel and entertainment expenses which are charged back to their shareholders as constructive dividends. The Service makes a concerted effort to enforce all their available travel and entertainment rules against closely held corporations in an attempt to curb the abuse which they feel exists.

Notwithstanding any suggestions made in this chapter, the practitioner must be cautioned to weigh the facts and circumstances in his own case before adopting one or more of the tactics described. Sometimes it may be more advantageous just to accept the agent's proposed adjustments—especially where he has overlooked or accepted other items where potential exposure exists.

The following areas will be discussed:

1. How to take advantage of the mistake most agents make when they propose constructive dividend issues

2. Proving a constructive dividend was or wasn't received

3. How to determine the strength of the IRS's case

4. How to negotiate the settlement of a constructive dividend issue

5. How to reduce the amount of a constructive dividend based upon personal use of a corporation's automobile

6. Defeating the agent's contention that unsubstantiated petty cash expenditures also represent constructive dividends

7. Business gifts and constructive dividends

8. Handling T & E expenses charged on credit cards

9. Stockholder's use of a corporate apartment is not automatically a constructive dividend

10. Summary: What you should remember even if you don't remember anything else

---

## How to take advantage of the mistake most agents make when they propose constructive dividend issues

Most agents will seek to make as many corporate adjustments as possible into constructive dividends. However, in their haste to do so it is the author's experience that agents frequently neglect to develop properly the constructive dividend aspect of the case. They assume that because the corporate expenditure cannot be adequately substantiated the disallowance automatically constitutes additional income to the shareholder.

When it appears that an agent will disallow a corporate expenditure it is usually best not to bring unnecessary attention to the issue by arguing with the agent. Rather, make note of the proposed disallowance and do not discuss it again until such time that the agent has completed his examination and has presented all his proposed adjustments. By proceeding in this manner you will not be giving the agent any added incentive to ask questions about the expenditure. In addition your absence of objection at this point may lull the agent into feeling that you have acquiesced to his determination to disallow a particular expense. As a result he will be less likely to develop the facts so as to build up his case. If the facts aren't developed during the examination it is most unlikely that the agent will go back and do it later after you have reviewed his proposed adjustments and have indicated your unwillingness to recommend that your client agree to them.

## Proving a constructive dividend was or wasn't received

The technical and legal aspects of a constructive dividend should be briefly reviewed.

The premise of a constructive dividend is the fact that a shareholder has received a distribution of earnings and profits if the corporation makes certain payments for the benefit of the shareholder, or if the shareholder makes personal use of corporate property without adequate payment.

The taxpayer/shareholder must be able to disprove the presumption that an unsubstantiated or personal expenditure made by a corporation constitutes a constructive dividend. Once the presumption is rebutted, the IRS must be able to show that the shareholder benefited from a corporate expenditure or made use of corporate property. If the agent has neglected to develop this aspect of the case, that is, to show that an economic benefit was derived, the government's case is considerably weakened.

The mere fact that an expenditure cannot be proven deductible by the corporation because of inadequate record-keeping does not automatically classify that amount as a constructive dividend. In fact, the tax court (Henry Schwartz Corp., 60 TC 728, Dec. 32,098) has gone so far as to rule that an estimate, based on the facts and circumstances of each case, of those charges which were probably incurred for business purposes, but which cannot be substantiated, should not be attributed to the shareholder as a constructive dividend.

## How to determine the strength of the IRS's case

After the agent has identified those items which he has determined constitute unallowable deductions, his next step normally is to bring these items to the practitioner's attention. The agent will probably offer general reasons for the position he has taken. For instance, the usual reasons offered T & E adjustments are noncompliance with substantiation requirements or the taxpayer's failure to prove that the expenditure was related to business.

At this point it is important to ascertain the strength of the agent's case so that the practitioner can decide how to proceed. The practitioner should do the following:

1) Review the items which have been proposed by the agent to determine how the agent arrived at his figures. Then segregate those items which are obviously unallowable and constitute constructive dividends. For instance, those charges identified by the agent which were incurred by the shareholder's spouse and not related to business should be segregated. By following this procedure the practitioner can determine the extent of his client's liability and have an informed foundation from which to negotiate.

2) Next, make the agent commit himself as to why he wants to make an adjustment with respect to *each* item. Don't accept general and broad reasons such as "The expenses are no good."

During the agent's discussion of the issues the practitioner should not challenge each statement that the agent makes but rather he should listen quietly without saying anything. Any arguing at this point will have the effect of discouraging the agent from explaining his position. While the agent is talking the practitioner should make careful notes as to the reason for the disallowance of each expense. Many times the reason that the agent has initially thought an amount to be unallowable may not be valid. For instance, in the course of his examination he may have found an expense that should not be deductible, and as a result of that one instance may have assumed that every similar amount is also nondeductible. By going through each item with the agent the obviously incorrect adjustments can be eliminated and the number of items in dispute can be reduced.

By forcing the agent to give actual reasons for disallowing each expenditure and attributing it to the shareholder as a constructive dividend, you are fulfilling a twofold purpose. First, you are telling him in a subtle way that you are not going to accept any proposed adjustment unless he is able to justify his position to you completely. Most agents will then be reluctant to raise issues merely for bargaining purposes. With the nonsense issues eliminated you will be able to trade important issues. Also, the process of going through each expenditure is very time-consuming and exhausting. Many agents will realize that if the practitioner is going to go through the trouble of questioning each and every proposed disallowed item the agent might be better off offering a settlement of a reduced amount rather than trying to disallow an entire amount. If such an offer is made the practitioner should be ready to evaluate it immediately and either accept or refuse. Remember, the first step was to review the items for yourself to determine their nature and to ascertain the extent of your client's liability.

Second, having the agent review each item with you lets you determine whether the agent has a handle on the amounts he wants to disallow. Does he really have a case or is he taking a swipe at a particular expenditure with the hopes of getting the largest adjustment he can? When the agent tells you why he is disallowing each item you will also be able to tell how much he knows. For example, does he actually know that the shareholder's spouse incurred a certain expense for a nonbusiness purpose or does he only suspect that the situation exists?

## How to negotiate the settlement of a constructive dividend issue

At this point in the tax examination the agent has informed you of his proposed adjustments, you have reviewed them to determine the extent of your client's exposure, and you have also questioned the agent about the basis for his disallowing each and every expense he has proposed. Now the practitioner must carry the ball by directing future conversations to a point of compromise.

The practitioner should present his client's position with respect to each item the agent has proposed to disallow and attribute to the stockholder as a constructive dividend. Hopefully, some of the issues will be resolved immediately.

The practitioner should next solicit a response from the agent as to whether he would consider compromising the remaining issues which are open for the sake of closing the case on an agreed basis. (It is usually a good tactical move to let the agent know first that your client would never agree to all of the remaining issues.) A proposal should be presented to the agent which constitutes a fair compromise. It should contain terms that both sides will be able to live with. Unless the character of the agent is such that it appears that the only way to achieve a compromise with him is to tell him you refuse to agree to any of his adjustments, you are usually better off proposing a sincere and reasonable offer.

One way to compromise a constructive dividend issue is to tell the agent that you will not fight about other corporate adjustments he has proposed if he agrees not to treat certain travel and entertainment disallowances as constructive dividends. Of course, you must have a reasonable argument for the agent's not assessing a constructive dividend as a result of the T & E adjustment. Always keep in mind that it will be easier for you to reach a compromise when you have taken the time to think up various arguments the agent can rely on in these instances. Agents will more readily accept a compromise when they are confident that their determination will be able to withstand the various levels of review to which their work is subjected.

If a compromise cannot be reached the practitioner should state that he will have to discuss the matter with his client and that he will have to get back to the agent at a later date. Always wait for the agent to call you back and ask whether your client will agree to his proposed adjustments since time, itself, has a way of making most agents more amenable to compromise. Surprisingly, many cases which appear to be deadlocked can be worked out on the telephone, a month or two after the last meeting with the agent, in a last-ditch attempt to settle.

If you are unable to work out a compromise because the agent is reluctant or for other reasons, there is normally no benefit in discussing any specific items at length with the agent. To do so will invite more questions on his part, and he will use the answers to develop his case against your client. After he has informed you of his proposed adjustments simply tell him that you will have to discuss the matter with your client. This will put the issue to rest for the time being.

It should be emphasized that all negotiation should take place only after the agent has completed his examination of the books and records. There is normally no advantage to challenging the agent each time he requests a particular invoice or paid bill. Also, after the examination has been completed specific documents will not be available for the agent to refer back to should an inconsistency be raised by any of your arguments.

## How to reduce the amount of a constructive dividend based upon personal use of a corporation's automobile

A favorite manuever of many agents is to attribute a personal portion of the use of the company's car to the shareholder as a constructive dividend. In fact, many agents approach this area as a "given" adjustment not even subject to discussion.

More times than not accurate and precise mileage records will not have been maintained by the company for the business/nonbusiness use of the car. Agents will either take two-sevenths of the use of the car as personal (the two days being Saturday and Sunday) or arbitrarily arrive at a personal use percentage ranging up to an unrealistic 100 percent. Let's say that two-sevenths is selected by the agent. What are your arguments if the agent wants to set up a constructive dividend?

First, you will argue that the agent has failed to prove that the shareholder used the car for personal purposes. (Remember, even if records weren't maintained your position would be that, while the car can't be proved to be an ordinary and necessary business expense, that doesn't prove that the shareholder used it.) This sort of argument will probably not work when the shareholder is the only employee or when the shareholder has no automobile at home which would be available for commutation purposes.

The agent, in determining the amount of the constructive dividend, will normally apply the disallowance percentage he has arrived at against the following categories of expenses: gasoline, insurance, repairs, and depreciation. For purposes of this discussion it will be assumed that each category contains expenditures directly related only to the automobile in question. This fact should be verified by the practitioner to make sure that the percentage is not applied against an expense category which also contains charges for other corporate vehicles.

It must always be kept in mind that a constructive dividend is an amount equal to the fair market value of what the shareholder has received. With this in mind the area of depreciation becomes important. If the books and records indicate that an accelerated method of depreciation was used then the percentage applied to depreciation expense may, when added to other amounts, be greater than the true fair market value for the use of the automobile. Do a comparison of the cost of renting a similar car against the amount the agent proposes to charge as a constructive dividend to determine whether his figure is reasonable.

In those situations where the shareholder has another personal automobile available for his use the practitioner can argue that the agent has failed to prove the amount of personal use by the shareholder or whether, in fact, the shareholder has even used the automobile.

An agent may contend that a constructive dividend was paid in those instances where he notices that a shareholder's spouse is signing credit card charges for gasoline. The presumption is that the spouse made personal use of the automobile. The practitioner should remember that this presumption is rebuttable. The practitioner could point out that the signing for gasoline only indicates that the spouse drove the car from the residence to the gasoline station for the convenience of her husband and that such use was therefore related to the business use of the car.

Although the facts in each case will differ, in fighting a constructive dividend based on the personal use of a corporation's automobile there are numerous imaginative arguments to consider.

## Defeating the agent's contention that unsubstantiated petty cash expenditures also represent constructive dividends

Situations may arise when the amount of petty cash which has been charged off as a business expense cannot be completely substantiated. If the agent proposes to disallow the expense to the corporation and set up a constructive dividend to the shareholders as well, how should the practitioner proceed?

As the introductory remarks of this chapter indicated, the practitioner should review the amounts in issue and ascertain the relative strengths of his and the agent's positions. The facts may establish that checks were drawn by the company's bookkeeper and endorsed by her and then the proceeds placed into a petty cash fund. Thereafter, the company failed to maintain adequate records to establish how the money was spent.

At this point there is no evidence, unless otherwise established, which would prove that a shareholder derived any personal benefit from these funds. This case would be strengthened by the fact that petty cash is normally disbursed to various employees.

## Business gifts and constructive dividends

When the issue of disallowed business gifts is raised it is usually done for one of the following reasons: either the recipient cannot be verified as having a business relationship with the corporation, or else the amount of the gift exceeds the statutory limit of twenty-five dollars.

If the gift is being disallowed because it is over the twenty-five dollar limit there is little justification for the agent to hold that the excess constitutes a constructive dividend which should be attributed to a shareholder.

In those instances where the recipient of a gift happens to be a party related to a shareholder, the agent may take the position that the gift was constructively made to the shareholder first, who then made it a gift to the related party. The practitioner could maintain, if the facts warrant, that the gift was authorized and paid for by the corporation and it was as such that the gift was made. Accordingly, the money was not effectively paid to the shareholder first and the shareholder received no economic benefit.

## Handling T & E expenses
## charged on credit cards

Although credit cards inherently provide most of the proof required properly to substantiate a travel or entertainment deduction, they can likewise be fatal in showing that a particular expenditure is not deductible or that it should be back to a shareholder as a constructive dividend.

Suppose a situation exists where there has been a failure properly to record the business purpose of a particular charge. If the agent takes the position that the expenditure constitutes a dividend to the shareholder the practitioner should carefully examine the items in dispute before recommending that his client agree to the proposed adjustment. As part of this review the following should be considered:

1) Were any of the disallowed credit card charges signed by employees who are not also shareholders? If so, these amounts could not normally be attributed to the shareholder as a constructive dividend, for the requirement that the shareholder must receive an economic benefit is not present. In certain cases it may be to the practitioner's advantage to contend that the proposed disallowed credit card charge constitutes additional compensation to the employee who received the benefit of the expense. The corporation would still be entitled to a deduction for this amount.

## Stockholder's use of a corporate apartment is not automatically a constructive dividend

Some companies maintain an apartment in the city so that employees will not have to commute on evenings on which they have late appointments. In the usual case of the small, closely held corporation only the shareholders and top executives will be permitted to use the apartment. An agent may maintain that all undocumented use of the apartment constitutes a constructive dividend to one or more of the shareholders.

In those situations where more than one shareholder had the apartment available for his use and records were not maintained which indicated who used the apartment on which day, an effective argument can be used to avoid a constructive dividend issue. Remember, if no records were maintained the practitioner would have only a weak argument that the corporation is entitled to take a deduction for the apartment's cost. However, the lack of records, in the appropriate circumstances, may be the key element in avoiding the imposition of a constructive dividend. The most effective argument in such a case is simply to tell the agent that you agree that the shareholder used the apartment on occasion but there is absolutely no way to tell how many times it was used because of the time elapsed since the use occurred. (The tax return will probably not be audited for one and a half to two years after the end of its accounting period.) Accordingly, the agent will normally be unable to prove that the shareholder derived any personal benefit at all which should be charged back to him as a constructive dividend.

## Summary: What you should remember even if you don't remember anything else

For the practitioner, the most important thing to know when faced with a potential constructive dividend issue is when to stop discussing the matter with the agent. You must not encourage the agent to develop the facts essential for the government to show that a constructive dividend was received. Once the case leaves the agent's hands it is most unlikely that other IRS personnel will spend the time and do the leg work required to build up the case. Rather, the chances are that the next person to review the case will realize that the agent failed to take the necessary steps to make an open and shut case and will therefore be more willing to settle the matter.

# CHAPTER 15

# How to Represent a Client at a Specialty Audit

The IRS designates certain revenue agents to handle only specific types of audits. Agents assigned to specialty groups develop expertise in a limited area of the tax law. Because of the infrequent involvement with these areas of the law the general tax practitioner may find that he is at a distinct disadvantage when it comes to representing a client at such an audit.

Why? The revenue agent in the specialty group is not only familiar with seldom cited provisions of the Code but is also up to date on the applicable rulings issued in the area.

This chapter will serve to remove some of the mystique of representing a client at a specialty audit by guiding the practitioner through some of the areas usually highlighted by the agents doing these audits. Three typical specialty audits are:

1. Tax shelter audits

2. Estate and gift tax audits

3. Audits of tax-exempt organizations

## Tax shelter audits

In recent years the IRS has placed much emphasis and committed much manpower to auditing what they deem to be "abusive" tax shelters. Generally, these are investments which generate large deductions relative to the actual amount a taxpayer has at risk. Also, these investments lack economic substance.

### "Abusive" tax shelter characteristics

1) Accelerated depreciation
2) Mismatching of income and deductions
3) Substantial nonrecourse financing

4) Novel financing techniques which do not conform to standard commercial practices

5) Property whose value is subject to substantial uncertainty

6) The marketing of the investment as a tax shelter

7) An unlikely prospect of future cash flow

If your client has invested in a tax shelter with these kinds of attributes the chances are good that if audited the deductions will not be allowed.

### The agent will ask to see everything and allow nothing

All documents pertaining to your client's tax shelter investment will be requested. This includes copies of the offering memorandum, notes, bank guarantees and appraisals. The chances are that the agent may already have copies of much of what your client has in his possession. Once the IRS has identified an abusive tax shelter they will find out, from the promoter, the identity of the participants. All adjustments which will be proposed to your client are pro forma. The IRS has, in fact, probably already disallowed the same items on every investor's tax return.

### How do you fight it?

There is not too much the practitioner can do, at the IRS level, to challenge a proposed adjustment successfully. From experience, it has been found that the appellate division is summarily sustaining the agent's determinations and recommending that notices of deficiency be issued. Accordingly, the best advice to give a client who is caught up in a tax shelter audit is not to spend too much money or time fighting the issue with the agent. It is more practical to join together with other investors in tax court and split the cost of litigation (it is very expensive).

### Backlog in tax court

Because literally thousands of tax shelter deductions are being disallowed, ranging from movies to farm losses to leasing deals, an equally large number of taxpayers are filing tax court petitions. District counsel of the IRS has not yet issued a formal statement of how they intend to deal with the bureaucratic nightmare created by their own agency.

### Conclusion

You really can't help your client too much at the IRS level. Don't waste too much time with the agent as the chances are excellent that he will disallow all deductions regardless of the merit of your position if your client's investment has the attributes of an abusive tax shelter.

## Estate and gift tax audits

Estate and gift tax audits are handled by agents who are attorneys, specially trained in the field. Unless you are well versed in the Code sections affecting estate and gift taxes you may be at a distinct disadvantage in representing a client at such an audit.

### Answer questions carefully

If you are asked a question and you do not know the consequences of the answer, what should you do? Simply say, "Why are you asking me this question?" Follow by saying, "What are the consequences of saying yes or no?"

Refuse to answer any questions until the agent tells you why he is asking the question or until you can research the issue he is attempting to develop.

### Valuation issues

One of the most touched-upon issues when dealing with an estate and gift tax agent is that of valuation. The agent generally wants to raise the value of a reported item whereas you will want to sustain the value originally ascertained. Since complete texts have been written on the subject of valuing various types of assets no attempt will be made to do that here.

### Some tips

1) Prepare for the audit by assembling those documents which will tend to prove that you took a reasonable approach in valuing the asset on the tax return. Appraisals from qualified experts are best. If not available, then assemble a common-sense argument.

2) Review documentation carefully *before* you submit it to the agent to support your position. Make sure it doesn't contain information which the agent can twist around and use against your client. For instance, a financial statement may show a poor net worth which will support your having placed a low value on a business. However, the same statement may show that the operating loss was caused by an extraordinary item.

### Don't support the agent

It generally does not pay to agree with the agent if he proposes a substantial adjustment based upon a difference of opinion with respect to the proper valuation of an asset. Unless literally tremendous amounts of money are involved it is unlikely that the agent will be able to secure the services of expert appraisers.

If your client has the ability to secure experts to testify at trial the chances of being successful are substantially increased.

*Pointer:* The agent and the appellate conferee can say whatever they want to about the proper value of an asset. But if their only justification is their feeling as to what something is worth, their case is very weak. Take a hard-line approach and push for an acceptable compromise!

## Audits of tax-exempt organizations

The tax examinations of tax-exempt organizations present the practitioner with a unique situation. Generally, it will not matter (within limits) if an expense was or was not properly deducted since the organization is exempt from tax. For example, there is not much consequence if an expense was deducted instead of being capitalized.

### Why does the IRS audit these entities?

Essentially, the IRS examines tax exempt organizations to promote compliance with the provisions of the Code which requires that the activities of the entity merit the tax-exempt status bestowed upon it. Since the IRS granted tax-exempt status based on certain representations made in the organization's application for such status, it is incumbent upon the IRS to confirm that the organization is carrying out its stated mission.

### What will the agent ask for?

Chances are that the agent will not concentrate on the financial aspects of the organization. Usually, only a cursory review will be made of the books and records. Instead, the agent will ask for documents pertaining to the organization's activities. Brochures, pamphlets, and other publications distributed by the organization will be of particular interest.

*A good idea:* Read all materials before handing them over to the agent. Does the literature promote the exempt purpose of the organization?

# CHAPTER 16

# Deciding Whether to Agree to an Agent's Proposed Adjustments

There comes a point at the end of every tax examination when the practitioner is faced with a dilemma: should he recommend to his client that the agent's proposed adjustments be accepted?

Before coming to a decision about what to recommend the practitioner should be aware of the options available to him and his client. The following areas will be covered in this chapter:

1. The importance of reviewing the agent's work papers

2. How to negotiate with an agent

3. What to do if an issue is 100 percent against your client

4. How to help the agent see things your way

5. Factors to consider before agreeing to the agent's proposals

6. Should you agree to a proposed negligence penalty?

## The importance of reviewing the agent's work papers

After the agent has told you the amounts that he proposes to adjust it is incumbent upon you to find out how he arrived at the amounts.

Go through each issue with the agent, one issue at a time. First, ascertain what numbers he added up to arrive at the proposed adjustment. (Did he miss something he should have found?) Then, discuss law, theory, and the facts.

### What to look for

In the course of conducting an examination the agent may tend to make generalizations about certain things and then summarily make disallowances.

Revenue Agent Jackson did a test check of certain charge card receipts and noticed that the taxpayer's wife signed some vouchers. He says to himself that some of the charge card expenses deducted must therefore be of a personal nature. (He never discussed the issue with you.) In the course of preparing his work papers and arriving at a proposed adjustment he summarily disallows 45 percent of all charge card expenses.

Now is the time to determine what the agent has actually uncovered. The strengths and weaknesses of his case should be determined. Don't just argue blindly over an issue which he proposes to adjust—make the agent reveal every detail of his case.

Go through every single adjustment. You give yourself a psychological advantage when you make the agent explain why he disallowed each and every item. You are putting him on the defensive and making him justify what he did. Questioning every issue also wears down his stamina.

*Ploy:* Spend more time arguing about small and insignificant adjustments first. Give the agent the impression that he is winning the negotiation. Then, when it is time to discuss the larger items he may be more willing to compromise knowing that he has already won something.

*Travel and entertainment issues:* Pressure the agent to explain to you why each and every individual expense he proposes to disallow is not a valid deduction. After half an hour of this he will not be able to go on much farther and will be more willing to listen to your offer for compromise. (Remember: challenge every contention or assumption he makes!)

*Extra benefit:* If you review the agent's work papers he will be less likely to add new adjustments after he goes back to his office since he knows that you know exactly what he proposed to disallow. (Technically, there is really nothing to stop him from changing his mind about the amount of adjustments until his report is actually submitted.)

## How to negotiate with an agent

The IRS will never officially admit it, but agents are encouraged to be flexible and to compromise under most circumstances. The exception is when the IRS wants to push a specific compliance project, like tax shelters which are abusive.

Management knows that taking a too hard-nosed approach in every case will create chaos. Cases will not be closed agreed and the system could not possibly absorb the phenomenal number of appeals.

"Let's make a deal."

It is not tactful actually to say to an agent "Let's make a deal." Such a statement will probably be construed as a bribe offer. The agent will thereafter not even consider compromising his position for fear that he is being set up.

**What should you say?**

Tell the agent that:

1) Certain assumptions he has made are unfounded and cannot be proved.

2) He is being unreasonable.

3) Your client will never agree to his proposed adjustments.

Now, follow this up by saying:

"I insist that you reconsider your position about _____. Let's talk about what would be a fair adjustment."

*Consider this:* You do not always have to state emphatically that you will not agree to any adjustment. Let the agent feel he is correct in that an adjustment should be made—but not in an amount as large as he proposes.

"I agree, [Revenue Agent] John, that there was some personal use of the automobile. It was probably not more than ten percent—not the seventy percent figure you seem to feel is correct."

*The agent's strategy:* He knows that he will have to give in on certain issues. Either entirely or in part. Many times he will raise issues, which he knows he cannot adequately develop or win, for bargaining purposes only. (This is technically, absolutely, against the rules, but it is commonly done.)

*Counterstrategy:* Do not let an agent scare you if he proposes an exotic issue (unreasonable compensation, for example.) He knows that this type of issue will be dropped in the course of negotiation. Do not let him fool you into accepting all his other adjustments if he tells you he will be a nice guy and drop the issues he knows he cannot prove anyway.

## What to do if an issue is 100 percent against your client

There will be times when an agent has a seemingly "airtight" case. What should you do about it? Try to develop alternative theories about what happened. Speculate. But let the agent know that you are speculating! He may be inclined to go along with your version of the story even though none of what you say may be provable.

### A typical example

Suppose an agent proposes to disallow all of the salary paid to your client's wife because the agent says that she never came into the office. This would be your response:

"First of all, you really do not know if she comes into the office or not. Even if she never came into the office that does not mean that she didn't earn the money she was paid. There is no law that says you must be physically present in an office to be paid a salary. How do you know she doesn't spend time meeting with potential customers or reviewing correspondence or consulting on management problems?"

## How to help the agent see things your way

Even though an agent may be sympathetic to your position he may be reluctant to change his mind about a proposed adjustment for fear that either his group manager or the review staff will send the case back to him for correction.

Help the agent. How? By helping him write his work papers in a way that will avoid any question that what he did was correct. You have to take the initiative. Don't expect the revenue agent to allow a gray issue without your explaining the entire rationale necessary to support your position.

Revenue Agent Jackson proposes to disallow deductions generated from a ranching operation because, according to him, "The IRS is disallowing all tax shelters." Since this type of adjustment could have substantial financial ramifications to your client—think fast! Explain that your client's deductions have been generated from a business and not merely a tax shelter. Show the revenue agent that this type of deduction was not contemplated under the tax shelter program. Make sure that he can justify your entire position when he writes up his work papers. Review what he has written. Make suggestions on how to improve his narrative, if possible.

## Factors to consider before agreeing to the agent's proposals

Sometimes there are very good reasons for agreeing with the agent's proposed adjustments—even if part or all of it is wrong!

## Probability of other issues being raised

If the agent failed to identify and develop an issue which could result in a far greater tax deficiency than what he has proposed, it may be a good idea to agree with the agent—just for the sake of closing the case. The IRS can, although it ordinarily does not, raise new issues at the appellate level or even in tax court.

## Blatant errors

If a revenue agent should come up with his own theory as to what the tax law is (but is absolutely incorrect) you may want to file a pro-forma appeal just to move the case into the hands of someone more reasonable. Most times it will take no more effort than a telephone conversation to resolve the issue with an appellate conferee.

## Dollar amount involved

If the dollar amount of the extra tax proposed by the agent is nominal it is not usually economical for your client to appeal. The cost, in terms of time, necessary to appeal a case, will be greater than the extra tax the IRS is seeking.

But if the amount of the proposed adjustment is substantial then there may be no downside risk in appealing. Even if you think, at this point, that the agent's case is airtight, there may be room for negotiation. When thousands of dollars of tax are involved even a 10 percent reduction of tax can be worth the effort of preparing an appeal.

## Handling the situation where the agent has missed an important issue but has also proposed a large deficiency

One of my client's was faced with a unique problem. The agent had proposed a large deficiency, which if protested, could have certainly been substantially reduced. On the other hand, the agent had not pursued an issue which could have resulted in a $250,000 deficiency.

If an appeal was made to the appellate division or to the tax court there existed the possibility that someone down the line would try to set up the $250,000 issue.

The problem was solved in the following manner:

1) The agent was told that the client would not agree and that he should close the case on that basis.

2) No appeal was filed.

3) The IRS issued a ninety-day letter and my client did not file a tax court petition.

4) The case was routinely processed, a bill was mailed to my client, and the bill was paid.

5) Before the statute of limitations expired for filing a claim for refund a claim was filed.

Even if the IRS decides to disallow the claim it will be unable to collect any more tax in the event someone wanted to pursue the $250,000 issue.

## Should you agree to a proposed negligence penalty?

Unless there should exist a compelling reason to do so, do not agree to a negligence penalty at the agent's level. This penalty is more times than not an arbitrary determination made by the agent because he either dislikes or does not trust you or your client.

### What is negligence?

According to the *Internal Revenue Manual,* negligence is defined as follows (italics mine):

"Negligence, in the generally accepted legal sense, is the omission to do something which a reasonable person, guided by those considerations which ordinarily regulate the conduct of human affairs, would do, or doing something which a prudent and reasonable person would not do. Whether or not negligence has occurred in a particular income or gift tax case is necessarily a factual determination that calls for taking into account the standard of conduct that can reasonably be expected from a taxpayer and the exercise of sound judgment by the examiner, supervisor, and reviewer. *The negligence penalty should be invoked if there has been negligence or an intentional disregard of published rulings and regulations in the preparation of returns, as distinguished from a mere error or a difference of opinion on some controversial question* and a willful intent to evade is not present or cannot be substantiated."

The following are examples of cases in which negligence may exist according to the *Manual:*

1) The taxpayer continues to make substantial errors in reporting income and claiming personal deductions year after year, even though these mistakes have been called to his attention in previous reports.

2) The taxpayer fails to maintain proper records after being advised through inadequate-records procedures to do so, and subsequent errors are filed.

3) The taxpayer makes careless and exaggerated claims of deductions unsubstantiated by facts.

4) The taxpayer fails to offer any explanation for the understatement of income, and for the failure to keep books and records.

### Don't be afraid to take the blame

An almost absolute defense to relieve your client of a negligence penalty is to acknowledge that you or some other practitioner advised your client that a certain tax deduction had some basis. You may suffer some embarrassment but the IRS will generally not levy the negligence penalty where it knows that the taxpayer relied on the advice of his accountant or attorney. (Caution: Be careful not to phrase your acceptance of the blame in such a manner that your client can sue you for malpractice.)

### Summary

The first step in deciding whether to agree to the agent's proposed adjustments is to determine how much he really knows about all of the potential issues. Review his work papers with him. Negotiate the best deal possible. Offer suggestions and alternative theories if you see that the agent is reluctant to change his mind.

Be sure that, before you take a stance with respect to appealing the proposed adjustments raised by the agent, you and your client are fully aware of any potential risks in making that decision. If you appeal the agent's determination then the cost of the appeal must be weighed against the possible gain, as well as the potential risk that additional issues may be raised.

# CHAPTER 17

# Taking a Case
# to the Appeals Division

The IRS fully recognizes that every case may not be settled at the examining agent's level. Accordingly, there exists a single level of administrative appeal within the IRS known as the appeals division. This office is usually staffed by veteran examiners who are quick to get to the merits of the case—be it your client's or the government's. Generally, the taxpayer and his representative receive fair treatment in what will amount to a mutual effort to resolve the case.

There may be circumstances when your client should not pursue the course of an administrative appeal, as previously unraised issues technically can be developed at the appeal stage. This chapter discusses the following items of interest to the practitioner contemplating an appeal:

1. Traps and benefits of taking a case to the appeals office

2. The leverage that appeals officers may apply and how to deal with it

3. Rev. Proc. 79-59

4. Pro-Forma Petition

## Traps and benefits of taking a case to the appeals office

### What are the traps?

Suppose you and the revenue agent have agreed on some issues but disagree on others. If you take your client's case to the appeals office can the IRS reopen issues you already thought were settled? Or worse, raise new issues?

The answer is yes, they can!

### There are guidelines

The official IRS position is that new issues should not be raised casually, indiscriminately, or haphazardly and should never, under any circumstances, be raised for bargaining purposes. The commissioner cautiously warns the appeals officers that to raise frivolous new issues would circumvent the stated mission of the appeals office which is "to resolve tax controversies, without litigation, on a basis which is fair and impartial to both the government and the taxpayer and in a manner that will enhance voluntary compliance and public confidence in the integrity and efficiency of the Service."

According to the *Internal Revenue Manual* a new issue should not be raised by appeals to the taxpayer's detriment unless grounds for such action are substantial (strong, possessing real merit) and the potential effect on tax liability is material.

*Important:* "Substantial" means that there must be some good reason *already existing in the record or known to the appeals officer* to raise the issue. Mere suspicion or a guess that something might be wrong is not "substantial."

For example, if the district director disallowed a claimed farm loss solely on the ground that it was a hobby and made no comment concerning the items making up the loss, there would not be substantial grounds for raising a new issue concerning the amount of loss, amount of any item making up the loss, or nature of any item making up the loss simply because the appeals officer merely suspected or guessed that the items had not been verified. On the other hand, if the district director's examination had indicated and his report had stated that these items had not been verified, there would be good reason for the appeals officer, if he believed such action was necessary, to refer the case back to the district director for such verification.

### Forget the guidelines if you anticipate a problem

Regardless of the guidelines which indicate that new issues will not be raised unless there is a substantial reason, do not take a case to the appeals office if it is obvious that the examining agent has overlooked a potential issue. The chances are that even if the appeals officer does not raise a new issue he or she may very well use it as leverage to make you agree to the adjustments presently on the table. For instance, you may be presented with the following option: "Mr. Practitioner, we both know that the revenue agent should have raised issue X but didn't. I'll tell you what I'm going to do—I won't raise the new issue even if the case should go unagreed. However, I'll only reduce the proposed adjustment by a nominal amount."

You may have a better shot of having the proposed adjustments compromised by filing a tax court petition instead of going to the appeals office.

### Benefits of going to the appeals office

The Appeals Office has something called "settlement authority" which means that they have the ability to compromise issues in an effort to close cases. Where the facts and circumstances in a given case indicate that there is a substantial uncertainty in event of litigation as to how the courts would interpret and apply the law or as to how the court will assess the facts in a particular case, the appeals office will be amenable to compromise issues.

### Split-issue settlements

A split-issue settlement is a form of mutual concession settlement of an issue which, if litigated, would result in a decision completely for the government or the taxpayer. The distinguishing feature of a split-issue settlement is that the agreed result would not be reached if the case was tried.

For example, the appeals office can split an exemption. Regardless of which spouse may be entitled to a particular exemption, each will be given one-half the value of the exemption.

*General guideline:* It generally is in your client's interest to bring his case to the appeals office when you don't think the revenue agent made a fair decision!

If you should have the unfortunate experience of dealing with a revenue agent who proposes unfair adjustments you will not be totally out of luck. The appeals officers are usually experienced agents themselves and know when something unreasonable has been suggested by the revenue agent at the district office level.

Unless both the issues involved and the facts of your client's case are such that there is absolutely no room for compromise, you can expect to come out with a better "bottom line" with the appeals office than you were presented with by the agent.

## The leverage that appeals officers may apply and how to deal with it

Appeals Officers may attempt to apply pressure in an effort to close the case on an agreed basis. One way is to imply that they may raise a new issue unless you agree to their proposals. If this is the case then a protest should be registered with both the appeals officer and his group manager. Treat such an implication as a threat and make it known that you will not stand for such treatment.

An appeals officer may think that he can pressure your client into agreeing to a particular issue based on the fact that the cost of appealing to the tax court would be prohibitive. How to counter: Explain that the cost of filing a tax court petition is only sixty dollars and that you will represent your client for nothing to see that justice is done. The filing of a tax court petition permits the case to be heard by an IRS attorney *before* anybody even goes to court.

## Rev. Proc. 79-59

The practitioner should be aware of the provisions of Rev. Proc. 79-59 as they relate to the role of the appeals office in cases docketed in tax court when the taxpayer did not first seek an administrative review in the appeals office.

If you let the thirty-day period expire without filing a protest the IRS will issue a notice of deficiency, requiring that a tax court petition be filed. Once the tax court petition is filed the case is sent back to the appeals office in an attempt to settle the case. The appeals division will have exclusive jurisdiction for a period of four months over the case. If the case cannot be settled then the case is returned to the regional counsel's office for trial preparation.

### Strategy

Depending upon the merits of each individual case, you may find that the appeals officer you are dealing with will make every effort to reach a settlement. Because of the IRS's self-imposed period of four months there generally is not time for the appeals officer to delve into all the facets of your client's case. Accordingly, you may be able to push successfully for a compromise now, although such a compromise may not have been possible had the case been routed to the appeals division pursuant to a formal protest.

## Pro-forma petition

A formal written protest must be filed with the district director in all cases except where:

1) The proposed increase or decrease in tax, or claimed refund, does not exceed $2,500 for any of the tax periods involved in a field examination.

2) The examination was conducted by a tax auditor or by correspondence.

If a written protest is required, it must be filed within the thirty-day period after the issuance of the agent's examination report.

# Sample Petition

[Date]

District Director
Internal Revenue Service
New York, NY 10008

Re:  Jack Jones
1979–1040
153-09-8764

AU:F 30D

Dear Sir:

This letter represents a formal written appeal of the findings of the examining offi-cer; a copy of his report is enclosed. It is requested that this protest be considered by the regional director of appeals.

The following adjustments were proposed to which our client takes exception:

| | |
|---|---|
| Real estate taxes | $3,000 |
| Business expenses | $9,673 |

## STATEMENT OF FACTS

[Set forth those facts supporting your position in any contested factual issue.]

## STATEMENT OF LAW

[Set forth the law or other authority upon which you rely.]

A Power of Attorney executed by the taxpayer is enclosed.

Under penalties of perjury, I declare that I have prepared this protest and accompa-nying documents and personally know that the statements of fact contained in the protest and accompanying documents are, to the best of my knowledge and belief, true, correct, and complete.

Sincerely,

Allen Scott, Esq.

*Tip:* Keep the protest simple. It can, but does not have to, have the complete-ness of a brief. Many issues can be settled inexpensively on your client's behalf. Don't spend the time on researching and writing until you see that such time will be warranted.

# CHAPTER 18

# How to Use the
# Freedom of Information Act

The Freedom of Information Act (FOIA) is a federal statute (5 USC 552) which, among other things, permits an individual access to records maintained by a government agency. Although the FOIA provides for disclosure of certain statistical data and operational procedure information about a particular federal agency, the scope of this discussion will be limited to the practical application of the law by practitioners when dealing with the IRS.

The following topics will be covered:

1. When would you use the FOIA?

2. What records are not available under the FOIA?

3. Form request letter

## When would you use the FOIA?

1) You have just been retained by a new client who is in the middle of a tax examination and you want to know exactly what the agent does and does not have in his work papers.

2) You are preparing an IRS appeal or a tax court petition and you want to see the agent's work papers to determine the rationale he is using to support his position on various issues.

## What records are not available under the FOIA?

There is presently much litigation in the area of what records are exempt under the Freedom of Information Act. "Investigatory records" compiled for law enforcement do not have to be provided if their disclosure would:

1) interfere with enforcement proceedings

2) deprive a person of a fair trial or adjudication

3) constitute an unwarranted invasion of personal privacy

4) disclose the identity of a confidential source

5) disclose investigative techniques and procedures

6) endanger the life or safety of law enforcement personnel

Generally, the IRS will be reluctant to provide any information during a criminal investigation citing as its reason that the documents requested are investigatory records whose disclosure would interfere with enforcement proceedings.

## Form request letter

[Date]

Disclosure Officer
Internal Revenue Service
120 Church Street
New York, N.Y. 10008

Re:  Jack Smith
1979–1040
104-56-7653

Dear Sir:

This letter represents a formal request pursuant to the provisions of the Freedom of Information Act for access to and copies of all work papers, correspondence, memoranda, internal documents, and all other papers maintained by the Internal Revenue Service with respect to the above captioned taxpayer's 1979 income tax examination.

The taxpayer authorizes you to incur expenses in an amount no greater than twenty-five dollars for search and copying charges. If the fee should exceed this amount, please contact the undersigned for further authorization.

It is requested that if you should determine that any of the information requested is exempt from disclosure, the taxpayer be provided with a detailed description of those documents not furnished.

A Power of Attorney executed by the taxpayer is enclosed.

Sincerely,

Allen Scott, Esq.

# CHAPTER 19

# Waiving the
# Statute of Limitations

The statute of limitations generally provides that the IRS has a time limit of three years after a tax return is due or filed, whichever is later, to examine a tax return and to make an assessment. Because of this congressionally imposed deadline the IRS finds it necessary to ask the taxpayer to extend the statute of limitations from time to time. The granting of an extension permits the IRS more time to determine if an assessment should be made and also permits the taxpayer access to the IRS appeals system.

This chapter answers many of the questions that come up when the IRS solicits an extension of time of the statute of limitations:

1. What happens if your client does not sign a waiver to extend the statute of limitations?

2. When shouldn't your client sign a waiver to extend the statute of limitations?

3. Requesting a limited or restricted waiver

## What happens if your client
## does not sign a waiver to extend
## the statute of limitations?

If the statute of limitations is about to expire and the IRS is still in the process of examining a tax return it will ask for a consent to extend the time that an assessment may be made. Unfortunately for the taxpayer, the IRS takes a "heads I win, tails you lose" attitude about its request for a waiver to extend the statute of limitations. If your client signs the waiver then the IRS has additional time to make an assessment. On the other hand, if your client refuses to sign the waiver the IRS will make an arbitrary assessment to protect its interest and issue a notice of deficiency. At that point, a tax court petition must be filed within ninety days to avoid paying the assessed tax and interest.

### Jeopardy assessments not permitted

The refusal to execute a waiver to extend the statute of limitations should not result in a jeopardy assessment. Jeopardy assessments, which must be approved by the district director, are only made if one or more of the following conditions exist:

1) The taxpayer is or appears to be planning to depart the United States quickly or to seek concealment.

2) The taxpayer is or appears to be quickly planning to place property beyond the reach of the government either by removing it from the United States, concealing it, dissipating it, or transferring it to other persons.

3) The taxpayer's financial solvency is or appears to be imperiled, other than in cases where the taxpayer becomes insolvent by the accrual of the proposed assessment of tax, penalty and interest.

### Don't let the agent threaten you

If the agent attempts to pressure you into having your client execute a waiver by threatening to propose an unrealistically high assessment "to protect the government's interest," immediately register a written complaint with the group manager and send a copy of your protest to the district director.

## When shouldn't your client sign a waiver to extend the statute of limitations?

There are certain circumstances where it would be in your client's best interest *not* to sign a waiver extending the statute of limitations.

### Potential issues

If the agent has failed to develop a significant issue it may be a good idea to tell the agent your client refuses to waive the statute of limitations. He will either be pressured to close the case at that point or recommend a proposed deficiency based on what he has already found. If an arbitrary amount of tax is assessed it should not be very difficult to have this eliminated at the tax court level.

### Unreported income

If you suspect that your client may not have reported all of his income, refusing to sign the waiver may be an appropriate step. Generally, there will be no further investigation into the matter. An assessment will be generated which your client will be happy to pay—considering the alternative of a complete criminal investigation if the agent had time to develop the case more fully.

## Requesting a limited or restricted waiver

The IRS may be willing to limit or restrict the terms of your client's waiver of the statute of limitations. But *you must ask for and then insist on a limitation/ restriction or else you will not get it!*

### Length of extension

There are two kinds of waivers:

1) *Fixed date, flexible expiration.* This type of waiver expires on the earlier of the date specified in the consent or the date of assessment of the tax.

2) *Open-ended consent.* This type of waiver extends the statute of limitations until ninety days after either the taxpayer or the IRS decides to end activity on the case.

*Tip:* Limit the length of a waiver to six months. If longer, the IRS has no incentive to work on the case and end it.

*Reverse strategy:* Give an open-ended consent and the case may just sit and get old without any work being done.

### Restricted waivers

Suppose you have completed the audit and the agent has proposed one or two issues to which you do not agree. Since the statute of limitations is about to expire the agent will solicit a waiver from you so that the appellate division will be able to review the case. Insist on receiving a waiver which is limited to the unagreed issues only.

This way, the appellate division is locked into the one or two issues which are the subject of the appeal and will be unable to raise new issues.

# CHAPTER 20

# Notice of Deficiency and
# Tax Court Practice and Procedures

## Notice of Deficiency

Before the IRS can assess a tax they must issue a notice of deficiency, also known as a "ninety-day letter," (see accompanying sample) which informs the taxpayer of the amount claimed to be due, the reason(s) why the tax has been proposed and the fact that the proposed adjustment in tax liability must be contested by filing a tax court petition within ninety days or else the tax will be assessed.

The notice of deficiency must be annexed to the tax court petition when it is filed. Without an issued notice of deficiency the tax court generally lacks jurisdiction to hear a case.

### Technical requirements

The notice of deficiency must be mailed by registered or certified mail to the taxpayer's last known address.

### Expiration of 90-day period

A problem faced by many practitioners is the following: *What do you do if the 90-day period to file a tax court petition has expired and nothing was done?*

This problem could arise for any number of reasons. Perhaps you are retained by a new client who does not remember receiving a notice of deficiency or received it but didn't realize the importance of the ninety-day period. In other cases a new client may have retained an accountant to handle his audit but that accountant never showed up and all deductions were summarily disallowed. In fact, you may have forgotten to file a tax court petition for one of your own clients. What do you do now?

Technically, the IRS can make your client pay the tax which is owed and then have him file a claim for a refund. Since an erroneous tax assessment could be very large it may be virtually impossible for your client to come up with the money and then have to wait for the IRS to process his claim.

Department of the Treasury
P.O. BOX 3100, CHURCH STREET STA.

Date: July 16, 1981

Social Security or
**Employer Identification Number:**
003-76-9998
Tax Year Ended and Deficiency:

12/31/78    $1,187.00

▷    Robert and Susan Smith
114 East 72nd Street
New York, N.Y.  10022

**Person to Contact:**
E:90D:R:  E. Jones
**Contact Telephone Number:**
264-7198

Dear Sir and Madam:

We have determined that there is a deficiency (increase) in your income tax as shown above. This letter is a NOTICE OF DEFICIENCY sent to you as required by law. The enclosed statement shows how we figured the deficiency.

If you want to contest this deficiency in court before making any payment, you have 90 days from the above mailing date of this letter (150 days if addressed to you outside of the United States) to file a petition with the United States Tax Court for a redetermination of the deficiency. The petition should be filed with the United States Tax Court, 400 Second Street NW., Washington, D.C. 20217, and the copy of this letter should be attached to the petition. The time in which you must file a petition with the Court (90 or 150 days as the case may be) is fixed by law and the Court cannot consider your case if your petition is filed late. If this letter is addressed to both a husband and wife, and both want to petition the Tax Court, both must sign the petition or each must file a separate, signed petition.

If you dispute not more than $5,000 for any one tax year, a simplified procedure is provided by the Tax Court for small tax cases. You can get information about this procedure, as well as a petition form you can use, by writing to the Clerk of the United States Tax Court at 400 Second Street NW., Washington, D.C. 20217. You should do this promptly if you intend to file a petition with the Tax Court.

If you decide not to file a petition with the Tax Court, we would appreciate it if you would sign and return the enclosed waiver form. This will permit us to assess the deficiency quickly and will limit the accumulation of interest. The enclosed addressed envelope is for your convenience. If you decide not to sign and return the statement and you do not timely petition the Tax Court, the law requires us to assess and bill you for the deficiency after 90 days from the above mailing date of this letter (150 days if this letter is addressed to you outside the United States).

If you have any questions, please contact the person whose name and telephone number are shown above.

Sincerely yours,

Roscoe L. Egger, Jr.
Commissioner
By

Enclosures:
Copy of this letter
Statement
Envelope

District Director

Letter 531(DO) (Rev. 3—81)

## Reconsideration

The IRS has an informal policy called "Reconsideration" whereby they will give a taxpayer what amounts to another chance to justify the deductions claimed that were disallowed. Generally, reasonable cause must exist to warrant the IRS to invoke the reconsideration policy. This action by the IRS is purely discretionary and the taxpayer has no recourse if his request is denied.

A letter should be written to the district director which explains the reasonable cause, and which should invoke the reconsideration policy. The letter should request that an appointment be scheduled to afford your client the opportunity to prove the amounts which were originally disallowed.

# Tax Court Practice
# and Procedures

This section will focus on the initial step which must be taken by the practitioner after his client receives a notice of deficiency. That is, deciding whether a tax court petition should be filed. Filing a petition is a relatively simple procedure which will enable the practitioner to discuss the merits of his client's case with at least one new person (an IRS attorney) before the case ever goes to court.

The following topics concerning tax court practice and procedure will be discussed:

1. Why should a tax practitioner want to be admitted to tax court?

2. What is the procedure for being admitted?

3. Why should you go to tax court?

4. Filing a petition

## Why should a tax practitioner want to be admitted to tax court?

The rules of the United States Tax Court permit a person who is not an attorney to represent a client. All practitioners who regularly represent clients before the Internal Revenue Service should attempt to become admitted to practice before the tax court. The fact that the IRS employee you are negotiating with knows that you are personally capable of pursuing the case to court provides you with an additional bit of leverage.

Filing a petition with the tax court does not mean that you will necessarily ever go to trial, file briefs, or do anything else for that matter. Generally, cases are settled before trial. By qualifying to be admitted to practice before the tax court you are providing your client with an additional opportunity to have his case heard by more people in an attempt to eliminate or at least reduce the amount of tax the IRS says he owes. The time needed to prepare a standard petition is nominal and much negotiation towards settlement can even be done over the telephone.

### What is the procedure for being admitted?

The official tax court rules provide for the following procedure:

1) An applicant, not an attorney at law, must file with the admissions clerk a completed application accompanied by a fee of ten dollars. In addition, such an applicant, as a condition of being admitted to practice, must give evidence of his qualifications satisfactory to the court by means of a written examination given by the court, and the court may require such person, in addition, to give similar evidence by means of an oral examination. Any person who has thrice failed to give such evidence by means of such written examination shall not thereafter be eligible to take another examination for admission.

2) An application for admission to practice before the court must be on the form provided by the court. Application forms and other necessary information will be furnished upon request addressed to the Admissions Clerk, United States Tax Court, 400 Second Street NW, Washington, D.C. 20217.

3) An applicant for admission by examination must be sponsored by at least three persons theretofore admitted to practice before the Court, and each sponsor must send a letter of recommendation directly to the admissions clerk of the court, where it will be treated as a confidential communication. The sponsor shall send his letter promptly, stating therein fully and frankly the extent of his acquaintance with the applicant, his opinion of the moral character and repute of the applicant, and his opinion of the qualifications of the applicant to practice before the court. The court may in its discretion accept such an applicant with less than three such sponsors.

4) Written examinations, for applicants other than attorneys at law, will be held no less often than every two years. By public announcement at least six months prior to the date of the examination, the court will announce the time and place at which he is to present himself for examination, and the applicant must present that notice to the examiner as his authority for taking an examination.

## Why should you go to tax court?

In most situations the tax court is the last step your client has to fight a proposed assessment by the IRS. Remember, the tax court is not part of the IRS. As such, the tax court does not always agree with the IRS interpretation of the Internal Revenue Code.

*Two extra chances to reduce the proposed assessment! (if the case wasn't taken to the appeals division):* Filing a petition is relatively simple and inexpensive. By filing the petition you will have the opportunity to settle your case twice before trial. Once with an appellate conferee and second with the IRS attorney who will represent the government in court.

After the case is docketed it is immediately sent back to the appellate division in an effort to resolve the case. If no agreement can be obtained then you will be contacted by the IRS attorney before he begins to prepare the case for trial.

*Inside information:* Regardless of official IRS statements, the people you will be dealing with after the tax court petition is filed will try to settle the case. The appellate conferee looks good to his superiors if he can close the case agreed and the IRS attorney will have one less case to prepare for trial. This rationale works especially well where no technical issues are involved, for example, where deductions for travel and business expenses have been disallowed. If your client's case has some sort of notoriety attached to it or the issue is "hot" (e.g. tax shelters) the prospects of settlement are substantially reduced.

*Caution:* You cannot file a tax court petition for a frivolous reason or merely as a delaying tactic!

*No money has to be paid to the IRS.* If you go to tax court the proposed assessment contained in the notice of deficiency does not have to be paid until the court renders a decision. Typically, one to two years could pass before your client will be required to pay the tax, if he loses.

### What about other forums?

The United States District Court and the Court of Claims may have already decided your client's issue favorably, whereas the tax court may not yet have had the issue presented. Alternatively, you may find that the tax court always sides with the government when it is presented with the facts and circumstances of your client's case. In order to take a case into either the district court or Court of Claims the tax your client owes must generally be paid.

As a practical matter, many practitioners favor tax court because of the ability to defer the time that the amount of disputed tax must be paid.

### The down side of going to tax court

In their answer to your petition the IRS can increase the amount of tax they think your client should pay. Although this does not usually happen it should be considered by the practitioner when his client's initial audit failed to uncover other areas which may have exposure.

*What should you do if you are afraid the IRS may increase the tax if you go to tax court?*

1)  Pay the tax instead of going to tax court.
2)  File a claim for refund with the IRS one week before the statute of limitations expires.
3)  Assuming the IRS will disallow the claim for refund, take the case to the district court or the Court of Claims. Even if the IRS should successfully claim that you owe more tax they will not be able to collect it since the statute of limitations has expired.

### Electing the small tax case procedure

Where a tax deficiency in any one year is $5,000 or less the tax court permits the taxpayer to elect to have the case conducted under an informal trial procedure. Rules of evidence are somewhat relaxed and formal trial practice is dispensed with.

If you lose in a small tax case procedure there is no appeal.

If a client does not want to incur the professional fees for representation in tax court then the following material could be used as your guide for preparing a petition at a nominal expense to your client with the understanding that if you cannot reach a settlement of the case before trial he can go to court himself and try his luck.

## Filing a petition

The mechanics of filing a tax court petition are very easy. There are only a few technical rules to know:

1) The IRS must have issued a statutory notice of deficiency, also known as a "ninety-day letter." A copy of the notice of deficiency must be annexed to the petition. The tax court will not accept a petition unless the IRS has formally issued a notice of deficiency.

2) The petition must be filed not later than ninety days after the notice of deficiency was mailed (150 days if the notice is addressed to a person outside the United States). Ninety days means ninety days—not three months!

3) File an original and four conformed copies of the petition.

4) Complete Tax Court Form #4 which allows you to choose the city of the trial. File an original and two copies.

5) Enclose a sixty-dollar check made payable to "Clerk, U. S. Tax Court."

6) Mail the petition, request for place of trial, and check via certified mail, return receipt requested.

# UNITED STATES TAX COURT

(FIRST)         (MIDDLE)        (LAST)

JOHN    J.    SMITH
(PLEASE TYPE OR PRINT)      Petitioner(s)

v.

COMMISSIONER OF INTERNAL REVENUE
         Respondent            Docket No.

## PETITION

1. Petitioner(X) disagree(s) with the tax deficiency(X) for the year(X) __1979__ , as set forth in the NOTICE OF DEFICIENCY dated __MARCH 1, 1981__ , A COPY OF WHICH IS ATTACHED. The notice was issued by the Office of the Internal Revenue Service at __BROOKLYN , NEW YORK__
(CITY AND STATE)

2. Petitioner(X) taxpayer identification (e.g. social security) number(X) is (X) __012-34-5678__ .

3. Petitioner(s) dispute(s) the following:

| Year | Amount of Deficiency Disputed | Addition to Tax (Penalty), if any, Disputed | Amount of Over- payment Claimed |
|---|---|---|---|
| 1979 | $4562.00 | | |
| | | | |
| | | | |

4. Set forth those adjustments, i.e. changes, in the NOTICE OF DEFICIENCY with which you disagree and why you disagree.

1. THE COMMISSIONER ERRED IN DISALLOWING $9450.00 OF ORDINARY AND NECESSARY BUSINESS EXPENSES WHICH WERE PROPERLY DEDUCTED PURSUANT TO INTERNAL REVENUE CODE SECTIONS 162 AND 274.

Petitioner(s) request(s) that this case be conducted under the "small tax case" procedures authorized by Congress to provide the taxpayer(s) with an informal, prompt, and inexpensive hearing at a reasonably convenient location. Consistent with these objectives, a decision in a "small tax case" is final and cannot be appealed to higher Courts (the Courts of Appeals and the Supreme Court) by the Internal Revenue Service or the Petitioner(s). *

| SIGNATURE OF PETITIONER | DATE | PRESENT ADDRESS—STREET, CITY, STATE, ZIP CODE—TELEPHONE NO. |
|---|---|---|

| SIGNATURE OF PETITIONER (SPOUSE) | DATE | PRESENT ADDRESS—STREET, CITY, STATE, ZIP CODE—TELEPHONE NO. |
|---|---|---|

Sam Smith, CPA

45 COURT STREET
BROOKLYN, N.Y. 11020
212-484-3000    4-18-81

SIGNATURE AND ADDRESS OF COUNSEL, IF RETAINED BY PETITIONER(S)    DATE

* If you do not want to make this request, you should place an "X" in the following box.

T.C. Form 2
(Rev. Feb. 1979)

UNITED STATES TAX COURT

JOHN J. SMITH                          )
                Petitioner(s),         )
                                       )
                                       )    Docket No.
            v.                         )
                                       )
                                       )
COMMISSIONER OF INTERNAL REVENUE,
                Respondent.

REQUEST FOR PLACE OF TRIAL

        Petitioner(s) hereby request(s) that trial of this case be
held at _____NEW YORK , NEW YORK_____
                (City and State)

                        Sam Smith, CPA
                Signature of Petitioner or Counsel

                Dated: APRIL 18 , 19 81

                                        Form 4
                                        (Rev. 11/76)

## Form Tax Court Petition

### UNITED STATES TAX COURT

_____, Petitioner

v.

Commissioner of Internal
Revenue, Respondent

Docket No. _____

### PETITION

The petitioner hereby petitions for a redetermination of the deficiency [or liability] set forth by the Commissioner of Internal Revenue in his notice of deficiency [or liability] [Service symbols, found in deficiency letter to left of "person to contact"] dated _____, 19 __, and as the basis for his case alleges as follows:

1) The petitioner is [set forth whether an individual, fiduciary, corporation, etc., as provided in Rule 60] with legal residence (or principal office) now at _____ [street], _____[city], ____[state], _____[zip code]. Petitioner's taxpayer identification number [e.g., social security or employer identification number] is _____. The return for the period here involved was filed with the Office of the Internal Revenue Service at _____[city], _____[state].

2) The notice of deficiency [or liability] (a copy of which, including as much of the statement and schedules accompanying the notice as is material, is attached and marked Exhibit A) was mailed to the petitioner on _____, 19 __, and was issued by the Office of the Internal Revenue Service at _____[city and state].

3) The deficiencies [or liabilities] as determined by the Commissioner are in income [estate, gift, or certain excise] taxes for the calendar [or fiscal] year 19 __, in the amount of $ _____, of which $ _____, is in dispute.

4) The determination of tax set forth in the said notice of deficiency [or liability] is based upon the following errors: [Here set forth specifically in lettered subparagraphs the assignments of error in a concise manner and avoid pleading facts which properly belong in the succeeding paragraph].

5) The facts upon which the petitioner relies, as the basis of his case, are as follows: [Here set forth allegations of fact, but not the evidence, sufficient to inform the court and the commissioner of the positions taken and the bases therefor, in orderly and logical sequence, with subparagraphs lettered, so as to enable the commissioner to admit or deny each allegation].

Wherefore, petitioner prays that [here set forth the relief desired].

[Signature] _____
["Petitioner" or "Counsel"]
[Post Office address]
[Telephone number]

[Date]

# CHAPTER 21

# The *Internal Revenue Manual* and Other Research Tools

In the course of preparing their case against your client, revenue agents may use various research tools. The *Internal Revenue Manual (IRM)* is the place for the practitioner as well as the agent to ascertain the "official" policy the IRS will take in a given situation. The *IRM* contains policies, procedures, and guidelines for every function of the IRS. Although certain provisions of the *Manual* are not public record, a significant portion has been released.

This chapter discusses how the practitioner can use for his client's benefit much of the same information available to the agent from the *IRM* and other sources.

The following topics will be covered:

1. How to utilize the *Internal Revenue Manual*

2. Organization of the *Manual*

3. Actions on Decisions

4. Bulletin Index-Digest System

## How to utilize the *Internal Revenue Manual*

Questions like these are often raised: "Can the IRS take this action under these facts and circumstances? If so, then how do they go about it? How long will it take?"

By reviewing the *IRM* the practitioner will obtain a sense of the "official" way a matter will be treated. If this is advantageous to your client then you will have some leverage if the IRS employee you are dealing with decides to make up his or her own rules.

### Example

The *IRM* provides that in the case of a repetitive audit the tax auditor (in office audit) must requisition the taxpayer's tax return, if the taxpayer does not have a copy, for a prior year if the taxpayer claims he was audited and there was a no change. I have been told by many tax auditors that "unless your client is able to produce his or her copy of the prior year return the client will be forced to waive the repetitive audit provisions." This is obviously untrue! Just insist that the tax auditor read the *Internal Revenue Manual.* The *IRM* controls, not the personal whim of the employee you are dealing with.

*Many IRS employees don't know the provisions in their own manual.* Use this lack of knowledge to your client's advantage. If the IRS employee you are dealing with proposes any type of adverse action (especially in the collection area) just see what the *IRM* says he or she can really do. Don't rely on what the particular IRS employee says is the rule.

## Organization of the *Manual*

The *IRM* is organized into various parts. Each part represents a particular function of the IRS. Those parts which are commonly referred to are:

| | |
|---|---|
| Part I | Administration |
| Part IV | Audit |
| Part V | Delinquent Accounts and Returns |
| Part VI | Taxpayer Service |
| Part VII | Employee Plans and Exempt Organizations |
| Part VIII | Appellate |
| Part IX | Criminal Investigation Division |
| Part X | Inspection |
| Part XI | Technical |

### Research aids

In addition to a table of contents the *Manual* contains an index called the keyword-in-context (KWIC) which allows the user to identify quickly the source of the answer when taking a problem approach.

## Actions on Decisions

How to find out what the chief counsel says about a case the IRS lost

Actions on Decisions (AODs) are legal memoranda which are prepared by attorneys in the tax litigation division and directed to the chief counsel whenever the IRS loses a case in the tax court, a federal district court, the Court of Claims, or the United States Court of Appeals.

The AODs set forth the issue which was decided against the government, a brief discussion of the facts and the reasoning of the attorney behind his or her recommendations that the commissioner either "acquiesce" or "nonacquiesce" in a decision of the tax court or of a federal district court. The reported decisions of the tax court as carried in the AODs are published in the *Internal Revenue Bulletin*. However, the full text of an AOD is not published in the *Internal Revenue Bulletin*.

### Disclosure of AODs

The IRS has lost a case in the United States Court of Appeals: *Taxation With Representation Fund v. Internal Revenue Service*, 81-1 USTC 9252. The Court held that AODs that recommend no appeal and that explain the IRS's legal position on a particular issue are not protected from disclosure. AODs are now available from various publishers.

## Bulletin Index-Digest System

The IRS publishes a research tool called the *Bulletin Index-Digest System* which can be extremely useful to practitioners.

The *Bulletin Index-Digest System* provides a method for researching matters published since 1952 in the *Internal Revenue Bulletin*. The *Internal Revenue Bulletins* contain announcements of official rulings and procedures of the Internal Revenue Service and of Public Laws, Treasury Decisions and other items of general interest. The *System* is divided into four parts:

- Service No. 1: Income Tax, Publication 641 (Rev. 12-78)
- Service No. 2: Estate and Gift Taxes, Publication 642 (Rev. 12-78)
- Service No. 3: Employment Taxes, Publication 643 (Rev. 12-78)
- Service No. 4: Excise Taxes, Publication 644 (Rev. 12-78)

## What will you find in these publications?

The major portion of the *Bulletin Index-Digest System* consists of brief summaries of revenue rulings and revenue procedures alphabetically arranged under topical headings and subheadings, along with brief summaries of Supreme Court decisions, adverse tax court decisions on cases involving tax issues in which the commissioner has announced acquiescence or nonacquiescence, executive orders, Treasury Department orders, delegation orders, and other miscellaneous items published in the *Internal Revenue Bulletins*.

# CHAPTER 22

# How Fraud Referrals
# Are Handled

A fraud referral is the first step the IRS takes in its effort to build a criminal case against your client. It is vital to what the revenue agent looks for and how he develops the information necessary to present a fraud referral to the criminal investigation division. This chapter focuses in not only on how the IRS handles fraud referrals but on what the practitioner can do about it.

The following areas will be covered:

1. Explanation of the fraud referral procedure

2. What is considered a good fraud referral

3. How to tell when a revenue agent suspects fraud—and what to do about it

4. Now that you know the revenue agent suspects fraud—what should you do?

5. How to tell if an agent has made a fraud referral

6. Why it can be fatal to the government's case if a fraud referral is not made promptly

## Explanation of the fraud referral procedure

As part of a revenue agent's training he is instructed to be cognizant of the existence of fraud. Although most revenue agents do not enter into an audit expecting to uncover fraud there are specific guidelines which require them to report the existence of fraud through proper channels.

For the purposes of this chapter revenue agents are referred to as the IRS employees who initiate fraud referrals. However, fraud referrals are also initiated by tax auditors (who conduct office audits) and revenue officers (collection division personnel).

After completing a report in which he describes those indications of fraud he has found, the agent routes the report to the criminal investigation division for its consideration. If the case is accepted a special agent will be assigned and a full-scale investigation will be initiated.

## What is considered a good fraud referral?

The criminal investigation considers the following facts:

1) How much tax is there? The more tax the better.

2) Does the fraud extend into two or three years?

3) What is the occupation, age, and health of the taxpayer? If the taxpayer is a professional (doctor, lawyer, etc.) or a small businessman then the referral is likely to be accepted even if the taxpayer is of advanced age or in poor health.

### Guidelines for referrals
### (taken from an IRS memorandum issued to all audit employees)

*Elements of fraud*

1) Fraud is generally defined as deception brought about by misrepresentation of material facts, or silence when good faith requires expression, resulting in material damage to one who relies on it and had the right to do so. It may be defined more simply as deception with the object of gaining by another's loss.

2) *The first basic fact to be proved is that the taxpayer failed to report his/her correct tax liability,* i.e., there was taxable income which was understated, or the taxpayer had income subject to tax but failed to file a return and report this tax liability. Proof may be obtained by direct evidence of specific items not properly reported on the return or indirectly by use of circumstantial evidence to show that the tax on the return is an understatement of the correct tax liability.

3) The government must prove not only that the tax liability reported was understated, *but that such understatement was the result of a deliberate or intentional design to knowingly evade tax.* A willful intent to evade tax is evidenced by an understatement based on deceit, concealment, subterfuge, or attempt to color or obscure the true facts. An intent to evade tax usually cannot be inferred solely from the fact that income was understated,

since proof that income was understated does not in itself establish that the omission was intentional. A failure to correctly report income may be due to mistake, inadvertence, reliance on technical advice, honest difference of opinion, negligence or carelessness, all of which may negate a willful intent to defraud. It is incumbent upon the audit examiner to attempt to ascertain the reason(s) for the understatement before a referral is made.

## How to tell when a revenue agent suspects fraud—and what to do about it

Since a fraud referral is the first step of a criminal investigation the practitioner should be aware of any clues which may lead him to believe that the revenue agent suspects fraud.

Once the revenue agent has gathered all the information he needs to assure himself that your client has committed fraud it is usually too late to protect important information from getting into the hands of the IRS.

The following steps are supposed to be taken by the revenue agent before a case is referred to the criminal investigation division:

1) Discover the potential fraud.

2) Document the alleged fraud.

3) Establish if a pattern of fraud exists.

4) Question the taxpayer concerning the fraud.

5) Account for significant discrepancies or explanations given by the taxpayer.

6) Determine if any indications of fraud still remain.

**You'll know that the revenue agent suspects fraud when he:**

1) Asks questions about cash expenditures your client made.

2) Schedules cancelled checks.

3) Asks for photocopies of gross receipts, sales, and accounts receivable records.

4) Tries to establish the amount of cash your client has on hand at the beginning of the year.

5) Spends too much time on the audit.

If you see that the revenue agent is conducting the audit as described above there is a good likelihood that he may suspect fraud.

*Good idea:* Look over the revenue agent's shoulder now and then during the audit to see what he is doing and writing down. If you see that he is scheduling pages and pages of information ask him what he is doing and why he is doing it. If there is any possibility that your client may have committed fraud tell the agent that the audit is over for today and that you will get back to him to set up another appointment. Make sure he does not take any records with him (especially records he may have photocopied earlier with your permission).

## Now that you know the revenue agent suspects fraud—what should you do?

The first thing you want to do is ask the revenue agent: "Why do you want to know about cash expenditures?" "Why do you want to make photocopies of cancelled checks or invoices?"

If a satisfactory answer is not forthcoming then merely continue to ask questions in the same vein: "Why are you asking me these questions?" If he tells you that he has found what he thinks is fraud tell him that you will discuss the matter with your client and get back to him. Don't discuss it further or offer any additional information.

If the revenue agent persists in being obstinate then tell him that you will have to discuss the matter with your client and that the audit is over for today. (Don't tell the revenue agent that you will not provide him with the information he is asking for.) At this point you have to carefully examine your client's records to ascertain what the revenue agent has found. If there is a problem then you should consider not showing the agent any more records by asserting your client's Fifth Amendment privilege against self-incrimination. (There may be a technical problem about raising the Fifth Amendment at this time since it is not yet officially a criminal case and the Fifth Amendment is not applicable to civil matters—but it is better to be safe than sorry.)

Never let the revenue agent get to the point where he has all the information he needs to develop his suspicion of fraud completely. The practitioner has an obligation to be aware of those things the revenue agent does that indicate that he suspects a problem.

## How to tell if an agent has made a fraud referral

You can generally tell when a revenue agent has made a fraud referral because he will not contact you to make another appointment for about six to nine months. During this time the criminal investigation division is evaluating the referral to determine if they should accept the case.

If you should happen to call the revenue agent to schedule an appointment he will give you any number of reasons why he can't meet with you. If you are concerned that he may have made a fraud referral simply ask him "Did you make a fraud referral?" Generally, the revenue agent will not lie—he'll probably say yes.

At this point it would be advisable to ask him why he thinks fraud exists. Don't give any answers to any questions he may ask, for if the case is accepted this information may incriminate your client.

*What should you do?* Arrange to retain an attorney with criminal tax experience in case he is needed.

## Why failure to make a prompt fraud referral can be fatal to the government's case

If your client's case becomes a criminal investigation then the IRS is required to notify your client of that fact. They are also required to inform your client of his "Miranda" rights, that is, that anything he says can be used against him in court.

What happens in practice is that the revenue agent usually identifies the fraud and then continues to solicit additional information without giving the proper notice to the taxpayer that he has certain Fifth Amendment rights. If this fact can be proved then it may be possible to exclude from evidence certain incriminating information which the revenue agent has obtained.

There are three primary ways in which a revenue agent can jeopardize a potential prosecution. They are:

1) solicit an agreement

2) solicit and receive a delinquent return

3) obtain advice and direction from the criminal investigation division prior to referring the case

*Tip:* Always request a copy of the revenue agent's "Activity Record" which lists dates of appointments and meetings. Did he speak to a special agent before the referral was made? Did he contact third parties which would have given him the information he needed to make a referral but continued to solicit information from the taxpayer anyway?

# CHAPTER 23

# IRS Summons Power
# and Third-Party Contacts

Perhaps the strongest weapon in the IRS arsenal is the power to issue a summons. Generally, no court order has to be obtained before the IRS can serve you or your client with a summons.

The IRS will normally resort to a summons when information they have requested is not forthcoming. It is unusual for a summons to be issued in a civil case unless there are compelling reasons (for example, the IRS agent may think he is on to fraud). Any person summoned has the right to contest the summons in court before complying with its provisions. As a rule, the IRS will be the one who decides whether they will enforce a summons. If they do not seek enforcement then the person summoned does nothing but notify them of his intention to contest the summons if and when enforcement proceedings are commenced.

This section covers the following areas which are typical in the area of summons:

1. Summons enforcement procedure

2. Notice provisions of summons issued to certain third parties

3. Contesting a summons in a criminal case

4. At what point should the practitioner give up his client's records if he receives a summons?

## Summons enforcement procedure

Just because a client is served with a summons which requests that he testify or produce books and records does not mean that there is no recourse. In fact, there is an alternative. The important thing to remember is that some action must be taken upon the receipt of a summons even if that action is to only notify the IRS that your client will not comply with the summons.

### Failure to obey a summons is a crime

"Any person who, being duly summoned to appear to testify, or to appear and produce books, accounts, records, memorandum, or other papers, neglects to appear or to produce such books, accounts, records, memorandum, or other papers, shall, upon conviction thereof, be fined not more than $1,000, or imprisoned not more than one year, or both, together with costs of prosecution."

If it is determined that the summons was not issued in good faith or was for purposes of harrassment rather than the determination of the correct tax liability in a particular case then your client has the right to contest the summons. *Notify both the agent who served the summons and the district director of your intention to contest the summons.*

At this point the IRS must decide whether it wants to enforce the summons in federal court. Unless there was a good reason for having issued the summons in the first place, it is likely that somewhere in the IRS chain of command the decision will be made not to enforce the summons.

With respect to civil cases, it is likely that the agent's desire to make you comply with the terms of the summons will not be upheld unless there are compelling reasons. Accordingly, if you should happen to be working with an agent who tells you that "You better show me such and such records or else I will issue a summons" tell him to "Do whatever you have to do!" (The chances are that the agent will ultimately just disallow whatever deduction you would not provide the support for or else he may impute an income figure which has no basis.)

Generally, if the summons is enforced your client will have the opportunity to present his side of the case to the judge. The worst that will probably happen is that the court will order compliance with the summons. At that point your client will be no worse off having contested the summons and lost than he would have been if he had complied with the summons initially.

## Notice provisions of summons issued to certain third parties

If a summons is served on a third-party recordkeeper (defined below) which requires the production of any portion of records made or kept of the business transactions or affairs of your client, then the IRS must tell your client. At that point your client has fourteen days from the date he is notified to advise the person summoned, in writing, not to comply with the summons. If the IRS decides to bring a summons enforcement action against the third-party recordkeeper your client will have the right to intervene and present objections as to why the summons should not be enforced. A *copy of a notice to a third-party recordkeeper not to comply with the summons must be mailed to the IRS at the address shown on the summons.*

## Who is a third-party recordkeeper?

Generally, a bank, consumer reporting agency, a stockbroker, an accountant or an attorney.

## Contesting a summons in a criminal case

A taxpayer who is the subject of a criminal investigation has an absolute right not to comply with an IRS summons. If a special agent should present your client with a summons you should respond, in writing, that your client refuses to testify or produce books and records based on his privilege against self-incrimination. The only recourse the special agent will have will be to recommend that the summons be enforced. Generally, enforcement action will not be taken against the taxpayer since even the IRS recognizes the privilege afforded by the Fifth Amendment.

It may be more difficult to sustain a stay of compliance of a summons issued to a third-party recordkeeper but the practitioner should institute the appropriate notice to the third party and the IRS to protect his client's interest.

## At what point should the practitioner give up his client's records if he receives a summons?

There is a tremendous amount of controversy and substantial litigation over the right of the IRS to examine the practitioner's work papers. Major CPA firms have been in the forefront of this litigation in an effort to keep their internal analysis of a particular tax problem outside the reach of the Service.

No effort will be made to discuss the various legal arguments available to the practitioner who is faced with the problem of having been served with a summons. However, before complying with the terms of the summons the practitioner should retain counsel to review the merits of withholding summoned information.

### Criminal cases

In criminal cases, return all records belonging to your client immediately. Generally, the practitioner lacks the ability to contest a summons based on the privilege against self-incrimination since the records are his client's and only the client can claim that privilege.

**When might you want the IRS to issue a summons?**

When some other party is in possession of records helpful to your client and that party will not turn them over to your client. Seek the agent's help by asking him to issue a summons!

---

# Third-Party Contacts

In pursuance of their mission the IRS is permitted to contact third parties in an effort to obtain information which is necessary to develop a particular case, be it civil or criminal.

Generally, notification of third parties that your client is under IRS investigation is not only embarrassing but can also disrupt business relationships. This section discusses the following areas:

1. When are third-party contacts initiated and what can you do about it?

2. Can the Privacy Act be used to restrain third-party contacts?

---

**When are third-party contacts initiated and what can you do about it?**

The IRS will resort to checking with third parties when required information is not readily available from the taxpayer. The following are typical situations when third-party contacts will be made:

1) when corroboration of a taxpayer's statement or records is necessary

2) when the taxpayer's records are in the possession of a third party and the taxpayer is unwilling or unable to obtain the records

3) when it is necessary for the IRS to obtain special expertise in areas such as appraisals, handwriting analysis, and voice identification

4) when the accuracy of information provided by the taxpayer needs to be verified or is in doubt

What can you do about it?

Generally, there is very little that the practitioner can do to prevent an IRS employee from making a third-party contact. The following steps could be taken to help make the best of a bad situation:

1) Notify those business and personal associates who will likely be contacted by the IRS. Explain to them what information will probably be requested and discuss their response. *Don't ever tell someone to lie or otherwise to "obstruct justice"!*

   Tell each person to call you as soon after they are contacted as possible. You will want to "debrief" them to find out exactly what was asked and how they answered. Request that they send you copies of whatever documents will be provided to the IRS.

2) Protest to the district director. Write a letter setting forth the reasons as to why the action being taken by the IRS personnel involved is unreasonable under the circumstances. Explain, if appropriate, how business relationships are being placed in jeopardy and the fact that such contacts are creating unwarranted anxiety for your client which is adversely affecting his health.

### Can the privacy act be used to restrain third-party contacts?

Unfortunately, the Privacy Act cannot be used to restrain third-party contacts unless there is a blatant violation. Internal Revenue Code section 6103(k)(6) provides that IRS employees are authorized to disclose return information to the extent necessary to gather data which may be relevant to a tax investigation. No authorization is needed to make investigative disclosures so long as the IRS employee is performing his official duty in an examination, collection activity, civil or criminal investigation, enforcement activity or action on another offense under the internal revenue laws.

It should be noted that the provision which permits disclosure of return information in the investigatory process does not authorize the disclosure of the taxpayer's tax return. When soliciting information from a third party, an IRS employee may not show a taxpayer's return to that third party. Pertinent data (such as the nature and amount of income, deductions and expenses) may be extracted, when necessary, from the tax return and used in questions to third parties.

# CHAPTER 24

# Dealing with a Special Agent

This chapter is "must" reading for any practitioner who contemplates representing a client before the criminal investigation division of the IRS. Any mistake made by the practitioner could literally result in his client's conviction for a tax crime. Whether your client is really guilty is not relevant. The essential fact is that in the eyes of the law he is innocent until proven guilty. The practitioner is generally not obligated to assist the government in its effort to meet that burden of proof.

The following topics are covered in this chapter:

1. The criminal investigation division and special agents

2. The things to do immediately if a special agent contacts your client

3. Client's questionnaire: special agent interview

4. What to say if a special agent walks into your office without an appointment

5. The first question to ask a special agent when he wants to talk to you about your client

6. Should you cooperate with a special agent?

7. Should the practitioner ever agree to let his client be interviewed by a special agent?

8. How to get a special agent to reveal his case against your client

9. How to respond if a special agent asks if he can tape record an interview

10. The right to be present at special agent's interview of third parties

## The criminal investigation division and special agents

The criminal investigation division of the IRS is charged with the responsibility of developing criminal tax cases—not prosecuting them. Special agents, those men, and now more frequently women, who work for the criminal investigation division, are specially trained accountant-investigators whose job it is to gather every piece of evidence available against your client.

For the most part special agents are very nice people and present a low-key image. Their unassuming posture tends to put those people who deal with them at ease, which is a great aid in helping them build a case.

The special agent's job is to put your client in jail! He receives recognition and gains promotions by doing his job—again, that is trying to gather all the available evidence which can be used by the U. S. attorney to convict your client of a tax crime.

Dealing with a special agent is a very serious matter, where a client's liberty may very well rest on decisions that the practitioner makes. Dealing with a special agent also takes a certain degree of experience. Such experience should be developed by retaining experienced cocounsel for the first few clients who come to you for assistance in a criminal tax matter.

## The things to do immediately if a special agent contacts your client

### Immediately hire an attorney

You should hire an attorney *with experience in criminal tax matters.* A person who is not an attorney does not have the privilege of maintaining confidences—there is no client privilege. Therefore, if your client tells you that he has been contacted by a special agent and you proceed to ask him questions (or he volunteers answers without being asked questions) you can be called upon in court to testify, under oath, about the conversation.

As a practical matter you will undoubtedly want to stay involved in the case since as the client's accountant you are familiar with his business and the types of records which are maintained. In order to protect your client's privilege it will be necessary for your client's attorney to retain your services. The fee paid by your client to the attorney will have to be an amount which also covers your fee. Therefore, the attorney will pay you and not your client.

A standard retainer agreement which provides that you are working for the attorney must be entered into before you get involved in the case. The accompanying sample form is an acceptable agreement.

## Sample Form of Agreement Whereby Attorney Employs Accountant in Course of an Internal Revenue Service Investigation

### AGREEMENT

THIS AGREEMENT entered into at _____, _____ this _____ day of _____, 19___, by and between _____ (hereinafter referred to as "the Attorney") and _____ (hereinafter referred to as "the Accountant").

### WITNESSETH:

WHEREAS, the Attorney has been employed by _____ (hereinafter referred to as the "Clients") to represent them in the matter of their federal income tax liabilities for the years 19 ___ to 19 ___, inclusive, in connection with an audit of their income tax returns presently being made by the Internal Revenue Service, and

WHEREAS, in carrying out his duties and responsibilities pursuant to such employment the Attorney will require accounting assistance in analyzing the books, records, papers and documents which have been delivered to him by the Clients and to have accounting assistance in preparing schedules, workpapers and other documents which when prepared will represent the product of the Attorney's work in preparing and presenting the case of the Clients.

NOW, THEREFORE, in consideration of the foregoing and the mutual promises and undertakings hereinafter set forth, the Attorney and Accountant do hereby agree as follows:

1. The Attorney employs the Accountant to assist the Attorney in analyzing the books, records, papers and documents of the Clients and the business, financial and personal affairs of the Clients insofar as the Attorney may deem such assistance to be necessary in the preparation and presentation of the Clients' case.

2. The Attorney agrees to pay the Accountant a reasonable fee for all such services actually rendered and performed by the Accountant pursuant to the Attorney's request.

3. (a) All books of account, records, papers and other documents belonging to the Clients and all memoranda, workpapers or other documents prepared by the Attorney which pertain to the affairs of the Clients which may be delivered by the Attorney to the Accountant in the course of the Accountant's employment shall be and remain the property of the Clients or the Attorney, as the case may be, and the Accountant shall be the gratuitous bailee thereof.

(b) All notes, workpapers, schedules, analyses and other documents prepared by the Accountant for use by the Attorney in the presentation of the Clients' case shall become the property of the Attorney immediately upon their preparation by the Accountant, whether or not

such documents are complete or incomplete and irrespective of who purchased or paid for the component parts thereof, in the same manner and to the same extent as though such documents had been prepared by the Attorney and the component parts thereof purchased and paid for by the Attorney, and the Accountant shall be the gratuitous bailee thereof.

(c) Under no circumstances shall the accountant permit anyone other than the Attorney to examine, inspect or copy or take possession of any of the records and documents referred to in paragraph 3(a) and 3(b) hereof.

4. The bailment to the Accountant of all records and documents referred to in paragraph 3 above shall be automatically revoked and the Accountant shall at once deliver to the Attorney all such records and documents upon the happening of any one of the following events:

(a) A request by the Attorney for the return of such records and documents;

(b) The exhibition to or surrender of any of such records and documents by the Accountant to anyone other than the Attorney;

(c) A request by anyone other than the Attorney (including, but without being limited to, a creditor of the Clients and a representative of any agency of the United States Government) to examine, inspect or copy any of such records and documents, or for the possession of any of such records and documents;

(d) Any attempt to serve, or the actual service of, any court order, subpoena or summons, or any administrative subpoena or summons upon the Accountant which requires or purports to require him to produce any of such records and documents.

5. Should any litigation result from the failure or refusal of the Accountant to comply with the requests, orders, subpoenas or summons referred to in paragraphs 4(c) and 4(d) hereof, the Attorney agrees, if requested by the Accountant, to defend the Accountant in such litigation at the Attorney's cost and expense.

IN TESTIMONY WHEREOF, witness the signatures of the parties hereto the day and year first above written.

_____
Attorney

Witnesses:

s/ _____    _____
s/ _____    Accountant

Witnesses:

s/ _____
s/ _____

Reproduced from Worksheet 11 of *Tax Management Portfolio 123–3rd*: "IRS Procedures—Production of Documents," with the permission of Tax Management, Inc., a subsidiary of the Bureau of National Affairs, Inc., Washington, D.C.

After these formalities take place you and the attorney will normally be working together during the investigatory stage of the case. You will be called upon to assemble various records and provide analysis of income and expense items.

### Immediately find out what happened with the special agent

If your client has been contacted in person by the special agent (which is usually the case since the element of surprise enables them to obtain information they probably would not get later) tell him not to talk to anyone from the IRS, FBI, etc. until an attorney is retained. If he should be contacted tell him to say "I have nothing to say, please call my attorney, Jim Jones, at 234-5678."

*A must:* Explain to your client that everything he has said to the special agent may be used to help the government develop its criminal case. Tell your client to sit down with a tape recorder *immediately* and describe the conversation he had with the special agent. Tell him to start with the time the special agent walked in the door.

The following questionnaire should be prepared and delivered to your client to assist him in remembering the events which transpired between him and the special agent. Chances are that he was very nervous during the interview and will not be able to recall much. These questions may refresh his memory. Impress upon your client the importance of sitting down with the tape recorder immediately. The facts that he can recall correctly can serve as a tremendous aid to the attorney in preparing a defense.

### Client's Questionnaire: Special Agent Interview

- On what date did the special agent meet with you?
- How many special agents were there?
- What were their names?
- What office were they from?
- Did they identify themselves as special agents?
- If so, how did they identify themselves? (Did they show you a badge?)
- Did they say anything to you before they identified themselves? What did they say? Did they ask you any questions before they identified themselves? What were the questions? What did you answer?
- Did they give you a Miranda warning?
- Did they read it from a card?

- Did they ask you any questions before they gave you the Miranda warning?
- If so, what were the questions? What did you answer?
- Did they tape-record the meeting?
- What questions did they ask you?
- How did you answer?
- Did you lie about anything? misrepresent something?
- Did they ask you if you reported all of your income? What did you say?
- Did they ask you where you maintain bank accounts? What did you say?
- Did they ask about the kind of car you own? if you go on vacation? if you own jewelry, antiques or collectables? How did you answer each question?
- Did they ask you if you ever receive cash? How did you answer?
- Did they ask you how much cash you had on hand at the beginning of any year? What did you say?
- How long did the interview last?
- Did you sign anything? If yes, do you have a copy?
- Did they ask you how you maintain your financial records? What did you say?

## Immediately caution your client

At this point it would be wise to inform your client of the seriousness of the involvement of the criminal investigation division in his case. Let your client know that the special agents have just one goal—to try to put him in jail!

The client should be instructed not to discuss the case with friends, relatives, employees, or business associates. The fewer people who know the IRS is investigating him, the better. He does not want to give anyone who may have a grudge against him the opportunity to vent it by supplying the IRS with unsolicited information.

## Immediately return all records to your client

All records in your possession are subject to an administrative summons which can be issued by the special agent. If personal (noncorporate) records are in your client's possession he can refuse to comply with a summons by asserting his Fifth Amendment privilege against self-incrimination. (See Chapter 23 dealing with how to fight an IRS summons.)

# What to say if a special agent walks into your office without an appointment

Special agents, as a rule, don't make appointments. They do not want the people they interview to have an opportunity to think about the questions they are likely to be asked and how answers should be formulated.

If a special agent should surprise you with a visit simply say "I have nothing to say at this time. I will get back to you in a day or two. What is your telephone number?"

The special agent will normally not accept such a response lightly but, rather, will try to pressure you into answering at least some of his questions. Just repeat: "I have nothing to say at this time. What is your telephone number?" *Do not lie! Don't make up excuses!* Just tell them that you will get back to him.

After the special agent has left, call your client to find out if they have contacted him. Then call an attorney to discuss the matter before you call the special agent back.

It cannot be stressed how important it is not to make statements to the special agent without knowing why he wants to know the information or how it is likely to affect your client. If you ultimately become involved in the representation of your client before the IRS then you have a duty not to incriminate your client!

# The first question to ask a special agent when he wants to talk to you about your client

The first thing to ask the special agent is: "Is my client the subject of a criminal investigation?"

If the answer is yes, then you must proceed cautiously. Anything you say which incriminates your client can be deemed to have been said by your client. At this point you should tell the special agent that you will get back to him. Follow the instructions set forth above.

If the special agent indicates that your client is not the subject of a criminal investigation, you still will want to know why he has approached you to ask questions. Was it because the special agent is investigating your client's business associates and your client's name merely appeared on some record? Or is the special agent trying to tie your client into a common scheme?

*Strategy:* You don't want to give any answers at this time which may be "potentially harmful" to your client's interest. Don't answer any questions at this time.

Rather, write down each question that is asked and tell the special agent that you will get back to him. After confirming with your client that he has no exposure it would be all right to supply the answers to the questions which were raised.

It is a good idea to write the following letter to the special agent confirming your conversation if he has told you that your client is not the subject of a criminal investigation:

[Date]

S/A John Jones
Internal Revenue Service
Criminal Investigation Division
120 Church Street
New York, N.Y. 10008

Re:  Joe Smith

Dear Mr. Jones:

This letter shall serve to confirm our conversation of today's date in which you stated that the above captioned taxpayer is not the subject of a criminal investigation by the criminal investigation division.

Sincerely,

A.B. Doe, CPA

In the event that the special agent has lied and your client really is the subject of a criminal investigation, there may be a potential Fifth Amendment violation which may serve to exclude evidence obtained by the special agent from being admitted into court at a later trial. Your letter serves the purpose of "creating a record" which can be used by the attorney at a later date.

## Should you cooperate with a special agent?

Generally, the answer is *no*!

There is normally no advantage to your client if you or he helps the government prove their case against him. *Remember: you are innocent until proven guilty*!

The Fifth Amendment of the United States Constitution clearly states that a person does not have to supply the government with evidence necessary to send him to jail. (Those are not the "exact" words of the Fifth Amendment but that's what they mean.)

The special agent will not like you if you make his job harder—but who cares? He will normally do the same amount of work whether he likes you or not. Special agents are very meticulous about covering all bases. By supplying the leads you are just cutting down on the amount of time the special agent has to spend on your client's case.

*Traps:* Don't fall into the trap of believing in the misconception that if you co-operate with a special agent he will "go away" or else "go easier on your client." Nothing could be farther from the truth.

If you are retained by a client who is involved with the criminal investigation division then you have an absolute moral and professional (and also legal) responsibility not to incriminate your client. You must defend him to the best of your ability.

### A common problem

What about other people who may cooperate with the special agent?

A representative and his client should be very careful about what they say to third parties. The general rule is that you can't tell someone else to do something or say something which constitutes the separate crime of "obstruction of justice." Obstructing justice is a subject which fills books all by itself. Suffice it to say, if you think that something you are telling another person to do or say could be construed as interfering with the government's investigation, then don't do it or say it!

Relatives, neighbors, employees, and business associates are all likely to be contacted by the special agent. The only thing you should tell "trusted" people is: "If anyone from the IRS contacts you please call me before you speak to them. Don't lie to the special agent. Just tell him that you will have to get back to him."

When the special agent is called back so that answers can be given to his questions, the practitioner should be present at the meeting as a witness.

## Should the practitioner ever agree to let his client be interviewed by a special agent?

Unless there is a compelling reason why it would be desirable to have your client meet the special agent (e.g. your client is innocent and the special agent is acting on an informant's allegation which is clearly erroneous) then no personal interview should ever be granted. Normally, there is nothing to be gained by exposing your client to a battery of questions designed to help the special agent build his case.

A special agent might tell you that unless you let him meet with your client he will issue a summons requesting that your client appear in his office. All you have to do to avoid such a confrontation is to advise the special agent, in writing, that your client wishes to exercise his privilege against self-incrimination and has no statement to make at this time.

### Sample Letter

[Date]

S/A John Jones
Internal Revenue Service
Criminal Investigation Division
120 Church Street
New York, N.Y. 10008

Re: Joe Smith

Dear Mr. Jones:

In response to your request for a meeting with the above captioned taxpayer, be advised that Mr. Smith wishes to exercise his Fifth Amendment right against self-incrimination and therefore will not make any statements at this time.

Sincerely,

A.B. Doe, CPA

## How to get a special agent to reveal his case against your client

It is very difficult, if not impossible, to find out everything the special agent knows and doesn't know about your client. Since they are professional investigators they do not want to tip their hand by telling you too much about the merits and/or weaknesses of their case.

In my experience, the easiest way to get a special agent to reveal at least part of his case is simply by telling him: "I can't tell whether you are right or not unless I see some figures." (Note: You should never tell the special agent he is right or wrong about anything!)

Sometimes it is advisable to set up a meeting (without your client) so that you can ask some questions. The questions you typically will ask and the types of responses you can expect are as follows:

PRACTITIONER: You think my client has committed fraud—is it because you think he has understated his income?

SPECIAL AGENT: Did he understate his income?

PRACTITIONER: Why don't you show me specific items of deposits or cash expenditures that make you think there is a problem? This way we can review each item together.

SPECIAL AGENT: Does your client receive cash?

PRACTITIONER: We may be able to close this case if you give my client the opportunity to explain certain transactions which bother you. I can't be of help unless you at least tell me what my client is being accused of.

Another scenario is likely to be as follows:

PRACTITIONER: Why do you think my client has committed a crime?

SPECIAL AGENT: Has your client filed tax returns for the past three years?

PRACTITIONER: Do you know that my client had a legal obligation to file a tax return? What monies do you feel he earned?

*Strategy:* Never lie or misrepresent anything! Don't allow yourself to get boxed into a corner by the special agent's questions. Always answer a question you don't want to answer with your own question.

In every case, if you are persistent, there is a good chance that you will come away from the meeting knowing more about the special agent's case than when the meeting started. Remember, the special agent is a professional and experienced investigator who knows how to ask the right questions. If you don't answer *any* of his questions then you can't jeopardize your client's case.

## How to respond if a special agent asks if he can tape record an interview

If you should be in a situation where you or your client is being questioned by a special agent, do not permit him to tape record the conversation. If he has to take notes on what was asked and answered, the number of questions will probably be reduced.

### Create your own record

From the minute you become involved in a criminal tax case you should start maintaining an activity record of every telephone call and meeting. After each call or meeting a "memo to the file" should be prepared which briefly outlines who said what.

The special agent will keep a similar record which may be introduced into evidence to highlight conflicting statements made by you or your client during the course of his investigation. If you have your own record the attorney will at least have some ammunition available which would be used to counter the special agent's damaging testimony about contradictory statements.

## The right to be present at special agent's interview of third parties

Recent court decisions have determined that a practitioner has a right to be present at interviews of third parties. The practitioner is not permitted to interfere or disrupt the interview but rather is given an opportunity to sit in and listen.

*The bad news:* Special agents do not encourage practitioners to attend such interviews and, in fact, will do everything possible to prevent you from doing so.

*What to do:* The third party must request your presence at the meeting. If anyone contacts your client to tell him the IRS has approached him, make it clear to the third party that you want to attend any interview as a witness.

Being present at a third-party interview is extremely valuable. You will have an opportunity to learn firsthand of any "new" problem areas you did not know existed. You will also be able to gain some insight as to the extent of the special agent's familiarity with your client's financial activities.

# CHAPTER 25

# The Preparer's Criminal Exposure and Preparer's Penalties

The IRS and the Justice Department have, in recent years, devoted an unusual amount of attention to the area of the preparer's or tax advisor's culpability. A public example will just as likely be made of a preparer or tax advisor who assists his client to commit a fraudulent act as the client himself. This chapter examines the preparer's potential criminal exposure in those situations where his client is the subject of a criminal investigation. The following topics will be discussed:

1. Do you need an attorney if your client is being investigated by a special agent?

2. What to say and what not to say when a special agent interviews you about a tax return you have prepared

## Do you need an attorney if your client is being investigated by a special agent?

A practitioner whose client is the subject of a criminal investigation will inevitably find the IRS at some point directing their attention to him in an effort to strengthen its case against the client. The extent of your involvement with your client's financial transactions will determine your exposure.

### What is your exposure?

It is possible for the IRS to take the position that you aided and abetted your client in the commission of a tax crime or otherwise were part of a conspiracy. Your client will undoubtedly offer the defense of "I don't know anything about recordkeeping—I rely on my accountant—I do everything he tells me to do." Such statements will, at least, cause the special agent to look into whether the practitioner had any knowledge of his client's effort to evade tax.

### Ascertaining the extent of your involvement

Exactly what have you done in the way of advising your client? Criminal exposure may exist if you:

1) counseled your client on how to avoid reporting cash sales

2) prepared a tax return knowing that a significant amount of income was omitted or that certain deductions claimed were fictitious

3) participated or had knowledge of the backdating of documents

4) structured a sham transaction for the purpose of evading tax

### The statutes

Conviction for fraud and false statements carries a potential $5,000 fine and/or three years imprisonment.

IRC 7206(1)   DECLARATION UNDER PENALTIES OF PERJURY
"Any person who willfully makes and subscribes any return, statement, or other document, which contains or is verified by a written declaration that it is made under the penalties of perjury, and which he does not believe to be true and correct as to every material matter."

IRC 7206(2)   AID OR ASSISTANCE
"Any person who willfully aids or assists in, or procures, counsels, or advises the preparation or presentation under, or in connection with any matter arising under, the Internal Revenue laws, of a return, affidavit, claim or other document, which is false as to any material matter, whether or not such falsity or fraud is with the knowledge or consent of the person authorized or required to present such return, affidavit, claim or document."

### Do you need an attorney?

If any possibility exists that you may become the target of a criminal investigation, an attorney should be retained. The time to involve the attorney is before you meet with a special agent to discuss your client's books and records. Statements which you may make in an effort to answer questions about your client may, in fact, be used against you in a later investigation.

The prosecution of tax practitioners is becoming more common. Generally, such criminal action is brought against those practitioners who have taken an active role in the evasion scheme or who have structured a plan to enable their clients to evade (not merely avoid) tax.

*To be safe:* Don't recommend anything to a client you couldn't justify (not rationalize) if you had to do so to the criminal investigation division.

# What to say and what not to say when a special agent interviews you about a tax return you have prepared

The practitioner whose client is the subject of a criminal investigation will be faced with a dilemma. That is, anything which he says with respect to his client's financial transactions could incriminate himself or the client.

## What the special agent is looking for

The special agent wants the practitioner's testimony as another piece of evidence to help build the government's case. The special agent wants to be able to prove that the client furnished all the data which was used in the preparation of his tax return and that the understatement of income was not a result of any error on the part of the practitioner, rather, the understatement was attributable to your client's willful and intentional act.

## Typical questions you will be asked

1) Did your client provide you with the amount of gross receipts earned by his business?

2) Did you make any adjustments for accounts receivable? If so, did your client provide you with a schedule of the accounts receivable at the end of the year?

3) Who maintains the accounting records at your client's place of business?

## Answering the questions

It is very difficult not to answer the special agent's questions regarding a tax return you have prepared unless you feel that by doing so you may be incriminating yourself. Typically, unless you were involved in a conspiracy with your client, you have no privilege against self-incrimination. Therefore, what you say could be used against your client.

Warning

Since you never know whether the IRS will try to tie you into a criminal act with your client it would be advisable to retain an attorney before statements are made about anything. If appropriate, the U.S. Attorney could be contacted to work out a grant of immunity in exchange for your testimony.

---

## Preparer Penalties

Various civil penalties can be assessed against a preparer of tax returns for any number of reasons. One of the primary reasons for the enactment into law of these penalties was to curb the abuses practiced by "store front" and "fly-by-night" tax return preparers. Essentially, operators would open up shop during tax season and advertise that they could secure refunds for people who went to them to have their tax returns prepared. The refunds, of course, were generated by overstating personal exemptions or by claiming fictitious deductions. The fee charged to customers would generally be a percentage of the refund.

This section will discuss preparer penalties and what you should know about them:

1. What are the penalties?

2. The one thing that your client can say at an IRS audit that can hurt you

3. Agreeing to a proposed preparer's penalty

4. Why you shouldn't correct a prior year's error with another error

---

## What are the penalties?

The following is a list of the civil penalties a preparer may be faced with:

• IRC 6694(a)   $100 penalty for the negligent or intentional disregard of rules and regulations

- IRC 6694(b) $500 penalty for the willful understatement of liability, reduced by the amount of the penalty paid by reason of IRC 6694(a)
- IRC 6695(a) $25 penalty for the failure to furnish a taxpayer with a copy of his return or claim for refund
- IRC 6695(b) $25 penalty for the failure to sign a return
- IRC 6695(c) $25 penalty for the failure to furnish an identifying number
- IRC 6695(d) $50 penalty for the failure to retain for three years after the close of the return period a copy of the return or claim or a list of names and identifying numbers of taxpayers for whom returns or claims were prepared (maximum penalty is $25,000)
- IRC 6695(e) $100 penalty for the failure to file a correct-information return and a penalty of $5 for each failure to set forth an item as required (maximum penalty is $20,000)
- IRC 6695(f) $500 penalty for the endorsement or negotiation of a check with regard to income taxes issued to a taxpayer

*Note:* These penalties are subject to change.

## The one thing that your client can say at an IRS audit that can hurt you

Preparer penalties are most commonly assessed at the office audit level. It is here that the practitioner may not always be present to represent a client. The tax auditor then has an opportunity not only to disallow a deduction which may not be substantiated but also to elicit damaging testimony from your client.

When asked why a particular deduction which cannot be proved was claimed, the client may say "My accountant told me it was all right to take the deduction even though he knew I couldn't prove it." The response may not be correct but it nevertheless provides the tax auditor with the ammunition he needs to proceed with a preparer penalty case.

## Agreeing to a proposed preparer's penalty

It is assumed for the purposes of this discussion that everyone who is reading this book is a professional tax practitioner—be it an attorney, accountant, or enrolled agent. Accordingly, you should vigorously contest the efforts of an overzealous IRS employee to propose a preparer penalty (even though the monetary sanction may be nominal). A preparer penalty constitutes a blemish on your professional reputation and should not be taken lightly.

*Remember:* Penalties under IRC 6695 will not be imposed if the failure is due to reasonable cause and not to willful neglect.

### Typical example

The IRS may propose a preparer penalty because it was determined upon audit that one of your clients could not substantiate a deduction claimed for travel expense. The IRS says that you were negligent in the preparation of the tax return for claiming the deduction without ascertaining whether the expense was proper.

*Your response:* You have no obligation to perform an audit of your client's records before preparing his tax return. If the client furnished you with a figure that he stated was the amount of the expense incurred (even though it was unusually high) and all you said was "You know, of course, that you are required to prove these deductions are business related if you are audited," then you have acted reasonably.

The standard of what constitutes negligence and/or an intentional disregard for the rules and regulations is ill defined. Accordingly, it is in the best interest of all persons engaged in the tax profession that only true abuses of the law are acknowledged and sanctioned.

## Why you shouldn't correct a prior year's error with another error

Correcting a prior year's error with another error when preparing the current year's tax return is a common practice. It may easily be rationalized but it nevertheless is grounds for the imposition of a preparer's penalty. The correct procedure for correcting a prior year mistake generally is to file an amended tax return.

### Common examples

1) claiming extra depreciation in the current year because the proper amount had not been deducted in earlier years (remember depreciation is allowed or allowable)

2) deducting expenses in the current year which were paid December 31 of the previous year because the former accountant failed to deduct them

3) correcting a transaction in the current year even though the proper procedure would be to file an amended return

# CHAPTER 26

# Failure to File

What do you do when a new client tells you he hasn't filed a tax return in three years? Ten years?

Every year at least three or four new clients come into my office and meekly declare, "By the way . . . I haven't filed a tax return for the past three years." Or five years, or 10 years.

By and large these clients cannot be characterized as tax evaders, but, rather, die-hard procrastinators. For a number of reasons they can never get around to gathering their records together to file a return. In fact, even when they finally do get to the point of coming into the office every once in a while, they never come back to claim their records or their completed tax returns.

This chapter will serve as a guide and checklist for dealing with a client who has failed to file a tax return and is not being investigated by the criminal investigation division.

1.  **Rule #1:** Insist on receiving one-half of your fee before starting any work

2.  Why don't people file tax returns?

3.  Failure to file is a crime!

4.  Guaranteed audit

5.  Assembling the records

6.  Preparing the return

7.  Married, filing separately, may cost more but may be cheaper

8.  Refunds may not be refunded

## Rule #1: Insist on receiving one-half of your fee before starting any work

Since nonfilers or late filers tend not to be terribly responsible in their finances, the practitioner should be concerned that it may not be easy to collect his fee. On top of everything else, the client will usually be faced with a tremendous bill for taxes, interest, and penalty after you have completed your work, making it likely that the client will (1) not have the ability to pay you, or (2) think you did a lousy job since he has a big tax bill. After all, the client may not have paid taxes for some time now and may have grown unaccustomed to the entire idea.

## Why don't people file tax returns?

Failure to file tax returns for one or more years could be attributable to any number of reasons. Some people may know they owe taxes but don't have the money to pay. Not filing allows them temporarily to alleviate their financial problem. Others may have innocently let April 15 slip by and then become scared to file late. This phobia compounds itself year after year. A common excuse for not filing which is offered is "If I file now the IRS will know that I haven't filed for the last few years." Rarely do you come across a client who doesn't file because he wants to evade paying taxes.

## Failure to file is a crime!

The first thing I do after a client has told me that he hasn't filed a tax return for one or more years is to explain clearly that he has technically committed a crime which is punishable by imprisonment.

Putting the fear of God into the client encourages him to cooperate in my effort to help him assemble the records which are necessary to file accurate returns as soon as possible.

Although no official policy exists which creates amnesty, the IRS will generally not recommend criminal prosecution where the taxpayer has filed all late returns before being notified of a failure to file.

## Guaranteed audit

Returns filed late are almost always audited. This being the case the practitioner should take more than usual care to insure that the correct amount of income has been reported and that all deductions can be substantiated. The IRS looks with suspicion upon tax returns filed late and it will serve no purpose to provoke an agent into recommending a fraud referral because substantial discrepancies are uncovered during the audit.

## Assembling the records

Again, due to the nature of the person you will be dealing with it is unlikely that his or her records will be complete. Reconstruction of both income and expenses will probably be necessary. Unfortunately, you will probably not be able to rely upon your client to do much of this reconstruction.

*Tip:* Encourage your client to bring in all his records in a shopping bag.
Look for leads to tax deductible items:

1) Checks paid for medical insurance indicate that charges (which may be missing) were incurred for doctors which were only partially reimbursed. Write to the insurance company and request a transcript of your client's activity.

2) Checks paid to finance companies and banks mean that interest expense was paid. Were any loans taken out in the year in question? If so, use the Rule of 78's rather than straight line to compute interest expense so as to obtain a larger deduction.

### Confirm gross receipts—always perform a "bank deposit analysis"

Identify all deposits made to savings, checking, and brokerage accounts. Can the source be explained? Does the deposit represent taxable income? After all taxable deposits have been determined add back all cash expenses. Cash spent for living expenses and for repayment of loans should not be overlooked.

## Preparing the return

After you have reviewed all the available information submitted by your client start thinking about tax items he has no records of or that haven't even occurred to him.

1) Can business expenses be reconstructed from available source documents like diaries or appointment calenders? Were any out-of-town business trips taken during the year?

2) Did your client have an investment in a partnership or Subchapter-S corporation? Was there a loss?

3) Could a position be taken that a bad-debt loss exists in the year in question?

4) Do any carryovers exist from net operating losses or capital losses?

5) Will income averaging save tax?

*Remember:* If you are filing a tax return which was due five years ago, use the tax law which existed five years ago!

## Married, filing separately, may cost more but may be cheaper

What? No I didn't make a mistake. Take the common situation where the husband earned the bulk of the income and neither spouse filed a tax return. If a large amount of tax is due and a joint return is filed the IRS can seize the largest asset the couple typically owns—their house. By filing as married, but filing separately, there may be some additional tax because of the wife's income, but the husband will generally have the greater liability.

Assuming that they own the house as Tenants by the Entirety, the IRS, in most states, can only get a lien against the husband's interest in the property, upon which they cannot foreclose. At the time of the husband's death, assuming he should die first, the lien essentially dissolves and the house passes to the wife free and clear.

By not filing jointly, if substantial tax is owned, the taint of "joint and several liability" is removed. The wife can continue to own property in her own name without fear that it may be confiscated to pay for her husband's tax liability. Joint returns can be filed in future years.

*Caution:* Make sure withholding is projected so that no refund is generated if a joint return is filed. It will be applied against the husband's liability!

## Refunds may not be refunded

Where tax has been withheld it will not be refunded if the return is filed more than three years late. Make sure that this potential ramification is considered before deciding whether or not to file jointly or separately.

*Query:* Can taxes which are not refunded be claimed as a charitable contribution on the grounds that your client let the federal treasury keep his refund?

# CHAPTER 27

# Problems in Preparing a Tax Return for a Client Who Is Engaged in Illegal Activities

A taxpayer with an illegal source of income faces some unique and special problems—both legal and tax—if he wants to file an income tax return. The practitioner who is not himself an attorney should arrange to have himself retained by an attorney for the purposes of protecting the attorney-client privilege. The practitioner then can do all the work he would otherwise do, under the attorney's umbrella of privilege.

This chapter will discuss the following areas which must be considered before proceeding to prepare a tax return for the client with an illegal source of income:

1. Filing a blank tax return

2. Filing a return using "net" figures

3. Determining income and expenses where no books or records have been maintained

4. Disclosing the client's source of income and occupation

5. Claiming the Fifth Amendment privilege

6. Preparer's responsibilities

7. How does the IRS detect unreported income?

---

Portions of this chapter appeared originally as an article written by the author for *The Practical Accountant*, published and copyrighted 1980 by the Institute for Continuing Professional Development, Inc. The material appears here with the institute's permission.

## Filing a blank tax return

Don't ever recommend that a client file a blank tax return! Filing a blank return will not fulfill a taxpayer's dual obligation under the law to report his income and pay the resulting tax. The courts have consistently held that the filing of a blank return or a return containing only the taxpayer's name, address, occupation, and signature constitutes a failure to file under Section 7203, subjecting the taxpayer to possible civil and criminal penalties. Moreover, the privilege against self-incrimination afforded by the Fifth Amendment does not extend to failure to file, except as to gamblers required to file an occupational and excise tax return.

## Filing a return using "net" figures

There may be adverse consequences in filing a return reporting only the "net income" from an illegal business (i.e., showing no gross receipts and no expense items). Various courts have held that a tax return that does not contain any information relating to the taxpayer's income from which the tax can be computed is not a return within the meaning of the Code or Regulations.

## Determining income and expenses where no books or records have been maintained

If a tax return is to be filed, a major problem is how to prepare the return when the books and records, if any, do not clearly reflect income and expenses.

Under Section 446, the commissioner has the authority to reconstruct income where a taxpayer keeps no books or records, or where the books and records are inadequate. Where a taxpayer has an inadequate record of income earned, but nevertheless wants to file a return, he can, in theory, utilize the bank-deposit or net-worth method to arrive at an income figure in much the same way as the commissioner would. An accurate reconstruction of income might rebut a subsequent assertion by the IRS that all income was not reported. However, an accurate reconstruction will usually be difficult where books and records are lacking.

### Expenses in conducting an illegal business are deductible

In general, ordinary and necessary business expenses incurred in the operation of an illegal enterprise are deductible. As a practical matter, however, most expenses incurred by an illegal business are paid in cash and are therefore difficult to substantiate. Nonetheless, the courts will often allow deductions for undocumented expenses of an illegal business if credible oral testimony is provided which can be supported by independent evidence. One court has permitted expense deductions that could not be substantiated by receipts where a bookmaker made a meticulous daily record of income and expenses. However, where the only available deductions were summary statements of expenses, with no records of original entry, no deduction was permitted.

## Keep daily records

The most appropriate advice, from a tax standpoint, would be to advise a client that records should be as detailed as possible and maintained on a daily basis.

# Disclosing the client's source of income and occupation

To what extent should a taxpayer with illegal income disclose his occupation or source of income? For example, can a narcotics dealer call himself a "salesman" or a prostitute report her income as being from "public relations"? Ignoring for the moment the application of the Fifth Amendment, the consequences of actually misstating one's occupation or source of income can be severe.

## A misstatement of source is a crime—even if the amount is correct

At least one federal court of appeals has ruled that a misstatement of the source of a taxpayer's income, even without a misstatement of the amount of the income, constitutes a crime. In that case, the taxpayer had reported that commission income had been paid to him by a certain corporation, whereas in fact he had never received income from that source. The court ruled that such a misstatement of income source constituted a material matter if it would have a tendency to influence the IRS in its normal processing of returns. The court reasoned that to allow taxpayers willfully to misstate and fabricate the source of their income would render virtually impossible the IRS's task of ascertaining whether the amount of reported income is accurate.

## False returns

Convictions for filing a false return have also been upheld where a loan shark reported collections of usurious interest as "miscellaneous income" and where a narcotics dealer indicated on his return that the source of money seized from him at the time of his arrest for narcotics violations was from "golf playing."

Whether the characterization of the taxpayer's occupation or source of income constitutes a willful and material misstatement would ultimately be a question that would have to be decided by the courts.

## Claiming the Fifth Amendment privilege

While the misstatement of occupation or income source can be a crime, what are the consequences if the taxpayer, on the advice of counsel, pleads the Fifth Amendment instead?

The Supreme Court has held that a taxpayer is permitted to exercise his Fifth Amendment privilege with respect to specific disclosures sought on a tax return. Therefore, he may refuse to answer questions on the return as to his source of income and perhaps even as to his occupation. The taxpayer would simply note on the appropriate line on the tax return "Fifth Amendment privilege exercised."

*Probable audit:* The IRS generally examines any tax return which pleads the Fifth Amendment.

### Dilemma still exists

Notwithstanding a taxpayer's right to claim the Fifth Amendment, the government may still attempt to prosecute for violation of Section 7203 (willful failure to file a return, supply information, or pay tax). The taxpayer contemplating claiming the Fifth Amendment is thus in the dilemma of facing possible self-incrimination (if he provides the information sought on the tax return) or risking the threat of prosecution (if he does not complete the return). Furthermore, if the taxpayer does make an incriminating disclosure on his tax return, instead of claiming the privilege as he has the right to do, he cannot take the position at a later date that his incriminating disclosure had been compelled. The Supreme Court has indicated that the taxpayer is better off taking the Fifth and risking prosecution, since a valid claim or even an erroneous good-faith claim of privilege would most likely result in acquittal if the issue did go to court.

## Preparer's responsibilities

There are certain guidelines regarding the accountant's responsibility when a taxpayer wants to pay tax on illegal income. The AICPA's *Statements on Responsibilities in Tax Practice*, Nos. 151 and 191, can be useful in formulating answers to the following questions:

1) Can estimates be used?

2) Must all questions on the return be answered before the return is signed?

Under the AICPA's guidelines, the use of estimates is permitted where precise information is not available. However, it is not permissible to present estimates in such a way as to imply greater accuracy than exists. A statement should be attached to the return disclosing that estimates have been used. Similarly, if all questions on the return have not been answered, a rider, attached to the return, should indicate the reasons why the return is not complete.

## How does the IRS detect unreported income?

A question that is most often asked is: "How would the IRS know if I did not report some of my income?"

The answer is that they may or may not be able to find out based on a combination of factors which include the amount, the source, the form of payment, and the method of disposition of the unreported income. For instance, a $1,000 dividend check from IBM which is deposited into a savings account is more likely to be uncovered by the IRS than a $50 tip that is received in cash and is used to purchase tickets to a Broadway show.

### Matching program

Recently, the IRS has stepped up its program of matching the amounts of interest and dividends reported on a tax return to the amounts reflected on 1099 statements which are issued by banks and corporations.

### Clue to unreported income

The IRS has access, through the use of its summons power, to bank account information. Specifically, they can examine checking account statements, cancelled checks, savings accounts, deposit and withdrawal tickets, and signature cards. By analyzing deposits that are made into bank accounts they may be able to reconstruct income. The IRS presumes that unless the taxpayer can adequately prove that a deposit made into one of his bank accounts does not represent a loan, gift, or other nontaxable source of funds, the amount constitutes income. Basically, the procedure that is followed is to add up all the deposits in all bank accounts and eliminate those deposits which can be identified as being from a nontaxable source. This net figure is then added to the amount of cash received during the year and not deposited. The sum is then compared to the amount of income reported on the tax return.

### Tricks people use (which the IRS already knows about!)

Common ploys which are used to hide unreported income are to deposit money into other people's bank accounts, deposit money in a bank in another state, or simply not deposit any of the unreported income. It is possible for the IRS to uncover these schemes in the following manner. Tax returns (and bank statements) of relatives and associates could also be audited—either in conjunction with the examination of the taxpayer's return or randomly based on the computer's selection. A savings account maintained out of state could be detected when the bank reports interest income, at the end of the year, to the IRS on Form 1099. On the other hand, a checking account could be uncovered through the use of a surveillance of your mail at the post office. Remember, checking account statements are usually mailed monthly. Local bank accounts are usually detected by "canvassing" those banks within a few miles of the taxpayer's home or place of business.

### How the money is spent counts

If the unreported income is not spent, but rather, placed in a safe deposit box or hidden in a mattress the chances of it being detected may be reduced. Safe deposit boxes require lease agreements and signatures. Thus, a trail exists which can be followed by an investigator with enough time and determination to check all possible leads. The mattress is a solution unless a person is concerned about a theft or a fire.

The very expenditure of unreported income could be the clue the IRS needs to detect its existence. The purchase of real estate, boats, and automobiles becomes a matter of public record because of statutory filing requirements. Title to real estate must be recorded and boats and automobiles must be registered. Jewelry or furs which are purchased with unreported income can be uncovered if they are insured. The use of unreported income to pay back bank loans and credit card purchases is similarly traceable. Also, cash used to pay for foreign vacations may be determined by an examination of a passport.

# CHAPTER 28

# How to Deal With
# the Collection Division

By law, after the IRS has made a demand for payment of unpaid tax it must be paid within ten days. The usual method of demand is made in the form of a bill. Accordingly, if no payment is made the collection process is commenced. Initially, payment is requested through a series of form letters and then eventually by a representative of the collection division. The personal contact is usually made by a revenue officer.

As a general rule any correspondence received from or contact made by the collection division should not be ignored in as much as a continual default will eventually culminate in some form of adverse action. In order to deal properly with and defend against the collection process it is vital that communication between the taxpayer and the government remain open. This communication will more often than not work to the advantage of the taxpayer because it will postpone immediate adverse action by the revenue officer. As a practical matter the longer the revenue officer has to keep a case open the more likely he will be to agree to negotiate a settlement and payment terms.

This chapter will explore those alternatives that are available once the collection division of the Internal Revenue Service has initiated action.

The discussion is divided into the following areas:

1.  Objective #1—"buying time" for your client

2.  Part payment arrangements

3.  Abatement of penalties

4.  Professional responsibility

5.  The seizure process

---

Portions of this chapter appeared originally as an article written by the author for *TAX-ES—The Tax Magazine*, published and copyrighted 1980 by Commerce Clearing House, Inc. and appear here with permission.

# Objective #1—"buying time" for your client

When a revenue officer is assigned a case his first objective is to close the case as soon as possible by collecting the tax. On the other hand, your objective is to enable your client to pay off his tax liability over such a period of time that will not leave him financially strapped. Since time priorities of your client and of the IRS are at opposite ends of the spectrum, it is vital for the practitioner to know how to proceed in order to buy as much time as possible before adverse collection actions, such as levy or seizure, are initiated.

The following checklist provides those steps that should be taken and the questions which should be asked after your client has notified you that a revenue officer has contacted him.

The outline also discusses certain basic defenses which are sometimes overlooked. Each potential defense normally takes time for you to prove and also time for the revenue officer to review. The amount of time it takes to complete this procedure can be substantial.

## 1. Telephone the revenue officer and explain that you are calling on behalf of your client

The revenue officer may be reluctant or even refuse to talk to you because he does not have a Power of Attorney in his possession from the taxpayer. This obstacle can usually be overcome by assuring him that a Power of Attorney will be mailed out at once and that you are sincerely interested in helping to resolve the matter.

If he still refuses to discuss the case with you, ask him not to take any collection action for the next few days until you are able to secure a Power of Attorney. Make sure to ask him for his mailing address.

## 2. Find out what years are involved and what kind of tax is owed

The years involved are important in order for you to determine whether the statute of limitations on collection has expired (six years from date of assessment). Similarly, it is important to determine whether the tax is income tax, payroll tax, gift tax, etc. For example, if payroll taxes are involved make sure to find out whether "trust fund" taxes are unpaid in order to determine the possibility of a 100 percent penalty assessment against your client.

## 3. To what extent are penalties and interest included in the amount claimed by the IRS to be due?

A breakdown should be requested of the total balance due. The component elements will be unpaid tax, penalties and interest.

Once the amount of unpaid tax is determined certain defenses can be considered. For example, has an amended return been filed which has reduced or negated the original tax? Similarly, thought could be directed to filing an amended return to take advantage of unused carryover or carryback items or to raise a new issue.

In addition to finding out the amount of the penalties involved, it is also necessary to pinpoint the type of penalty that has been assessed. Also, ascertain the dates the IRS has of depository tax payments and the date the tax return in question has been received. This information can be vital in the case of late payment and late-filing penalties. A late-payment penalty can be abated by producing cancelled checks which indicate that payments were, in fact, made timely. If you learn that a late-filing penalty has been assessed, there will exist an affirmative defense if the client can produce an extension.

As a general rule, no information should be accepted at face value from the revenue officer. Many times the revenue officer himself will be unable to verify the accuracy of information contained on IRS computer terminals and may be inadvertently relaying incorrect data. Accordingly, always attempt to inspect physically all documents which are in dispute.

*Tactic:* Request that the revenue officer produce the tax return which he claims was filed late so you can confirm the date of receipt by IRS. If he must requisition the return from the service center, a considerable period of time could elapse.

### 4. Have payments on account been properly credited to your client's account?

It is possible that prior payments made by your client have been credited against a wrong year or not credited at all. Verify that all tax refunds which have been withheld by the IRS were also properly recorded to your client's account.

### 5. Is the underlying tax assessment correct?

Determine from the revenue officer why the assessment was made. Did your client fail to file a return which resulted in the creation of an arbitrary assessment? If so, now would be the time to bring the correct facts and figures to the revenue officer's attention.

Assessments are also generated after an audit has taken place and the taxpayer has failed to file a tax court petition to protest the IRS adjustments. In some instances the client may never have shown up for the audit and all the questioned items may then have been summarily disallowed. Although the taxpayer is now technically required to pay the tax first before he can challenge the assessment, there is an informal procedure called "Reconsideration" which may be utilized. If reasonable cause exists, the case can be sent back to the audit division so that the taxpayer has another chance to present his substantiation. Situations in which reconsideration can be requested and will usually be approved are when the taxpayer relied on his accountant to handle the audit but the accountant failed to appear for a scheduled appointment or where the taxpayer never received a ninety-day letter informing him to file a protest with the tax court. It must be remembered that the reconsideration procedure is entirely discretionary on the part of the Service.

**6. Set up an appointment to meet with the revenue officer.**

After you have determined the above information, tell the revenue officer that you would like to discuss the matter with your client and that an appointment is requested.

Meeting with the revenue officer accomplishes certain very important objectives. Primarily, you can be fairly confident that no adverse action will be taken until after your meeting. This tactic "buys time" for the client which is your most important objective in dealing with the collection division. Secondly, a meeting affords you the opportunity to establish a personal rapport with the revenue officer. If he notes a sincere effort on your part to help resolve the situation, which will also help him to close his case, the necessary time needed by your client to raise cash may be granted.

A personal meeting should also help you determine the elements of the government's case against your client and ascertain its strengths and its weaknesses.

The above checklist represents the fundamental steps which must be taken in order to restrain collection activity temporarily. The purpose of raising defenses to challenge the tax or penalty assessment is twofold. First, the IRS may be entirely or partially incorrect in their factual assumptions in which case there would be an abatement. Second, even if the IRS is entirely correct various good-faith defenses can be raised which will serve to delay collection efforts.

It should be noted that the IRS is not bound to suspend collection efforts where the collection of the tax will be put in jeopardy or where the taxpayer has a history of tax delinquency.

## Part payment arrangements

Although all collection division employees are instructed to request full payment of the account, it is obvious that all taxpayers cannot comply with such a request. Since the goal of the collection division is after all to collect tax they will usually be willing to enter into a part payment plan. This arrangement is completely discretionary on the part of the IRS as there exists no statutory provision for allowing a taxpayer to liquidate a delinquent account over a period of time.

Before such a plan is agreed to the IRS will require that the taxpayer furnish a financial statement. The statement must reflect that the taxpayer is unable to make immediate payment in full.

The inherent drawback of providing a financial statement is that your client has informed the IRS of the amounts and whereabouts of his assets. Accordingly, should they reject his request for a partial payment plan their job of collecting the tax has been made easier. Clients should also be cautioned that they are better off not submitting a financial statement at all than submitting a fraudulently prepared statement.

Even if a part payment arrangement is entered into the IRS will still file a lien which may adversely affect your client's ability to obtain credit.

*Idea:* When entering into a partial payment plan, insist that all monies are first credited against interest owed and then tax. This way the client will be entitled to a tax deduction for the interest paid immediately.

## Abatement of penalties

The collection division will usually play some part in assessing penalties for failure to pay, failure to deposit and failure to file. Even if the penalty is automatically generated by the service center, the collection division will ultimately become involved if it goes unpaid. Various procedures can be followed in an attempt to abate the penalties once they have been assessed. Although this discussion will direct itself to achieving an abatement through collection division personnel, the same procedures can be followed when dealing with the service center.

When confronted with a penalty, the taxpayer must be able to prove that the reason he failed to pay, deposit, or file was due to a reasonable cause.

In general, the following reasons are considered by the IRS to constitute reasonable cause in all cases:

1) Death or serious illness of the taxpayer or a death or serious illness in his immediate family. In the case of a corporation, estate, trust, etc., the death or serious illness must have been of an individual having sole authority to execute the return or of a member of such individual's immediate family. In the case of the failure-to-pay penalty, the death or serious illness must be of an "individual having the sole authority to make payment."

2) Destruction by fire or other casualty of the taxpayer's place of business or business records.

3) Unavoidable absence of the taxpayer. In the case of a corporation, estate, trust, etc., the absence must have been of an individual having sole authority to execute the return. In the case of the failure-to-pay penalty, the absence must be of an "individual having sole authority to make payment."

4) The taxpayer is unable to obtain records necessary to determine the amount of tax due, for reasons beyond the taxpayer's control.

5) The facts indicate that the taxpayer's ability to pay has been materially impaired by civil disturbances.

6) The taxpayer is in a combat zone.

In addition to the aforementioned acceptable excuses IRS guidelines provide that in the following situations reasonable cause shall also exist:

## Failure to pay

1) The taxpayer shows that he exercised ordinary business care and prudence in providing for payment of his tax and he posts a bond or acceptable security coupled with a collateral agreement after showing further that he was unable to pay the tax when due or that payment on the due date would have caused undue hardship. Lack of funds, however, is not an acceptable reasonable cause unless it is shown that the taxpayer was unable to pay despite his exercise of ordinary business care and prudence.

2) Any other reason which establishes that the taxpayer exercised ordinary business care and prudence but still was unable to pay the tax when due.

## Failure to deposit

1) Tax liabilities for occasional months in a given quarter exceed the $200 or $2,000 deposit requirements by only a small amount.

2) Taxpayer requested the appropriate depositary form but one was not furnished in sufficient time to permit timely deposit of the taxes.

3) Seasonal changes resulting in sudden increases in the liability of a taxpayer not ordinarily required to make deposits.

4) Unusually large sales or increases in employment causing unanticipated increase in liability to an amount in excess of the $200 on $2,000 deposit requirements.

5) Taxpayer deposits collected excise taxes on the basis of taxes charged to customers rather than actual tax collections, and the deposit may be slightly more or less than the tax.

6) Taxpayer, in order to save clerical expense, uses a system of estimating the amount of his monthly or semi-monthly tax liability and achieves substantial compliance with the deposit requirements. For example, a large company with branches throughout the country uses as a basis for determining each deposit the same amount as was deposited in the corresponding period of the preceding year but adjusts the amount to reflect any change in

tax rate, employment conditions, etc., under which system the deposit for a given period would be slightly more or less than the tax.

## Failure to file

A taxpayer does not file a return upon the advice of a reputable accountant or attorney whom the taxpayer selected with reasonable and ordinary prudence, and the taxpayer in good faith supplied him with information which he could reasonably believe was sufficient. Such failure to file will be deemed to be due to reasonable cause. However, if a return is not timely filed because the taxpayer's accountants or attorney failed to prepare it in time, reasonable cause will not be presumed.

The facts and circumstances of your client's case should be presented in writing to the revenue officer for his consideration. The letter should state that in the event of an unfavorable determination, the client requests a hearing before a penalty appeals officer. The penalty appeals officer is normally a senior revenue officer who will review the protest and ask you to attend a meeting to discuss the case. If you are still unsuccessful at this point, the penalty must be paid and a claim for refund can then be filed.

The following is a sample letter which can be adapted for use in most instances where the practitioner is seeking to have a penalty abated on behalf of his client:

[Date]

Mr. Jones
Revenue Officer
Internal Revenue Service
120 Church Street
New York, N.Y. 10008

Attn: Group 6

Re:  Ajax Rentals, Inc.
13-1234567

Dear Mr. Jones:

The above captioned taxpayer has been assessed late filing, failure-to-deposit, and failure-to-pay penalties as follows:

| Kind of Tax | Tax Period Ending | Total |
|---|---|---|
| Form 941 | December 31, 1978 | $1,350 |
| Form 941 | June 30, 1979 | $ 750 |

The taxpayer feels that there was reasonable cause and these penalties should be abated.

[Set forth the reasons why reasonable cause exists]

In light of the above facts, we respectfully request that the aforementioned penalties be abated.

The taxpayer has authorized us to write this letter on his behalf. A copy of a Power of Attorney is enclosed.

It is requested that this petition be considered by the district penalty appeals officer in the event of an unfavorable determination.

Sincerely,

Bob Smith, CPA

## Professional responsibility

Certain questions arise as to the type of advice that should be given to a client who is faced with a collection problem. For example, should you instruct your client to withdraw funds from all of his present bank accounts and set up new accounts at a bank in a neighborhood which is not located near his home or business? Alternatively, should you tell a client to withdraw all his money or mortgage his home and then go to Las Vegas for the weekend so as to build up a case that all the cash was lost at the gambling tables?

Whereas the Las Vegas alternative clearly amounts to aiding and abetting your client to defraud the government, the transferring of bank accounts may be permissible.

Although conduct of attorneys and certified public accountants is governed by their respective codes of professional responsibility, they, together with enrolled agents, are subject to the regulations prescribed by Treasury Department Circular No. 230. This document sets forth the responsibilities of those persons who practice before the IRS.

Section 10.23 specifically provides that the practitioner shall not unreasonably delay the prompt disposition of any matter before the IRS. Section 10.20(a) further provides that the practitioner shall not interfere with any lawful effort by an IRS employee to obtain records or information.

Whether specific guidance given to a client does or does not constitute a violation of the IRS Rules of Practice could only be determined on an individual basis.

# The seizure process

One of the collection division's strongest enforcement tools is the power to seize property in satisfaction of a taxpayer's outstanding liability. Although this power is awesome, the practitioner should not be intimidated by a revenue officer who threatens seizure unless the full liability is paid immediately. By examining the seizure process it will be possible to evaluate intelligently whether the seizure of your client's property is or is not imminent and how you should proceed.

There are two types of seizures: levy of property in the possession of third parties, and levy of property in the taxpayer's possession. Seizure of property in the hands of third parties (banks, for instance) is more routine and will be discussed later. Concentration will be focused on seizure of property in the taxpayer's possession, which is usually a more drastic step.

The practitioner must first consider the odds that seizure will be used against property in his client's possession. The latest figures compiled by the comptroller general of the United States indicate that the following groups of taxpayers are most likely subject to seizure:

1) those who owe payroll taxes withheld from employee's wages

2) those who have a history of untimely filing of their tax returns

3) those who have more than one delinquent account

4) those who have an outstanding tax liability in excess of $8,800.

Even if it appears that the Service will eventually take the seizure route, no adverse action is usually taken until about ten months after the date of the assessment.

In the event the matter cannot be resolved with the revenue officer, an appeal of the decision to go through with the seizure may be taken to his supervisor. As a practical matter this appeal will usually not result in overturning the revenue officer's decision since the supervisor has most likely been involved with the case for some time and probably also initially approved of the seizure as a means of closing the case. However, an appeal does give the taxpayer some additional time with which to raise the money to pay the tax.

Clients are normally concerned about what type of property can be seized. The answer is that almost anything they own can be seized, including their home, automobile, and jewelry.

The following items are the only categories of property which are exempt from seizure. (Property exempt from execution under state law is, nevertheless, subject to levy by the United States for the collection of its taxes.)

### Property exempt from levy by federal law

1) wearing apparel, and school books (However, expensive items of wearing apparel, such as furs, are luxuries and are not exempt from levy.)

2) fuel, provisions, furniture, and personal effects, not to exceed $500 in value

3) books and tools used in one's trade, business or profession, not to exceed $250 in value (As a matter of policy, the Service generally excludes $1,500 in personal effects and $1,000 in business property from levy.)

4) unemployment benefits

5) undelivered mail

6) certain annuity and pension payments

7) workmen's compensation

There is also an exemption for minimum amounts of wages, salaries, or other income determined in accordance with a prescribed formula.

### Property generally not levied on

As a matter of policy, some types of property are generally not levied on, or are levied on only in flagrant and aggravated cases of refusal to pay. These include, for example, the following:

1) social security benefits

2) Medicare payments

3) welfare payments

4) payments under the Manpower Development and Training Act of 1962 or the Area Redevelopment Act

5) cash loan value of insurance policies

6) death benefits

7) pension plan proceeds

8) contributions to individual retirement accounts (IRAs) and Keogh accounts

9) household property, for a head of household, up to $1,500 and business property up to $1,000

If the taxpayer was able to borrow against his property before a tax lien was filed against it, the probability of seizure is reduced. If the salable equity interest of the property is minimal, the IRS will normally not be interested in taking it as the inherent costs involved will not justify the tax collected.

Pursuant to a Supreme Court decision that held that the search warrant requirement applied to searches conducted to seize the property of delinquent taxpayers, the IRS has revised its procedures for seizing property in private premises by requiring its revenue officers to obtain either (1) a taxpayer-signed statement that waives the taxpayer's Fourth Amendment rights, or (2) a court order permitting entry.

### Levy of bank accounts

One of the first assets a revenue officer will attempt to seize is the balance in a bank account. The procedure is relatively simple and the results are usually good.

As soon as your client has notified you that the collection division has contacted him, certain defensive action should be initiated immediately. The client should be instructed (see discussion of professional responsibility earlier in this chapter) that before he makes any more deposits he should confirm with the bank whether a notice of levy has been served on them by the IRS. If you expect a levy to be served, then the money should not be deposited into the account. An additional step to take would be to open up a new bank account at a small, out-of-town bank or simply refrain from using a bank.

Bargaining power is effectively lost once the IRS has seized a client's money. They will normally not return the money in return for a promise to make payments pursuant to a part payment arrangement. An exception may exist only when a bond is obtained or other assets are pledged as security.

### What to do after property has been seized

Even if the collection division seizes your client's property, it is possible to have the property returned.

A taxpayer has a right to redeem his property prior to the time of sale. However, he must pay the tax and also all expenses of the seizure, which could include storage charges and insurance. Real estate may be redeemed at any time within 120 days after the sale by paying the purchaser the amount he paid for the property plus interest of 20 percent per annum.

Certain procedural requirements must be followed by the IRS prior to the sale of the seized property. Unless these steps are taken, grounds may exist to set aside the sale as unlawful.

Once the property has been seized, the IRS must provide written notice to the owner. Furthermore, the time, place, and manner of the sale of the property plus a description of the property must be published in a newspaper generally circulated within the county in which the property was seized.

The sale must take place not less than ten days or more than forty days from the time public notice is given. Furthermore, the sale must take place in the county in which the property was seized unless the district director feels that a substantially higher bid could be obtained elsewhere.

Notwithstanding the aforementioned time limits an adjournment of the sale is possible, but not later than one month after the date fixed in the original notice of sale, if the district director feels that a postponement will serve the best interests of either the government or the taxpayer.

The IRS is required to set a minimum price before the sale. If no person offers that amount at the sale, the property is deemed to have been purchased by the United States.

### Seizing the wrong person's property

On occasion the wrong person's property is levied upon. In such a case a written request for the return of the property must be made.

A wrongful levy can take place in a situation where a corporate bank account has been set up with a bank but the corporation never filed a copy of a resolution with the bank authorizing the account. It may be possible to allege, under these circumstances, that the proceeds in the corporate bank account do not belong to the corporation. Accordingly, any levy placed on the account may have to be released.

CHAPTER 29

# How to Make
# Offers in Compromise

## What is an offer in compromise?

"Offers in Compromise" is the procedure whereby the IRS will entertain an offer to compromise the payment of a tax liability. A tax liability can cover more than one period and can also include penalties and interest.

Once an agreement is reached, neither the government nor the taxpayer can reopen the case unless there was falsification or concealment of assets, or a mutual mistake of a material fact was made which would be sufficient to set aside or reform a contract.

## How likely is it that an offer
## will be accepted by the IRS?

Although general guidelines exist, which will be explained, whether your offer in compromise will be accepted depends on the facts and circumstances in your particular case. Let's face it—if your client can succeed in preventing the collection division from liquidating his liability for a year or two and the government cannot see any prospect of satisfying the debt in the near future, they'll be receptive to an offer. Normally, it is not advisable to make an offer until you are satisfied that the collection division has tried and failed to collect the tax owed by your client. The IRS will feel no necessity to compromise if they do not already know that they will not be able to locate and seize a sufficient amount of your client's assets. A premature offer would force your client to reveal the amount and location of his assets and would also give the Service insight into possible future sources of income that they may rely on for a complete satisfaction of the debt.

239

## General guidelines—what can you expect from the IRS?

The compromise of a tax liability can only rest upon doubt as to liability, doubt as to collectability, or doubt as to both liability and collectability. The Internal Revenue Code (section 7122) does not confer authority to compromise tax, interest, or penalty where the liability is clear and there is no doubt as to the ability of the government to collect. This rules out, as ground for compromise, equity or public policy considerations peculiar to a particular case, individual hardships and similar matters which do not have a direct bearing on liability or ability to pay.

The stated position of the Service is not to accept an offer for only a portion of taxpayer's unpaid liability. All unpaid liabilities should be included in the offer or otherwise be satisfied before acceptance of an offer.

## Preparing an offer

All offers in compromise must be submitted on Form 656 (see accompanying sample). The original and one copy is filed with the service center servicing the district office where the taxpayer's liability is, regardless of where the taxpayer resides or has his place of business.

## How much should you offer?

The practitioner should approach an offer in compromise as he would any other type of negotiation. Start off with a low offer and be prepared to increase it, if necessary.

An unreasonably small offer in proportion to the amount of tax owed cannot be summarily dismissed by the IRS. Service policy is to consider the maximum collection potential rather than the difference between the amount of the offer and the unpaid liability (see Policy Statement P-5-84). However, offers which are frivolous or have been submitted for the purpose of delaying collection will be rejected.

Offers that are small as compared to the outstanding balance are justifiable in certain cases. Examples of these include the following situations:

1) An individual taxpayer submits a realistic future income collateral agreement as additional consideration

2) An individual taxpayer's age and/or physical condition precludes him from returning to significant income producing activities

3) A corporation submits a realistic future income collateral agreement as additional consideration for its offer

4) A corporation is defunct and its prospects of acquiring new assets are remote.

As a general rule there is not much to be gained by making an incredibly small offer. If done, the IRS official assigned to the case will most likely form an unfavorable impression as to your client's sincerity in attempting to resolve the outstanding tax liability. As such, the conceived lack of good faith could be the stumbling block which ultimately interferes with the ability to reach a compromise.

A possible way to ascertain the amount that you could suggest to your client to offer initially is to determine the maximum amount of money your client has available and then offer 20 percent of this amount.

## Do you have to send money with the offer?

Although the IRS would like to have a check accompany the offer it is permissible to make no payment at the time the offer is filed. The amount of the offer can be paid after the offer is accepted. This period of time should be as short as possible, but the IRS does permit an extended period, as long as six years, when the taxpayer can justify such a period of time.

*Idea:* If the IRS pressures for a larger payment argue that a forced sale of your client's assets would bring less money or that it is not fair to ask the client to sell assets which are subject to fluctuating prices if the offer may not ultimately be accepted.

In theory, the IRS is required to return all monies paid with the offer if the offer is not accepted. However, an aggressive collection division officer could come up with a dozen reasons why the money should not be returned but should be applied against your client's tax liability. For this reason, only a token payment should be made with the offer.

Form **656**
(Rev. July 1979)

Department of the Treasury – Internal Revenue Service

## Offer in Compromise

To be Filed in Duplicate

Names and Address of Taxpayers

Social Security and Employer Identification Numbers

To: **Commissioner of Internal Revenue**

Date

1. This offer is submitted by the undersigned proponents (persons making this offer) to compromise a liability resulting from alleged violations of law or failure to pay an internal revenue liability as follows:

*(State specifically the alleged violation involved, the kind of unpaid tax liability, and each period involved)*

2. The total sum of $ _____ _____ paid in full or payable on a deferred payment basis as follows:[1]

with interest at the annual rate as established under section 6621(a) of the Internal Revenue Code (subject to adjustments as provided by Code section 6621(b)) on the deferred payments, if any, from the date the offer is accepted until it is paid in full, is voluntarily tendered with this offer with the request that it be accepted to compromise the liability described above, and any statutory additions to this liability.

3. In making this offer, and as a part of the consideration, it is agreed (a) that the United States shall keep all payments and other credits made to the accounts for the periods covered by this offer, and (b) that the United States shall keep any and all amounts to which the taxpayer-proponents may be entitled under the internal revenue laws, due through overpayments of any tax or other liability, including interest and penalties, for periods ending before or within or as of the end of the calendar year in which this offer is accepted (and which are not in excess of the difference between the liability sought to be compromised and the amount offered). Any such refund received after this offer is filed will be returned immediately.

4. It is also agreed that payments made under the terms of this offer shall be applied first to tax and penalty, in that order, due for the earliest taxable period, then to tax and penalty, in that order, for each succeeding taxable period with no amount to be allocated to interest until the liabilities for taxes and penalties for all taxable periods sought to be compromised have been satisfied.

5. It is further agreed that upon notice to the taxpayers of the acceptance of this offer, the taxpayers shall have no right to contest in court or otherwise the amount of the liability sought to be compromised; and that if this is a deferred payment offer and there is a default in payment of any installment of principal or interest due under its terms, the United States, at the option of the Commissioner of Internal Revenue or a delegated official, may (a) proceed immediately by suit to collect the entire unpaid balance of the offer; or (b) proceed immediately by suit to collect as liquidated damages an amount equal to the liability sought to be compromised, minus any deposits already received under the terms of the offer, with interest on the unpaid balance at the annual rate as established under section 6621(a) of the Internal Revenue Code (subject to adjustments as provided by Code section 6621(b)) from the date of default; or (c) disregard the amount of the offer and apply all amounts previously deposited under the offer against the amount of the liability sought to be compromised and, without further notice of any kind, assess and collect by levy or suit the

balance of the liability, the right of appeal to the United States Tax Court and the restrictions against assessment and collection being waived upon acceptance of this offer.

6. The taxpayer-proponents waive the benefit of any statute of limitations applicable to the assessment and collection of the liability sought to be compromised, and agree to the suspension of the running of the statutory period of limitations on assessment and collection for the period during which this offer is pending, or the period during which any installment remains unpaid, and for 1 year thereafter. For these purposes, the offer shall be deemed pending from the date of acceptance of the waiver of the statutory period of limitations by an authorized Internal Revenue Service official, until the date on which the offer is formally accepted, rejected, or withdrawn in writing.

7. The following facts and reasons are submitted as grounds for acceptance of this offer: _____

_____

*(If space is insufficient, please attach a supporting statement)*

8. It is understood that this offer will be considered and acted upon in due course and that it does not relieve the taxpayers from the liability sought to be compromised unless and until the offer is accepted in writing by the Commissioner or a delegated official, and there has been full compliance with the terms of the offer.

[1] *If this offer is paid in full at the time it is filed, show in item 2 the amount only. If this is a deferred payment offer, show (a) the amount deposited at the time of filing this offer; (b) any amount deposited on prior offers which are applied on this offer; (c) the amount of each deferred payment, and the date on which each payment is to be made. (Amounts payable after the filing date of the offer, including amounts payable upon notice of acceptance, are deferred payments.)*

| | |
|---|---|
| I accept the waiver of statutory period of limitations for the Internal Revenue Service. | Under penalties of perjury, I declare that I have examined this offer, including accompanying schedules and statements, and to the best of my knowledge and belief it is true, correct and complete. |
| Signature of authorized Internal Revenue Service official | Signature of Proponent |
| Date | Signature of Proponent |
| Title | |

Form **656** (Rev. 7-79)

## For Office Use Only

| Liability Incurred By *(List taxpayers included under same account no.)* | Kind of liability *(Complete description)* |
|---|---|

| Date Notice of Lien Filed | Place Notice of Lien Filed | Was Bond Filed? *(If yes, attach copy)* ☐ Yes ☐ No |
|---|---|---|

| Were Assets Pledged as Security? *(If yes, attach complete information)* ☐ Yes ☐ No | Periods Involved and Dates Returns Filed for Offers Involving Delinquency Penalties Only | Were Tax Collection Waivers Filed? *(If yes, attach copies)* ☐ Yes ☐ No |
|---|---|---|

**Attach Transcript of Accounts**

243

Terms of a typical offer

"I offer to pay $10,000 to be paid as follows:

— $1,000 with this offer

— $3,000 within thirty days after notice that the offer was accepted, and

— $6,000 to be paid in equal monthly installments of $200 commencing ninety days after notice of the acceptance of this offer."

Reason for making an offer

Simply state, "I am unable to pay the total liability in full."

## Financial statements must be filed!

A taxpayer seeking to compromise a tax liability based on doubt as to collectability must submit Form 433, "Statement of Financial Condition and Other Information" (see accompanying sample).

Since this form must be signed under penalties of perjury, your client must be warned that it is a crime to make any false or fraudulent statements. Depending upon the circumstances, it may be more prudent not to offer to compromise the tax liability since doing so may expose your client to other problems.

An offer will be immediately rejected if a taxpayer refuses to submit Form 433.

## Adverse collection action is stayed

When an offer is submitted and there is no reason to believe that collection of the tax liability sought to be compromised would be jeopardized, adverse collection activity is normally suspended.

## What constitutes "inability to pay"?

To be considered adequate, an offer to compromise a legally due tax liability must reflect the taxpayer's maximum capacity to pay. That is, all that can be collected from the taxpayer's equity in assets and income, present and prospective.

In addition to the taxpayer's equity in his assets, his earning capacity will also be evaluated before an offer is accepted. Information about the taxpayer's education, profession, trade, age and experience, health, past and present income and

DEPARTMENT OF THE TREASURY – INTERNAL REVENUE SERVICE
## STATEMENT OF FINANCIAL CONDITION AND OTHER INFORMATION
(To be filed in duplicate with offer in compromise)

Please submit information requested on this form with your offer in compromise, if offer is based wholly or partly on inability to pay the liability. If you need help in preparing this statement, contact your local office of District Director of Internal Revenue. It is important that all applicable questions be answered fully. The careful filling out of this form will expedite the consideration of your offer.

| 1A. NAMES OF TAXPAYERS | 1B. SOC. SEC. NO. | 1C. EMPLOYER IDENT. NO. |
|---|---|---|
| 1D. BUSINESS ADDRESS | 1E. BUS. TEL. NO. | 2. NAME AND ADDRESS OF REPRESENTATIVE, IF ANY |
| 1F. HOME ADDRESS | 1G. HOME TEL. NO. | |

3. If proponent is not taxpayer

| 3A. NAME OF PROPONENT | 3B. ADDRESS OF PROPONENT | 3C. RELATIONSHIP TO TAXPAYER (partner, president, father, etc.) |
|---|---|---|

| 4. Kind of tax involved | Taxable period | Amount offered | Unpaid liability |
|---|---|---|---|
| 4A. | | | |
| 4B. | | | |
| 4C. | | | |
| 4D. | | | |
| 4E. | | | |

5. Due and unpaid federal taxes, except those covered by this offer in compromise

| KIND OF TAX | TAXABLE PERIOD | UNPAID LIABILITY |
|---|---|---|
| 5A. | | |
| 5B. | | |
| 5C. | | |

6. List names of banks and other financial institutions you have done business with at any time during past 3 years.

| NAME AND ADDRESS | NAME AND ADDRESS |
|---|---|
| 6A. | 6B. |
| 6C. | 6D. |

6E. DO YOU RENT A SAFETY DEPOSIT BOX IN YOUR NAME OR IN ANY OTHER NAME? (If "yes" give name and address of bank)
☐ YES ☐ NO

7. If income withholding or employment tax involved, complete 7a through 7f inclusive

7A. WERE THE EMPLOYEES' INCOME WITHHOLDING OR EMPLOYMENT TAXES, DUE FROM EMPLOYEES ON WAGES RECEIVED BY THEM WITH RESPECT TO EMPLOYMENT, DEDUCTED OR WITHHELD FROM THE WAGES PAID DURING ANY PERIOD MENTIONED ABOVE?   ☐ YES   ☐ NO

| 7B. IF SO, WAS THE TAX PAID TO INTERNAL REVENUE SERVICE OR DEPOSITED?<br>☐ YES ☐ NO | 7C. IF DEDUCTED BUT NOT PAID OVER, WHAT DISPOSITION WAS MADE OF THE AMOUNTS DEDUCTED? |
|---|---|

| 7D. HAS BUSINESS IN WHICH YOU INCURRED SUCH TAXES BEEN DISCONTINUED? | 7E. IF DISCONTINUED, WHEN? (Date) |
|---|---|

7F. WHAT DISPOSITION WAS MADE OF ASSETS OF DISCONTINUED BUSINESS?

8. Offer filed by individual

| 8A. NAME OF SPOUSE | 8B. AGE OF SPOUSE | 8C. AGE OF TAXPAYER |
|---|---|---|

| 8D. DEPENDENT CHILDREN OR RELATIVES   NAME | RELATIONSHIP | AGE |
|---|---|---|
| (1) | | |
| (2) | | |
| (3) | | |
| (4) | | |
| (5) | | |
| (6) | | |
| (7) | | |

Furnish your most recent financial information in separate columns below the cost and fair market value of each asset. List all assets directly or indirectly owned and all interests in estates, trusts, and other property rights, including contingent interests and remainders.

| 9. Statement of assets and liabilities | | THIS STATEMENT IS AS OF *(Date)* |
|---|---|---|
| **9A. ASSETS** | COST * | FAIR MARKET VALUE |
| (1) CASH | $ | $ |
| (2) CASH SURRENDER VALUE OF INSURANCE *(See item 10)* | | |
| (3) ACCOUNTS RECEIVABLE *(See item 12A)* | | |
| (4) NOTES RECEIVABLE *(See item 12B)* | | |
| (5) MERCHANDISE INVENTORY *(See item 13)* | | |
| (6) REAL ESTATE *(See item 14)* | | |
| (7) FURNITURE AND FIXTURES *(See item 15)* | | |
| (8) MACHINERY AND EQUIPMENT *(See item 15)* | | |
| (9) TRUCKS AND DELIVERY EQUIPMENT *(See item 16)* | | |
| (10) AUTOMOBILES *(See item 16)* | | |
| (11) SECURITIES *(See item 17)* | | |
| (12) | | |
| (13) | | |
| (14) | | |
| (15) | | |
| (16) | | |
| (17) | | |
| (18) | | |
| (19) | | |
| (20) | | |
| (21) | | |
| (22) | | |
| (23) | | |
| (24) | | |
| (25) | | |
| (26) | | |
| (27)                          Total assets | $ | $ |

| **9B. LIABILITIES** | AMOUNT | |
|---|---|---|
| (1) LOANS ON INSURANCE *(See items 10 & 11)* | $ | |
| (2) ACCOUNTS PAYABLE | | |
| (3) NOTES PAYABLE | | |
| (4) MORTGAGES *(See item 14)* | | |
| (5) ACCRUED REAL ESTATE TAXES *(See item 14)* | | |
| (6) JUDGMENTS *(See item 18)* | | |
| (7) RESERVES *(Itemize)* | | |
| (8) | | |
| (9) | | |
| (10) | | |
| (11) | | |
| (12) | | |
| (13) | | |
| (14) | | |
| (15) | | |
| (16) | | |
| (17) | | |
| (18) | | |
| (19) | | |
| (20) | | |
| (21) | | |
| (22)                          Total liabilities | $ | |

*(Less depreciation, if any)*

FORM **433** (PAGE 2)(REV. 1-70)

**10. Life insurance policies now in force with right to change beneficiary reserved**

| NUMBER OF POLICY | NAME OF COMPANY | AMOUNT OF POLICY | PRESENT CASH SUR-RENDER VALUE PLUS ACCUMU-LATED DIVIDENDS | POLICY LOAN | DATE MADE | AUTOMATIC PREMIUM PAYMENTS* | DATE MADE |
|---|---|---|---|---|---|---|---|
| 10A. | | $ | $ | $ | | $ | |
| 10B. | | | | | | | |
| 10C. | | | | | | | |
| 10D. | | | | | | | |
| 10E. | | | | | | | |
| 10F. | | | | | | | |
| 10G. | | | | | | | |
| 10H. | | | | | | | |
| 10I. | | | | | | | |
| 10J. | | | | | | | |

*Show only those made prior to date notice of levy was served on the insurance company.*

**11. Life insurance policies assigned or pledged on indebtedness**

·If any of the policies listed in item 10 above are assigned or pledged on indebtedness, except with insurance companies, give the following information with respect to each policy:

| NO. OF POLICY AS-SIGNED OR PLEDGED | NAME AND ADDRESS OF PLEDGEE OR ASSIGNEE | AMOUNT OF INDEBTEDNESS | DATE PLEDGED OR ASSIGNED |
|---|---|---|---|
| 11A. | | $ | |
| 11B. | | | |
| 11C. | | | |
| 11D. | | | |
| 11E. | | | |
| 11F. | | | |
| 11G. | | | |

**12. Accounts and notes receivable**

| NAME | BOOK VALUE | LIQUIDATION VALUE | AMOUNT OF INDEBT-EDNESS IF PLEDGED | DATE PLEDGED |
|---|---|---|---|---|
| 12A. ACCOUNTS RECEIVABLE | | | | |
| (1) | $ | $ | $ | |
| (2) | | | | |
| (3) | | | | |
| (4) | | | | |
| (5) | | | | |
| (6) | | | | |
| (7) | | | | |
| (8) | | | | |
| (9) | | | | |
| (10) | | | | |
| (11) | | | | |
| (12)          Total | $ | $ | $ | |
| 12B. NOTES RECEIVABLE | | | | |
| (1) | $ | $ | $ | |
| (2) | | | | |
| (3) | | | | |
| (4) | | | | |
| (5) | | | | |
| (6) | | | | |
| (7) | | | | |
| (8) | | | | |
| (9) | | | | |
| (10) | | | | |
| (11)          Total | $ | $ | $ | |

FORM **433** (PAGE 3) (REV. 1-70)

247

**13. Merchandise inventory**

| DESCRIPTION | COST | FAIR MARKET VALUE | LIQUIDATION VALUE | AMOUNT OF INDEBTEDNESS IF PLEDGED | DATE PLEDGED |
|---|---|---|---|---|---|
| 13A. RAW MATERIAL | $ | $ | $ | $ | |
| 13B. WORK IN PROGRESS | | | | | |
| 13C. FINISHED GOODS | | | | | |
| 13D. SUPPLIES | | | | | |
| 13E. OTHER (Specify) | | | | | |
| 13F.              Total | $ | $ | $ | $ | |

**14. Real estate**

| DESCRIPTION | COST* | FAIR MARKET VALUE | BALANCE DUE ON MORTGAGE | DATE MORTGAGE RECORDED | UNPAID INTEREST AND TAXES |
|---|---|---|---|---|---|
| 14A. | $ | $ | $ | | $ |
| 14B. | | | | | |
| 14C. | | | | | |
| 14D. | | | | | |
| 14E. | | | | | |
| 14F. | | | | | |
| 14G. | | | | | |
| 14H. | | | | | |
| 14I.              Total | $ | $ | $ | | $ |

**15. Furniture and fixtures — Machinery and equipment**

| DESCRIPTION | COST* | LIQUIDATION VALUE | AMOUNT OF INDEBTEDNESS IF PLEDGED | DATE PLEDGED |
|---|---|---|---|---|
| 15A. FURNITURE AND FIXTURES (Business) | $ | $ | $ | |
| 15B. FURNITURE (Household - residence) | | | | |
| 15C. MACHINERY (Show type etc., specify) | | | | |
| 15D. | | | | |
| 15E. | | | | |
| 15F. | | | | |
| 15G. EQUIPMENT (Except trucks and automobiles — specify) | | | | |
| 15H. | | | | |
| 15I. | | | | |
| 15J. | | | | |
| 15K.              Total | $ | $ | $ | |

**16. Trucks and automobiles**

| | COST | LIQUIDATION VALUE | AMOUNT OF INDEBTEDNESS IF PLEDGED | DATE PLEDGED |
|---|---|---|---|---|
| 16A. TRUCKS | $ | $ | $ | |
| 16B. | | | | |
| 16C. | | | | |
| 16D. | | | | |
| 16E. | | | | |
| 16F. | | | | |
| 16G. AUTOMOBILES (Personal or used in business) | | | | |
| 16H. | | | | |
| 16I. | | | | |
| 16J. | | | | |
| 16K. | | | | |
| 16L. | | | | |
| 16M.              Total | $ | $ | $ | |

*(Less depreciation, if any)

FORM 433 (PAGE 4) (REV. 1-70)

**17. Securities** *(Bonds, stocks, etc.)*

| NAME OF COMPANY | NO. OF UNITS | COST | FAIR MARKET VALUE | AMOUNT OF INDEBTEDNESS IF PLEDGED | DATE PLEDGED |
|---|---|---|---|---|---|
| 17A. | | $ | $ | $ | |
| 17B. | | | | | |
| 17C. | | | | | |
| 17D. | | | | | |
| 17E. | | | | | |
| 17F. | | | | | |
| 17G. | | | | | |
| 17H. | | | | | |
| 17I.          Total | | $ | $ | $ | |

**18. Judgments**

| NAME OF CREDITOR | AMT. OF JUDGMENT | DATE RECORDED | WHERE RECORDED |
|---|---|---|---|
| 18A. | $ | | |
| 18B. | | | |
| 18C. | | | |
| 18D. | | | |
| 18E.          Total | $ | | |

**19. Statement of income — Corporation**

IMPORTANT: If corporation submits offer in compromise, furnish information requested below from income tax returns, as adjusted, for past 2 years and from records for current year from January 1 to date.

| 19A.  GROSS INCOME | 19 | 19 | JAN. 1 TO | 19 |
|---|---|---|---|---|
| (1) GROSS SALES OR RECEIPTS *(less returns and allowances)* | $ | $ | $ | |
| (2) COST OF GOODS SOLD | | | | |
| (3) GROSS PROFIT - TRADING OR MANUFACTURING | | | | |
| (4) GROSS PROFIT - FROM OTHER SOURCES | | | | |
| (5) INTEREST INCOME | | | | |
| (6) RENTS AND ROYALTIES | | | | |
| (7) GAINS & LOSSES *(From Sched. D)* | | | | |
| (8) DIVIDENDS | | | | |
| (9) OTHER INCOME *(Specify)* | | | | |
| (10)          Total income | $ | $ | $ | |
| **19B. DEDUCTIONS** | | | | |
| (1) COMPENSATION OF OFFICERS | $ | $ | $ | |
| (2) SALARIES & WAGES *(Not deducted elsewhere)* | | | | |
| (3) RENTS | | | | |
| (4) REPAIRS | | | | |
| (5) BAD DEBTS | | | | |
| (6) INTEREST | | | | |
| (7) TAXES | | | | |
| (8) LOSSES | | | | |
| (9) DIVIDENDS | | | | |
| (10) DEPRECIATION AND DEPLETION | | | | |
| (11) CONTRIBUTIONS | | | | |
| (12) ADVERTISING | | | | |
| (13) OTHER DEDUCTIONS *(Specify)* | | | | |
| (14) | | | | |
| (15)          Total deductions | $ | $ | $ | |
| 19C.          Net income (loss) | $ | $ | $ | |
| 19D.          Nontaxable income | $ | $ | $ | |
| 19E.          Unallowable deductions | $ | $ | $ | |

**20. Salaries paid to principal officers and dividends distributed — Corporation**

IMPORTANT: If corporation submits offer in compromise, show salaries paid to principal officers for past 3 years and amounts distributed in dividends, if any, during and since the taxable years covered by this offer.

| 20A. SALARIES PAID TO (Name and Title) | | 19 | 19 | 19 |
|---|---|---|---|---|
| (1) | , PRESIDENT | $ | $ | $ |
| (2) | , VICE PRESIDENT | | | |
| (3) | , TREASURER | | | |
| (4) | , SECRETARY | | | |
| (5) | | | | |
| (6) | | | | |
| (7) | Total | $ | $ | $ |

| 20B. | YEAR | DIVIDENDS PAID | | YEAR | DIVIDENDS PAID | | YEAR | DIVIDENDS PAID |
|---|---|---|---|---|---|---|---|---|
| (1) | | $ | (8) | | $ | (15) | | $ |
| (2) | | | (9) | | | (16) | | |
| (3) | | | (10) | | | (17) | | |
| (4) | | | (11) | | | (18) | | |
| (5) | | | (12) | | | (19) | | |
| (6) | | | (13) | | | | | |
| (7) | | $ | (14) | | $ | (20) | Total | $ |

**21. Statement of income — Individual**

IMPORTANT: If individual or estate submits offer in compromise, furnish information requested below from income tax returns as adjusted for past 2 years.

| 21A. GROSS INCOME | 19 | 19 |
|---|---|---|
| (1) SALARIES, WAGES, COMMISSIONS | $ | $ |
| (2) DIVIDENDS | | |
| (3) INTEREST | | |
| (4) INCOME FROM BUSINESS OR PROFESSION | | |
| (5) PARTNERSHIP INCOME | | |
| (6) GAINS OR LOSSES (From Sched. D, Form 1040) | | |
| (7) ANNUITIES AND PENSIONS | | |
| (8) RENTS AND ROYALTIES | | |
| (9) INCOME FROM ESTATES AND TRUSTS | | |
| (10) | | |
| (11) | | |
| (12) | | |
| (13) | | |
| (14) | | |
| (15) Total income | $ | $ |

| 21B. DEDUCTIONS | | |
|---|---|---|
| (1) CONTRIBUTIONS | $ | $ |
| (2) INTEREST PAID | | |
| (3) TAXES PAID | | |
| (4) LOSSES BY FIRE, STORM, ETC. | | |
| (5) MEDICAL EXPENSES | | |
| (6) BAD DEBTS | | |
| (7) | | |
| (8) | | |
| (9) | | |
| (10) | | |
| (11) | | |
| (12) Total deductions | $ | $ |

| 21C. | Net income (loss) | $ | $ |
|---|---|---|---|
| 21D. | Nontaxable income | $ | $ |
| 21E. | Unallowable deductions | | $ |

| 22. Receipts and disbursements — Individual | FROM | TO |
|---|---|---|

If offer in compromise is submitted by an individual or on behalf of an estate furnish below a complete analysis of receipts and disbursements for the past 12 months.

**22A. RECEIPTS**

| DESCRIPTION | SOURCE FROM WHICH RECEIVED | AMOUNT |
|---|---|---|
| (1) SALARY | | $ |
| (2) COMMISSIONS | | |
| (3) BUSINESS OR PROFESSION | | |
| (4) DIVIDENDS | | |
| (5) INTEREST RECEIVED | | |
| (6) ANNUITIES OR PENSIONS | | |
| (7) RENTS AND ROYALTIES | | |
| (8) SALE OF ASSETS (Net Amt. Rec'd) | | |
| (9) AMOUNTS BORROWED | | |
| (10) GIFTS | | |
| (11) | | |
| (12) | | |
| (13) | | |
| (14) | | |
| (15) | | |
| (16) | | |
| (17) | | |
| (18) | | |
| | Total receipts | $ |

**22B. DISBURSEMENTS**

| DESCRIPTION | AMOUNT |
|---|---|
| (1) DEBT REDUCTION | $ |
| (2) INTEREST PAID | |
| (3) FEDERAL TAXES | |
| (4) OTHER TAXES | |
| (5) INSURANCE PREMIUMS | |
| (6) MEDICAL EXPENSES | |
| (7) AUTOMOBILE EXPENSE | |
| (8) SERVANTS WAGES | |
| (9) GIFTS | |
| (10) LIVING EXPENSES (Itemize) | |
| | |
| | |
| | |
| | |
| | |
| | |
| | |
| | |
| | |
| | |
| | |
| | |
| | |
| | |
| | |
| | |
| Total disbursements | $ |

FORM 433 (PAGE 7) (REV. 1-70)

**23. Disposal of assets** – Have you disposed of any assets or property with a cost or fair market value at the time of sale, transfer, exchange, gift or other disposition in excess of $500, except for full value, from the beginning of the taxable period covered by this offer in compromise to the present date?

☐ YES ☐ NO *(If answer is "Yes" submit following information)*

| DESCRIPTION OF ASSET | DATE OF TRANSFER | FAIR MARKET VALUE WHEN TRANSFERRED | CONSIDERATION RECEIVED | RELATIONSHIP OF TRANSFEREE TO TAXPAYER |
|---|---|---|---|---|
| | | $ | $ | |
| | | | | |
| | | | | |
| | | | | |

**24. Interest in or beneficiary of estate or trust** – Have you any life interest or remainder interest, either vested or contingent in any trust or estate, or are you a beneficiary of any trust?

☐ YES ☐ NO *(If "Yes," furnish copy of instrument creating trust or estate – Also give the following information)*

| NAME OF TRUST OR ESTATE | PRESENT VALUE OF ASSETS | VALUE OF YOUR INTEREST | ANNUAL INCOME RECEIVED FROM THIS SOURCE |
|---|---|---|---|
| | $ | $ | $ |
| | | | |
| | | | |
| | | | |

**25. Grantor, donor, trustee or fiduciary** – Are you the grantor or donor of any trust, or the trustee or fiduciary for any trust?   ☐ YES

☐ NO *(If "Yes," submit copy of instrument creating trust. Also give value of corpus of trust at present time and any other information pertinent to your case.)*

**26. Any other assets or interests in assets** – Have you any other assets or an interest in assets either actual or contingent, other than those listed herein? *(i.e. Profit sharing plan and pension plan)*

☐ YES ☐ NO *(If "Yes," describe such assets fully)*

| 27A. ARE FORECLOSURE PROCEEDINGS PENDING AT THE PRESENT TIME ON ANY REAL ESTATE WHICH YOU OWN OR HAVE AN INTEREST? | 27B. IF "YES," GIVE LOCATION OF REAL ESTATE. | 27C. WAS THE GOVERNMENT MADE A PARTY TO THE SUIT? |
|---|---|---|
| ☐ YES ☐ NO | | ☐ YES ☐ NO |

| 28A. ARE BANKRUPTCY OR RECEIVERSHIP PROCEEDINGS PENDING? | 28B. IF A CORPORATION, IS IT IN PROCESS OF LIQUIDATION? |
|---|---|
| ☐ YES ☐ NO | ☐ YES ☐ NO |

**29.** If sum offered in compromise is borrowed money, give name and address of lender and list collateral, if any, pledged to secure the loan.

**30. Prospect of increase in value of assets or in present income** *(Give general statement)*.

### 31. Affidavit

Under penalties of perjury, I declare that the statements and information are to the best of my knowledge and belief true, correct, and complete and that I have no assets, owned either directly or indirectly, or income of any nature other than as shown in this statement.

| 31A. THIS STATEMENT IS AS OF *(Date)* | 31B. SIGNATURE |
|---|---|
| | |

U. S. GOVERNMENT PRINTING OFFICE : 1970 O - 379-619

future prospects will all be considered before the IRS determines that the amount they will accept in compromise is the maximum amount possible.

## Collateral agreements: the kicker for the IRS

Form 2261 (see accompanying sample) is used by the IRS as their last ditch effort to collect a tax liability.

Although collateral agreements are not supposed to be used by a taxpayer to enable him to submit an offer in an amount less than his financial condition would dictate, they are used in practice as effective bargaining tools. It is easier for a taxpayer to agree to give away something in the future, which he may or may not have, than it is to take money out of his pocket now.

The collateral agreement can be filed at the time the offer is made. However, it would probably be advantageous to wait until it is solicited by the IRS. This way you might gain some leverage for your client by not exposing to the IRS what you are prepared to offer them with respect to future income.

*Idea:* After you have filed the offer and have been contacted by the IRS, it is usually a good idea to volunteer that your client will be receptive to a collateral agreement (don't volunteer any numbers).

### Types of collateral agreements

Collateral agreements may provide for:

1) payments from future income
2) reduction in the basis of assets for computing depreciation and gain or loss for tax purposes
3) waiver of net operating losses or unused investment tax credit carrybacks or carryovers
4) waiver of bad-debt losses or other deductions

Collateral agreements are very flexible—anything you want to propose will be considered.

Collateral agreements usually run for a period of not more than five years.

## Collateral agreements for future income: what are you really agreeing to?

In addition to agreeing to pay over money based on an amount of future annual income, the collateral agreement has standard provisions which should be considered before advising a client to enter into one. If the provisions should be too

DEPARTMENT OF THE TREASURY — INTERNAL REVENUE SERVICE

# Collateral Agreement

Future Income — Individual

| Names and Address of Taxpayers | Social Security and Employer Identification Numbers |
|---|---|
| | |

**To: Commissioner of Internal Revenue**

The taxpayers identified above have submitted an offer dated _____ in the amount of $_____ to

compromise unpaid _____ tax liability, plus statutory additions, for the taxable periods _____

The purpose of this collateral agreement (hereinafter referred to as this agreement) is to provide additional consideration for acceptance of the offer in compromise described above. It is understood and agreed:

1. That in addition to the payment of the above amount of $ _____ , the taxpayers will pay out of annual income for the years _____ to _____ , inclusive

    (a) Nothing on the first $ _____ of annual income.

    (b) _____ percent of annual income more than $ _____ and not more than $ _____ .

    (c) _____ percent of annual income more than $ _____ and not more than $ _____ .

    (d) _____ percent of annual income more than $ _____.

2. That the term annual income, as used in this agreement, means adjusted gross income as defined in section 62 of the Internal Revenue Code (except losses from sales or exchange of property and the deduction allowed by Code section 1202 for long-term capital gains shall not be allowed), plus all nontaxable income and profits or gains from any source whatsoever (including the fair market value of gifts, bequests, devises, and inheritances), minus (a) the Federal income tax paid for the year for which annual income is being computed, and (b) any payment made under the terms of the offer in compromise (Form 656) for the year in which such payment is made. The annual income shall not be reduced by net operating losses incurred before or after the period covered by this agreement. However, a net operating loss for any year during such period may be deducted from annual income of the following year only. It is also agreed that annual income shall include all income and gains or profits of the taxpayers, regardless of whether these amounts are community income under State law.

3. That in the event close corporations are directly or indirectly controlled or owned by the taxpayers during the existence of this agreement, the computation of annual income shall include their proportionate share of the total corporate annual income in excess of $10,000. The term corporate annual income, as used in this agreement, means the taxable income of the corporation before net operating loss deduction and special deductions (except, in computing such income, the losses from sales or exchange of property shall not be allowed), plus all nontaxable income, minus (a) dividends paid, and (b) the Federal income tax paid for the year for which annual income is being computed. For this purpose, the corporate annual income shall not be reduced by any net operating loss incurred before or after the periods covered by this agreement, but a net operating loss for any year during such period may be deducted from the corporate annual income for the following year only.

4. That the annual payments provided for in this agreement (including interest at the annual rate as established under section 6621(a) of the Internal Revenue Code (subject to adjustments as provided by Code section 6621(b)) on delinquent payments computed from the due date of such payment) shall be paid to the Internal Revenue Service, without notice, on or before the 15th day of the 4th month following the close of the calendar or fiscal year, such payments to be accompanied by a sworn statement and a copy of the taxpayers' Federal income tax return. The statement shall refer to this agreement and show the computation of annual income in accordance with items 1, 2, and 3 of this agreement. If the annual income for any year covered by this agreement is insufficient to require a payment under its terms, the taxpayers shall still furnish the Internal Revenue Service a sworn statement of such income and a copy of their Federal income tax return. All books, records, and accounts shall be open at all reasonable times for inspection by the Internal Revenue Service to verify the annual income shown in the statement. Also, the taxpayers hereby expressly consent to the disclosure to each other of the amount of their respective annual income and of all books, records, and accounts necessary to the computation of their annual income for the purpose of administering this agreement. The payments (if any), the sworn statement, and a copy of the Federal income tax return shall be transmitted to:
    Address:

*(Over)*

Form **2261** (Rev. 4-77)

5. That the aggregate amount paid under the terms of the offer in compromise and the additional amounts paid under the terms of this agreement shall not exceed an amount equivalent to the liability covered by the offer plus statutory additions that would have become due in the absence of the compromise.

6. That payments made under the terms of this agreement shall be applied first to tax and penalty, in that order, due for the earliest taxable period, then to tax and penalty, in that order, for each succeeding taxable period with no amount to be allocated to interest until the liabilities for taxes and penalties for all taxable periods sought to be compromised have been satisfied.

7. That upon notice to the taxpayers of the acceptance of the offer in compromise of the liability identified in this agreement, the taxpayers shall have no right, in the event of default in payment of any installment of principal or interest due under the terms of the offer and this agreement or in the event any other provision of this agreement is not carried out in accordance with its terms, to contest in court or otherwise the amount of the liability sought to be compromised; and that in the event of such default or noncompliance or in the event the taxpayers become the subject of any proceeding (except a proceeding under the Bankruptcy Act) whereby their affairs are placed under the control and jurisdiction of a court or other party, the United States, at the option of the Commissioner of Internal Revenue or a delegated official, may (a) proceed immediately by suit to collect the entire unpaid balance of the offer and this agreement, or (b) proceed immediately by suit to collect as liquidated damages an amount equal to the tax liability sought to be compromised, minus any payments already received under the terms of the offer and this agreement, with interest at the annual rate as established under section 6621(a) of the Internal Revenue Code (subject to adjustments as provided by Code section 6621(b)) from the date of default, or (c) disregard the amount of such offer and this agreement, apply all amounts previously paid thereunder against the amount of the liability sought to be compromised and, without further notice of any kind, assess and collect by levy or suit (the restrictions against assessment and collection being waived) the balance of such liability. In the event the taxpayers become the subject of any proceeding under the Bankruptcy Act, the offer in compromise and this agreement may be terminated. Upon such termination, the tax liability sought to be compromised, minus any payments already received under the terms of the offer and this agreement, shall become legally enforceable.

8. That the taxpayers waive the benefit of any statute of limitations applicable to the assessment and collection of the liability sought to be compromised and agree to the suspension of the running of the statutory period of limitations on assessment and collection for the period during which the offer in compromise and this agreement are pending, or the period during which any installment under the offer and this agreement remains unpaid, or any provision of this agreement is not carried out in accordance with its terms, and for 1 year thereafter.

9. That when all sums, including interest, due under the terms of the offer in compromise and this agreement, except those sums which may become due and payable under the provisions of item 1 of this agreement, have been paid in full, then and in that event only, all Federal tax liens at that time securing the tax liabilities which are the subject of the offer shall be immediately released. However, if, at the time consideration is being given to the release of the Federal tax liens, there are any sums due and payable under the terms of item 1, they must also be paid before the release of such liens.

This agreement shall be of no force or effect unless the offer in compromise is accepted.

| Taxpayer's Signature | Date |
|---|---|
| Taxpayer's Signature | Date |

I accept the waiver of statutory period of limitations for the Internal Revenue Service.

| Signature and Title | Date |
|---|---|

harsh in your client's particular situation it would be advisable to negotiate to strike out an offending provision or introduce additional terms which would have the effect of mitigating an objectionable term.

The collateral agreement for future income provides that an individual will pay additional payments from future income. These payments are determined by multiplying various percentages times the taxpayer's "annual income." "Annual income" means adjusted gross income (except for losses from the sales or exchanges of property and the deduction allowed for long-term capital gains) plus all sources of nontaxable income including gifts, bequests, devices, and inheritances. A deduction is allowed for federal income tax paid for the year in which the amount of "annual income" is computed.

"Annual income" cannot be reduced by net operating losses incurred before or after the period covered by the collateral agreement. However, a net operating loss from any year during the period of the collateral agreement may be deducted from "annual income" of the following year only.

*Plan:* Take advantage of NOL carryovers by filing claims before entering into a collateral agreement.

Another standard provision of the collateral agreement for future income provides that certain monies earned by closely held corporations are deemed to have been received by the taxpayer for purposes of computing "annual income."

The amount agreed to under the terms of the collateral agreement must be paid, with interest, on or before the fifteenth day of the fourth month following the close of the taxpayer's year. Payments made under the agreement will be applied first to tax and penalty, in that order—and not to interest until such time that all the liabilities for tax and penalties for all years covered by the compromise have been satisfied.

*Idea:* Negotiate to have this provision reworded to provide that interest will be deemed to have been paid first.

The taxpayer waives his right to contest in court the amount of the liability sought to be compromised under the terms of the collateral agreement. For example, if the taxpayer defaults in the payment of any installment of principal or interest and the government revokes the agreement and seeks to collect the original tax liability (less payment already made) the taxpayer is out of luck.

The statute of limitations with respect to assessment and collection is waived for the period starting with the time that the offer in compromise is made until the time that any provision of the collateral agreement is not carried out in accordance with its terms, and for one year thereafter.

## Summary

The offer in compromise and the collateral agreement serve as effective tools for the taxpayer to use to help settle his problems with the IRS. It enables him to receive income without the fear that it will be subject to levy or attachment by the collection division. It should be noted that federal tax liens, which have been filed, will not be released until such time that all monies have been paid under the terms of the offer and collateral agreement. The existence of a federal tax lien will impair the ability to secure credit, but the offer in compromise can be used by your client to impress upon potential lenders that their funds will remain safe from the IRS as long as the terms of the agreed payment schedule are met.

# CHAPTER 30

# How to Handle
# 100 Percent Penalty Assessments

Congress has provided the Internal Revenue Service with an effective tool for recovering withheld payroll taxes which have not been paid over to the government. Section 6672 of the Internal Revenue Code provides that a penalty shall be assessed, in an amount equal to the tax not paid over (hence, the "100 percent"), against those persons who were required to pay over such tax. This provision enables the IRS to go after former officers and employees of defunct companies when there is reason to believe that these persons failed to account properly for withheld payroll taxes.

This discussion will focus upon the techniques used by revenue officers in conducting an investigation to determine who was a responsible person for the collection and payment of withholding taxes. In addition, various suggestions will be made to assist the practitioner in formulating defenses which may pertain to his client. The following subjects will be covered:

1. Who is liable for the 100 percent penalty assessment?

2. How to ascertain whether the computation of the 100 percent penalty is correct

3. What documents will the IRS want to look at and which documents should you be looking for?

4. Avoiding the 100 percent penalty even if your client was a responsible person.

5. How to protest a proposed 100 percent penalty assessment

6. How to take a tax deduction for the 100 percent penalty assessment if your client is held liable for withheld payroll taxes

## Who is liable for the
## 100 percent penalty assessment

To determine liability for the 100 percent penalty assessment the law provides for a twofold test. First, the person in question must have had the duty to account for, collect, and pay over trust fund taxes. Secondly, he must have willfully failed to perform this duty.

A "responsible person" is one who has the duty to perform or the power to direct the act of collecting, accounting for, and paying over trust fund monies. Such person may be an officer or employee of a corporation, or a member or employee of a partnership, or a corporate director or shareholder with sufficient control over funds to direct disbursement of such funds. In practice, the revenue officer will usually look to those persons with executive titles and summarily conclude that they were responsible persons. If possible, the practitioner's first rebuttal to a revenue officer's position should be that his client was merely an employee who was subject to the control of another person.

Many times it will be difficult, if not impossible, for the revenue officer to conduct a thorough investigation because of misplaced records, lack of cooperation, etc. In such a case the *Manual* authorizes the revenue officer to look to the officers of a company as constituting "responsible persons." Although the revenue officer should be able to establish a relationship between those persons whom he seeks to hold responsible for the failure to pay over payroll taxes and the actual responsibility they had, most times a "broad sweep" will be made so as to create liability for more than one person to increase the government's odds of recovering misappropriated monies.

The second part of the test, concerning willfulness, does not require a bad motive or evil intent. Rather, all that needs to be shown is that the responsible party was aware of the outstanding taxes and deliberately declined to pay them over. The most common example of willfulness is where money which was required to be withheld from employees as payroll taxes was knowingly and intentionally used to pay operating expenses of the business or other debts in lieu of being paid over to the government.

Practitioners should be cautioned from making statements such as "My client was able to keep X number of people employed by using the withheld payroll taxes—otherwise he would have had to shut the doors months earlier." This type of rationale is exactly what the revenue officer needs to help strengthen his case.

There is a substantial amount of litigation in the area of who qualifies as a "responsible person" under the statute. Since each case the practitioner deals with will be governed, to a large degree, by its own facts and circumstances, the best advice that can be given is to ascertain the strengths and weaknesses of the government's case as early as possible and then proceed by emphasizing the weak points when negotiating with the revenue officer.

It should be noted that the 100 percent penalty assessment is used by the IRS as a collection tool. Accordingly, if you know that some or all of the delinquent payroll taxes have already been paid this fact should be brought to the attention of the revenue officer. It is the policy of the Service to use the 100 percent penalty only as a collection device and not to collect the same tax twice.

## How to ascertain whether the computation of the 100 percent penalty is correct

The 100 percent penalty assessment is based only upon "trust fund" taxes which have been withheld from an employee's salary. The employer's share of FICA tax must be excluded from the base used in determining the amount of the penalty.

The underlying documentation used by the revenue officer in computing the penalty must be examined very carefully. There will be occasions when the hardest part of the government's case to prove is the correctness of the amount of the assessment. The following list should be reviewed each time the practitioner is handling a 100 percent penalty assessment case:

1) Determine how the revenue officer arrived at the amount of unpaid "trust fund" taxes by reviewing his work papers.

2) Have the payroll tax returns in question, Form 941, been prepared by the company or has this revenue officer or a previous revenue officer assigned to the case prepared them? If no payroll tax returns were originally filed, the revenue officer may prepare them for the purpose of generating an assessment.

3) Ascertain that the payroll tax returns, which are being used as a basis for the penalty, are correct. Tie in payroll cards and/or cancelled checks to confirm that the amount of withholding and employer's share of FICA reported on the 941s are accurate numbers.

4) Review the periods covered by the payroll tax returns to make sure that your client was associated with the company for that period of time. For example, if an assessment is based upon the unpaid trust fund taxes reflected on the 941s for the first and second quarters of a given year (January 1 through June 30), was your client involved with the company for the entire six-month period? If not, then after you establish the period he was with the firm it is necessary to ascertain the dates and amounts of each

payroll period. You might find that the bulk of the payroll was paid during that part of a quarter in which your client was not even associated with the company.

# What documents will the IRS want to look at and which documents should you be looking for?

The *Manual* provides the following checklist of records which revenue officers should examine before recommending a 100 percent penalty assessment:

## 1. Corporate records

A)  articles of incorporation showing duties of officers, directors, etc.

B)  changes of officers, directors, etc., and their duties as recorded in minutes

C)  appointment of officers, directors, etc.

D)  resignations of officers, directors, etc.

E)  in examining minute book, note—

   i)   diversion of funds to anything other than taxes, when taxes had already accrued

   ii)  borrowing of monies when taxes had already accrued, and monies borrowed not used to pay taxes

   iii) authority of persons to sign checks, deposit monies, obligate the corporation by borrowing, etc.

   iv)  responsibility of persons to file tax returns and pay same

   v)   issuance of stock to officers, assets transferred to officers, etc.

   vi)  any evidence of transfer of assets that appears questionable

F)  in examining cancelled checks and bank statements, if available, note—

   i)   diversion of funds to officers, members, etc.

   ii)  deposits and withdrawals of alleged loans to corporation by officers, directors, members, etc.

   iii) excessive salaries, expenses, etc.

   iv)  payment of other obligations when tax liability had already accrued

   v)   deposit record of monies received for sale of assets for less than full value

   vi)  deposit record of payments for stock in corporation, where it is believed less than full value was paid for stock

G) in examining payroll records and other records, note—

    i)   unreported payroll and other taxes

    ii)   evidence of any kind to support recommendation

## 2. Bank records

A) signature cards and supporting corporate resolutions, correspondence to the bank, relative to changes affecting signature cards, etc.

B) bank statements, if not available from corporation

C) financial statements submitted to bank

D) records of loans by bank to corporation, especially if made since accrual of tax liability

Revenue officers should have photocopied, if possible, those documents, minutes, checks, etc., that will help support the 100 percent penalty assessment recommendation.

Although the *Manual* suggests that the revenue officer look at numerous documents, in practice, this cannot usually be done since most records of the defunct company are usually lost or destroyed by the time the IRS gets involved. The records most likely have already passed through the hands of attorneys, creditors, and even the bankruptcy court. The most readily accessible document is normally the signatory cards maintained for bank accounts. The practitioner must always confirm the following before accepting a revenue officer's statement that "Your client must have been a responsible person—after all he was a signatory on the company's bank account":

1) Examine the signature cards. Did your client really sign them or did some other person sign your client's name? Did that other person also sign your client's name to checks?

2) Determine from the signature cards the dates the account was opened and closed.

3) Was the bank account(s) your client was the signatory on active? Try to establish that most deposits/withdrawals were made from other bank accounts over which your client had no authority. Look at bank statements.

4) Was a separate payroll account maintained? Did your client have check signing authority?

A copy of Form 4180 is presented below that reveals those questions the revenue officer particularly wants answers to. Practitioners should be advised to answer most carefully all questions asked. In fact, if there is any doubt as to whether or not you should respond to the questions at all it may be advisable to wait until a summons is issued. Revenue officers will generally not bother with summons since it is easier for them just to recommend the penalty assessment if they do not receive cooperation. Having your client interviewed by a revenue officer is normally advisable only in those instances where there is no doubt but that he or she was not a responsible person under the law. Cooperation under these circumstances would be helpful to your client since it may eliminate the possibility of the 100 percent penalty assessment.

## Avoiding the 100 percent penalty even if your client was a responsible person

The practitioner should always confirm that the statute of limitations on assessment of the 100 percent penalty has not expired. The *Manual* provides the following information to revenue officers with respect to this subject:

| Type of Tax | Taxable Periods | Statutory Assessment Period |
| --- | --- | --- |
| Withholding FICA | After 1954 | With respect to any taxable period within a calendar year, three years from the succeeding April 15 or from the date the return was filed, whichever is later. |
| Excise RRTA | After 1954 | Three years from due date of return or from date return was filed, whichever is later. |

## How to protest a proposed 100 percent penalty assessment

In the event that you are unable to persuade the revenue officer or his group manager that your client should not be assessed the 100 percent penalty, the IRS has two levels of appeal.

The first level is the special procedures staff (SPS). If an agreement cannot be reached at that level then a second appeal at the appellate division is available.

Although an appeal may be brought directly to the appellate division without first meeting with the conferee from the special procedures staff, there are at least two good reasons why a practitioner should contact both levels. First, the more people who hear your case, the more likely it will be that one of them may offer an attractive settlement. Second, even if you are completely unsuccessful in having the proposed penalty negated or reduced, you are "buying time" for your client.

## Report of Interview Held With Persons Relative
## to Recommendation of 100-Percent Penalty Assessments
*(Where question is not applicable, mark "N/A". Attach additional sheets if necessary)*

**Consult Exhibit 5500-8 Before Starting This Interview**

| 1. Person Interviewed | | *(b)* Age | Date of Interview |
|---|---|---|---|
| *(a)* Name | | | |

| *(c)* Address | Interview Conducted by |
|---|---|
| | *(e)* Social Security Number |

| *(d)* Dependent's Age and Relationship | *(f)* Telephone Number |
|---|---|
| | *(g)* Place of Employment |
| | *(h)* Income *(Approx.)* |
| | *(i)* Net Worth *(Estimated)* |

| 2. Taxpayer *(Corporation)* | *(a)* Address |
|---|---|

3. What status or official capacity have you hold with this corporation? *(Officer, employee, member, stockholder, etc.):*

4. What were your duties and responsibilities?

5. When did this corporation commence business? *(Date of incorporation, etc.):*

6. Who were the incorporators?

7. Who have been officers? *(Note dates of service.)*

8. Who have been directors? *(Note dates of service.)*

9. What is the present status of corporation? *(Operating, Bankrupt, Defunct, etc.)*

10. If not operating, when did the business cease to operate?

11. In your opinion, what caused this business to fail, cease to operate, etc.?

12. Are there any assets of the corporation available; if so, where are they located?

13. Was any property of the corporation sold, transferred, quit-claimed, donated, or otherwise disposed of, for less than full consideration, since accrual of the tax liability? *(Question particularly if any officers, members, employees, relatives, etc., received stock in corporation, expense accounts, property, etc., and did not render an adequate service in exchange.)*

14. Were minute books kept: if so, where are they?

Form **4180 Page 1** (Rev. 4-75)          Department of the Treasury — Internal Revenue Service.

15. Were meetings of any kind ever held by stockholders, officers, members, or other interested parties, regarding nonpayment of the tax liabilities?

    *(a)* Date(s) of such meetings:

    *(b)* Who was present?

    *(c)* What was discussed?

    *(d)* What decisions were reached?

    *(e)* Were any minutes taken at these meetings; are they recorded in the minute book?

    *(f)* If not recorded in minute book, who may have made a record of these meetings and now have this record in their possession?

16. When were the last wages paid?

17. Was employment tax withheld by the employer?

    *(a)* Who is the person who maintained the books and records?

18. During the time this delinquent tax was accruing, were all payrolls met?

19. If payrolls were not met during period tax was accruing, was money available to pay payrolls?

20. Did the taxpayer endeavor to set up a trust fund for the withheld and/or collected taxes?

21. If employment taxes are involved, has the income tax been paid by employees?

22. When did you first become aware that the tax liability was not paid?

    *(a)* What action did you take to see that the tax liabilities were paid?

23. Were any other obligations paid during period tax liabilities were accruing?

24. Who had authority or allowed these other obligations to be paid?

25. In your opinion, what is the reason the corporation did not pay the tax liability?

26. Who was responsible for filing Form 941 during the periods of delinquency?
    Name
    Title
    Periods

Form **4180 Page 2** (Rev. 4-75)

27. Who was responsible for paying withheld Federal taxes during the periods of delinquency?

Name

Title

Periods

28. Who was responsible for making Federal tax deposit (FTD) during the periods of delinquency?

Name

Title

Periods

29. Did you ever sign any returns or pay any tax for the corporation? If so, when?

30. Who had the right to sign the following? *(Indicate banks, dates, etc.):*

*(a)* Payroll checks?

*(b)* Other than payroll checks?

31. What banks or financial institutions did the corporation have dealings with?

32. Do you know of any person or organization that borrowed or otherwise provided funds to pay net corporate payrolls? If so:

(a) Who borrowed funds?　　　　(b) Who supplied funds?　　　　(See IRC 3505)

33. Are you aware of any employment or excise tax returns which have not been filed by the taxpayer?

34. Are you aware of any tax liabilities of this corporation, which have not been reported on a Federal tax return?

35. Is there a financial statement available for the corporation; if so, where?

36. Did the corporation submit a financial statement to anyone *(financial institution, etc.);* if so, to whom were these statements submitted?

37. Where are the following located?

*(a)* Payroll records?

*(b)* Cancelled checks?

*(c)* Remainder of the books and records?

38. With respect to excise taxes, were the patrons or customers informed that the tax was included in the sales price?

39. If the tax liability is one of the so-called "collected" taxes — admissions, transportation of persons or property, dues and initiation fees, safe deposit boxes, communications and cabaret as it relates to concessionnaires:

*(a)* Was the tax collected?

*(b)* Were you aware, during the period the tax accrued, that the law required the collection of the tax?

**Ask the person interviewed for any further comments he may care to make regarding the case. The person interviewed is not required to sign this form. However, he may be requested to do so.**

*(Additional remarks on reverse)*

| Interviewer's signature | Date |
|---|---|
| | |

Form **4180 Page 3** (Rev. 4-75)

Any delay between the time of the ultimate assessment and the initiation of adverse collection action will benefit your client.

## Filing a protest

Generally, a written protest must be filed within thirty days from the date of the IRS notice informing you of the proposed 100 percent penalty assessment (sixty days if the letter is addressed to a taxpayer outside the United States). If the amount of the proposed tax is not more than $2,500 for any of the tax periods or years involved, then no written protest is required. In such a situation the practitioner would be advised to write the following letter to "go on record" with his client's intention not to agree with the proposed penalty:

[Date]

Internal Revenue Service
Special Procedures Staff
120 Church Street
New York, N.Y. 10008

Re:  James Smith<br>111-22-3456<br>100 Percent Penalty<br>Assessment

Gentlemen:

Enclosed find a Power of Attorney.

On May 5, 1980, the above captioned client was notified that a 100 percent penalty assessment in the amount of $1,563 has been proposed.

My client does not agree with the proposed penalty. A conference is respectfully requested to discuss this matter.

Please call me to arrange for a meeting.

Sincerely,

Allen Scott, Esq.

A second letter, addressed to the appellate division, should be prepared if an agreement cannot be reached at the special procedures staff level.

If the amount of the proposed penalty is more than $2,500 for any of the tax periods or years involved a formal written protest must be prepared. This formal written protest is required whether you are appealing to the special procedures staff first or directly to the appellate division. If a formal written protest is filed for the special procedures staff conference a second written protest does not have to be filed again with the appellate division.

If a written protest is required, it must be submitted in duplicate within the thirty-day period described above and must contain:

1) a statement that you want to appeal the findings of the notice mailed to you to the special procedures staff or the appellate division

2) your name and address

3) the date and symbols of the letter

4) the tax periods or years involved

5) an itemized schedule of the findings with which you do not agree

6) a statement of facts supporting your position in any contested factual issue

7) a statement outlining the law or other authority on which you rely

A statement of facts (item 6) must be declared true under penalties of perjury. This may be done by adding to the protest the following signed declaration:

Under penalties of perjury, I declare that I have examined the statement of facts presented in this protest and in any accompanying schedules and statements, and, to the best of my knowledge and belief, they are true, correct, and complete.

The following is a sample formal protest:

[Date]

Special Procedures Staff
Internal Revenue Service
120 Church Street
New York, N.Y. 10008

Re: James Smith
14 Main Street
Yonkers, N.Y. 19405

111-22-3456

941-7709      $4,500

941-7712      $990

Gentlemen:

This letter represents a formal written protest of your notice dated May 5, 1980, in which the above captioned client was notified that a 100 percent penalty assessment in the amount of $5,490 has been proposed.

It is our position that James Smith was not a responsible person as defined by statute, who was required to collect, account for, and pay over withheld taxes of Ajax, Inc.

During 1977 Mr. Smith was employed by Ajax, Inc., in the capacity of General Manager. He was not an officer of Ajax, Inc., or a stockholder at any time during 1977. Although his duties included the payment of bills he was subject to the direction and control of Stanley Johnson during his period of employment. Mr. Johnson, a vice president of Ajax, Inc., told Mr. Smith which bills to pay and when to pay them. Mr. Smith was, at all times, acting in the capacity of a mere employee.

Mr. Smith did have check-signing authority of the "regular checking account" during the period October 8, 1977, to December 31, 1977. A separate payroll account and tax account was maintained by Ajax, Inc. Mr. Smith did not have check-signing authority over either of these accounts.

A review of the activity of all the bank accounts indicates that after salaries were paid from the payroll account the extra money which was supposed to be paid as taxes was transferred to the tax account. The money was later withdrawn from the tax account and deposited into the regular account. Mr. Smith did not have the authority to transfer any funds from either the payroll account or the tax account.

In light of the aforementioned facts it is requested that the determination to propose a 100 percent assessment against Mr. Smith be reconsidered as he was not a responsible person as required by law. Alternatively, even if you should continue to hold that he was a responsible person then he should only be liable for the 100 percent penalty assessment for those taxes which were not collected and paid over from October 8, 1977, to December 31, 1977, as that was the period of time that he was a signatory on the regular checking account.

It is requested that this protest be forwarded to the appellate division in the event a settlement in this matter cannot be reached.

Under penalties of perjury, I declare that I have examined the statement of facts presented in this protest and in any accompanying schedules and statements, and, to the best of my knowledge and belief, they are true, correct, and complete.

Sincerely,

Allen Scott, Esq.

# How to take a tax deduction
# for the 100 percent penalty assessment
# if your client is held liable
# for withheld payroll taxes

According to statute, penalties are not tax deductible. However, it may be possible to structure the payment of your client's liability for unpaid payroll taxes so that the amount paid becomes deductible.

Since the IRS has stated that the 100 percent penalty assessment will be used only as a collection device, it stands to reason that if the unpaid taxes are ultimately paid by the entity which incurred the liability, the 100 percent assessment levied against your client will be abated.

If the entity that incurred the payroll tax liability was a corporation then the practitioner may have certain alternatives available. If the corporation has not lost its state charter it may be advisable to have your client loan the corporation money in an amount equal to the unpaid tax liability. The corporation will make the tax payment, the 100 percent penalty assessment against your client will be abated and then a bad debt deduction can be claimed. In the event that the corporation has lost its charter because of unpaid corporate or franchise taxes, it may be to your client's advantage to have him loan the corporation those funds necessary to reinstate its charter.

If your client is a shareholder in the corporation and Section 1244 can be utilized, your client could contribute additional capital to the corporation in an amount equal to the tax owed and then take a Section 1244 loss when the stock is sold.

In both cases the amount that should be paid by the corporation is only the unpaid payroll taxes, exclusive of interest and penalties. It is the author's opinion that the 100 percent penalty against your client would not be sustained for interest and penalties where the total amount of withheld payroll taxes have, in fact, been paid over.

# CHAPTER 31

# Service Center Problems and the Problems Resolution Program

The regional service centers generate a tremendous amount of correspondence between the IRS and the taxpayer. Sometimes money claimed to be owed is not really due. A mistake has been made. For example, a payment may not have been properly credited or an assessment of a penalty, which has been abated, was never removed from your client's account.

Problems with the service center can be frustrating to resolve since you are dealing, more times than not, with a computer. Eventually, things get straightened out, so do not be overly concerned if certain form letters which are contained in this chapter receive no immediate response. The trick in dealing with the service center is to respond initially with a letter answering their bill and then just send photocopies of your original letter with every notice that is subsequently received. The time saved using this procedure can be substantial.

## Saving time when dealing with the service center

An increasing number of functions are handled by the various service centers throughout the country. This ranges from correspondence audits involving the disallowance of unallowable items reported on the tax return and the failure to report 1099 income to the billing and collection function normally associated with the service center. It is easy to limit the amount of time needed to resolve your client's problems when they are contacted by the service center.

### The first step

After receiving a call from your client informing you that he has received a notice from the service center tell him just to "Send me the notice, I will take care of it." Don't get involved in a prolonged discussion with your client at this point. Tell him that you will get back to him as soon as you have an answer.

The following are typical examples of service center correspondence which generally necessitate a response:

## 1. Error in computing tax or no record of payments

*Problem:* After filing his tax return your client receives a notice indicating that the amount of his refund has been reduced or that he owes additional tax. There may have been a mathematical mistake or the computer may have no record of estimated tax payments which have been made.

*Solution:* Draft the following letter:

[Date]

Internal Revenue Service
Holtsville, New York 00501
Stop:

Re:  Jim Smith
1980–1040
118-09-8765

Gentlemen:

Our office is in receipt of your notice, a copy of which is enclosed.

According to your notice no credit was given for the third quarter estimated tax payment which was made on or about September 15, 1980. Enclosed find a photocopy of our client's check for $545.

Please correct your records accordingly.

Sincerely,

Allen Scott, Esq.

## 2. A late filing penalty has been assessed

*Problem:* Your client filed a tax return late, but reasonable cause exists for having the penalty abated.

*Solution:* Draft the following letter.

[Date]

Internal Revenue Service
Holtsville, New York 00501
Stop:

Re:  Jim Smith
1980–1040
118-09-8765

Gentlemen:

Our office is in receipt of your notice, a copy of which is attached.

This letter represents a request for the abatement of the late-filing penalty as reasonable cause exists.

[Set forth facts]

The taxpayer has always relied upon his accountant to prepare the appropriate forms whenever it was necessary to request an extension of time to file his tax return. Due to an administrative failure within our office the taxpayer's extension was not filed. This fact was unfortunately not uncovered until three months after the due date.

As soon as we realized no extension had been requested the taxpayer's return was prepared and filed.

Due to the fact that the taxpayer exercised due diligence in retaining our firm the facts leading to the assessment of the penalty were beyond his control.

[Restate reasonable cause] Inasmuch as reasonable cause exists for the late filing it is respectfully requested that the penalty be abated.

[Unfavorable determination provision:] In the event of an unfavorable determination it is requested that this letter be forwarded to the penalty appeals officer.

A Power of Attorney executed by the taxpayer is enclosed.

Sincerely,

Allen Scott, Esq.

*Tips on writing "successful" letters to abate penalties:*

1) Always indicate at least twice in the letter that "reasonable cause" exists.

2) If possible, blame yourself or your firm—it usually works.

### 3. An unexpected letter is received indicating a balance due

*Problem:* Your client receives a notice indicating that a balance due is owed but neither you nor your client have any idea of what it is all about.

*Solution:* Draft the following letter.

[Date]

Internal Revenue Service
Holtsville, New York 00501
Stop:

Re:  Jim Smith
     1980–1040
     118-09-8765

Gentlemen:

We are in receipt of your notice, a copy of which is enclosed.

Our client does not know how the amount shown as a balance due was arrived at. Accordingly, it is requested that a transcript be provided of our client's account.

It is requested that all collection action be suspended pending resolution of this matter.

A Power of Attorney is enclosed.

Sincerely,

Allen Scott, Esq.

**Service center practice tips:**

1) Respond to all correspondence promptly. Send all letters "Return Receipt Requested."

2) Expect to receive additional computer-generated letters and bills. Just mail them back with a copy of your initial letter. At some point someone will answer you.

3) Always send a Power of Attorney with any letter which requires a response.

4) Try to get someone's name each time you have a service center problem. Keep your own directory and call next time you have a problem with another client in the same area.

## Problems resolution program

The IRS has instituted a service known as the Problems Resolution Program (PRP). This department's function is to act as a liaison between the taxpayer and the IRS when conventional efforts to resolve a problem have failed. Essentially, the PRP office cuts through the IRS's own red tape.

Before the PRP gets involved with a case it is necessary for the taxpayer or his representative to have attempted to resolve the problem through normal channels. In the event of no response or an inadequate response to a particular problem, contacting the PRP office is the next step.

### Emergencies

Contact the PRP office immediately if circumstances warrant, such as when a levy has been placed on your client's salary but the amount of tax he owed has already been paid.

A PRP office is maintained at the district office and also at the service center.

### Form letter to the PRP office

[Date]

Problems Resolution Program Officer
Internal Revenue Service
Holtsville, New York 00501

Re: Jack Smith
1980–1040
104-56-6572

Gentlemen:

This letter represents a request for your assistance on behalf of the above captioned taxpayer.

The taxpayer has received various notices from the service center, copies of which are enclosed, which request additional tax. All efforts to resolve this matter with the service center, to this point, have proved unsuccessful.

It is requested that the taxpayer be furnished with an explanation as to how the amount claimed to be owed was arrived at and that all collection action be suspended.

A Power of Attorney executed by the taxpayer is enclosed.

Sincerely,

Allen Scott, Esq.

## Service center organization

A chart of organization of the service center and a description of the various functions is included in Appendix I.

# CHAPTER 32

# Inspection Division and Internal IRS Security

The inspection division of the Internal Revenue Service is charged with the responsibility of maintaining internal security. This is a two-pronged function. First, as far as the practitioner is concerned, the inspection division monitors the conduct of all IRS employees and investigates offers of bribes. Its second major responsibility is to audit the physical operations of the IRS to insure that all procedural matters are handled in accordance with the established provisions of the *Internal Revenue Manual.* For example, the inspection division may audit the operations of a particular collection division to confirm that checks received from taxpayers, in payment of outstanding liabilities, are being processed correctly.

The investigation of bribe offers made to IRS employees will be the subject of this chapter. Absolutely no inference should be made that the author will make any effort to explain how "successfully" to bribe an IRS employee. Rather, the purpose is to educate the practitioner to those things he may innocently say or do which may be construed as a bribe by an IRS employee.

IRS employees, in general, and revenue agents, in particular, are incorruptible. Those taxpayers and/or their representatives who are convicted of bribery have apparently underestimated the integrity of the IRS employee they were dealing with.

*Caution:* Certain IRS employees may try to "set up" a practitioner even though they have no intention of accepting a bribe. It is done for purposes of personal glory and the hope of special recognition by their supervisors. There are always certain IRS employees who seem regularly to inform the inspection division of attempted bribe offers even though the vast majority of employees go through their entire career without ever being offered anything more than a cup of coffee.

This chapter focuses on the following topics:

1. What constitutes a bribe?

2. What are agents told to do if they suspect that they have been offered a bribe?

3.   When will an agent be "wired"?

4.   Taking the agent to lunch

---

## What constitutes a bribe?

Generally, a bribe is any offer of money or other consideration to an IRS employee in an effort to persuade him not to take certain action he would otherwise be required to take under the law.

*For practical purposes: A bribe offer is what the agent perceives it to be!* It doesn't mean he is right—but it can create unnecessary anxiety for you.

In order to avoid any inference that you are making an agent a bribe offer there are certain things which should not be said, even kiddingly.

**Don't say:**

1)   Why don't you take home one of these products my client manufactures? After all, it is only worth about twelve dollars. Nobody could ever say you were bribed for twelve dollars.

2)   What would it take for us to settle this case so that my client only has to pay a small amount of tax?

3)   Here are two tickets to the theater. My client gives them to all his customers.

4)   Would you like to borrow one of my client's cars for a few weeks while yours is being repaired?

## What are agents told to do if they suspect that they have been offered a bribe?

During training IRS agents are instructed in the procedure to follow if they think they have been offered a bribe. They are not supposed to accept or reject the offer. Rather, the idea is get out of the meeting as soon as possible and notify the inspection division of what has transpired. Agents are specifically instructed not to accept any offer of a bribe the first time it is made because there are no witnesses. It would be the agent's word against that of the practitioner or his client.

When will an agent be "wired"?

After a meeting with a representative of the inspection division the agent's account of the bribe offer will be evaluated to ascertain the merits of the agent's contention. It generally does not take much for the agent to convince the inspection division that he has been offered a bribe since this type of work is the inspection division's job and they could not possibly be overwhelmed with potential bribe offers.

Assuming that the inspection division decides to proceed they will have the agent arrange another appointment with the practitioner and/or his client. At this meeting the agent will be "wired" with a concealed radio transmitter. The agent will be instructed to elicit the offer from the practitioner and/or his client once again. If money is to be handed over the agent will intentionally count the money, out loud, to establish for the record that he has received something.

## Taking the agent to lunch

Are you allowed to buy the agent lunch?

Each district has its own policy with respect to whether its agents may allow a taxpayer or a practitioner to pay for lunch. The trend is not to permit agents to accept a free lunch since implications may be made that the agent is compromising his position in some fashion. Management generally takes the position that if no lunches are allowed the problems which otherwise exist in the area of conflicts of interest will be reduced.

There is usually no rule that says that the agent cannot eat lunch with you as long as he pays for his own share.

Don't offer to pay for lunch if you know that the agent is not allowed to accept it!

# CHAPTER 33

# Private Rulings

There are numerous occasions when a client asks a question as to the tax ramifications of a proposed transaction and no definitive authority exists on which to base an answer. The IRS has recognized this problem and has a procedure whereby a taxpayer may request, from the national office, a ruling. Based on the facts submitted the IRS will tell you how it will treat your client's transaction. This ruling is binding only between your client and the IRS. It cannot be relied on or cited as an authority or precedent by any other taxpayer.

The following topics will be covered in this chapter:

1. On what issues will the IRS not issue an advance ruling?

2. Requirements for obtaining a ruling

3. How to request a ruling

4. Closing agreements

## On what issues will the IRS not issue an advance ruling?

Because of the inherently factual nature of some specific problems, or for other administrative reasons, the service may not issue an advance ruling.

The following are areas in which rulings will not be issued:

### .01 Specific questions and problems

1) *Section 79.*—Group Term Life Insurance Purchased for Employees.— Whether a group insurance plan for ten or more employees qualifies as group term insurance if the amount of insurance is not computed under a formula that would meet the requirements of section 1.79-1(c)(2)(ii) if the group consisted of fewer than ten employees.

2) *Section 83.*—Property Transferred in Connection with Performance of Services.—Whether a restriction constitutes a substantial risk of forfeiture if the employee is a controlling shareholder.

3) *Section 105(h).*—Amount Paid to Highly Compensated Individuals under a Discriminatory Self-Insured Medical Expense Reimbursement Plan.—Whether, following a determination that a self-insured medical expense reimbursement plan is discriminatory, that plan had previously made reasonable efforts to comply with tax discrimination rules.

4) *Section 117.*—Scholarships and Fellowships Grants.—Whether an employer-related scholarship or fellowship grant is excludable from the employee's gross income if there is no intermediary private foundation distributing the grants, as there was in Rev. Proc. 76-47, 1976-2 C. B. 670.

5) *Sections 121 and 1034.*—One-Time Exclusion of Gain from Sale of Principal Residence by Individual Who Has Attained Age 55; Rollover of Gain on Sale of Principal Residence.—Whether at the time of its sale property qualifies as the taxpayer's principal residence.

6) *Section 162.*—Trade or Business Expenses.—Whether compensation is reasonable in amount.

7) *Section 170.*—Charitable Contributions and Gifts.—Whether a taxpayer who advances funds to a charitable organization and receives therefor a promissory note may deduct as contributions, in one taxable year or in each of several years, amounts forgiven by the taxpayer in each of several years by endorsements on the note.

8) *Section 264(b).*—Certain Amounts Paid in Connection with Insurance Contracts.—Whether "substantially all" the premiums of a contract of insurance are paid within a period of four years from the date on which the contract is purchased. Also, whether an amount deposited is in payment of a "substantial number" of future premiums on such a contract.

9) *Section 264(c)(1).*—Certain Indebtedness Incurred or Continued as Part of a Plan in Connection with Insurance Contracts.—Whether section 264(c)(1) of the Code applies.

10) *Section 269.*—Acquisition Made to Evade or Avoid Income Tax.—Whether an acquisition is within the meaning of section 269 of the Code.

11) *Section 302.*—Redemption of Stock.—Whether section 302(b) of the Code applies when the consideration given in redemption by the corporation consists entirely or partly of its notes payable, and the shareholder's stock is held in escrow or as security for payment of the notes with the

possibility that the stock may or will be returned to the shareholder in the future, upon the happening of specified defaults by the corporation.

12) *Section 302.*—Redemption of Stock.—Whether section 302(b) of the Code applies when the consideration given in redemption by a corporation in exchange for a shareholder's stock consists entirely or partly of the corporation's promise to pay an amount that is based on, or contingent on, future earnings of the corporation, or when the promise to pay is contingent on working capital being maintained at a certain level, or any other similar contingency.

13) *Section 302.*—Redemption of Stock.—Whether section 302(b) of the Code applies to a redemption of stock if after the redemption the distributing corporation used property that is owned by the shareholder from whom the stock is redeemed and the payments by the corporation for the use of the property are dependent upon the corporation's future earnings or are subordinate to the claims of the corporation's general creditors. Payments for the use of property will not be considered to be dependent upon future earnings merely because they are based on a fixed percentage of receipts or sales.

14) *Section 302.*—Distributions in Redemption of Stock.—Whether the acquisition or disposition of stock described in section 302(c)(2)(B) of the Code has, or did not have, as one of its principal purposes the avoidance of federal income taxes within the meaning of that section, unless the facts and circumstances are materially identical to those set forth in Rev. Rul. 56-556, 1956-2 C. B. 177, Rev. Rul. 56-584, 1956-2 C. B. 179, Rev. Rul. 57-387, 1957-2 C. B. 225, Rev. Rul. 77-293, 1977-2 C. B. 91, or Rev. Rul. 79-67, 1979-1 C. B. 128.

15) *Sections 311 and 336.*—Taxability of Corporation on Distribution; General Rule.—Upon distribution of property in kind by a corporation to its shareholders, in complete liquidation under section 331 of the Code (when under the facts a sale of the property by the corporation would not qualify under section 337), in partial liquidation under section 346, or in redemption of stock under section 302(a), followed by a sale of the property, whether the sale can be deemed to have been made by the corporation under the doctrine of *Commissioner v. Court Holding Company* [45-1 USTC ¶9215], 324 U. S. 331 (1945). Ct. D. 1636, 1945 C. B. 58.

16) *Section 312.*—Earnings and Profits.—The determination of the amount of earnings and profits of a corporation.

17) *Sections 331, 332, and 333.*—Effects on Recipients of Distributions in Corporate Liquidations.—The tax effect of the liquidation of a corporation preceded or followed by the reincorporation of all or a part of the business and assets when more than a nominal amount of the stock (that is, more than 20 percent in value) of both the liquidating corporation and the transferee corporation is owned by the same shareholders; or when a liquidation is followed by the sale of the corporate assets by the shareholders to another corporation in which such shareholders own more than a nominal amount of the stock (that is, more than 20 percent in value).

18) *Section 337.*—Gain or Loss; Certain Liquidations.—The application of this section to a corporation upon the sale of property, in connection with its liquidation, to another corporation, when more than a nominal amount of the stock (that is, more than 20 percent in value) of both the selling corporation and the purchasing corporation, and the purchasing corporation is owned by the same persons.

19) *Section 346.*—Partial Liquidation.—The amount of working capital attributable to a business or portion of a business terminated that may be distributed in partial liquidation.

20) *Section 351.*—Transfers to Controlled Corporation.—

   (A) That this section applies to a transfer by a shareholder of stock in one corporation (acquired) to another corporation (acquiring), in an exchange otherwise qualifying for treatment under this section, if the exchange is part of a larger transaction that fits a pattern common to acquisitive reorganizations, and after the transaction the acquiring corporation has control of the acquired corporation [within the meaning of section 368(c)], unless there is a continuing interest through stock ownership in the acquiring corporation on the part of the former shareholders of the acquired corporation that is equal in value to at least 50 percent of the value of all of the stock of the acquired corporation outstanding immediately before the overall transaction. For purposes of this determination, liabilities assumed or liabilities to which the property transferred is subject, will be considered to be part of the total consideration received. See Rev. Rul. 80-284, 1980-43 I. R. B. 8, and section 3.02 of Rev. Proc. 77-37, 1977-2 C. B. 568, 569.

   (B) That this section applies to a transfer by a corporation (acquired) of a substantial portion of its assets to another corporation (acquiring) in an exchange otherwise qualifying for treatment under this section, if the exchange is part of a larger transaction that fits a pattern common to acquisitive reorganization, unless there is a continuing interest through stock ownership in the acquiring corporation on the part of the acquired corporation or shareholders of the acquired corporation that is equal in value to at least 50 percent of the value of all of the stock of the acquired corporation outstanding immediately before the overall transaction. For purposes of this determination, liabilities assumed or liabilities to which the property transferred is subject, will be considered to be part of the total consideration received. In addition, for purposes of this revenue procedure, an acquired corporation shall be deemed to have transferred a substantial portion of its assets if the transferred assets constitute 15 percent or more of its gross assets. See Rev. Rul. 80-285, 1980-43 I. R. B. 9, and section 3.02 of Rev. Proc. 77-37.

21) *Section 451.*—General Rule for Taxable Year of Inclusion.—The tax consequences of a nonqualified unfunded deferred compensation arrangement with respect to a controlling shareholder employee eligible to participate in the arrangement.

22) *Sections 451 and 457.*—General Rule for Taxable Year of Inclusion; Deferred Compensation Plans With Respect to Service for State and Local Governments.—The tax consequences to unidentified independent contractors in nonqualified unfunded deferred compensation plans. This applies to plans established under section 451 of the Code by employers in the private sector and to eligible state plans under section 457. However, a ruling with respect to a specific independent contractor's participation in such a plan may be issued.

23) *Section 453.*—Revolving Credit Sales as Installment Sales.—Whether a proposed sampling procedure will be acceptable by the Service for the purpose of determining the portion of revolving credit balances to be treated as installment account balances. See Rev. Proc. 64-4, 1964-1 (Part 1) C. B. 644, and Rev. Proc. 65-5, 1965-1 C. B. 720.

24) *Section 642(c).*—Deduction for Amounts Paid or Permanently Set Aside for a Charitable Purpose.—Allowance of an unlimited deduction for amounts set aside by a trust or estate for charitable purposes when there is a possibility that the corpus of the trust or estate may be invaded.

25) *Section 704(b)(2).*—Partner's Distributive Share Determined.—Whether the allocation to a partner under the partnership agreement of income gain, loss, deduction, or credit (or an item thereof) has substantial economic effect.

26) *Section 704(e).*—Family Partnerships.—Matters relating to the validity of a family partnership when capital is not a material income producing factor.

29) *Section 856.*—Definition of a Real Estate Investment Trust.—Whether a corporation whose stock is "paired" with or "stapled" to that of another corporation will qualify as a real estate investment trust under section 856 of the Code if the activities of the corporations are integrated.

28) *Section 1221.*—Capital Asset Defined.—Whether specialty stock allocated to an investment account by a registered specialist on a national securities exchange is a capital asset.

29) *Section 1551.*—Disallowance of Surtax Exemption and Accumulated Earnings Credit.—Whether a transfer is within section 1551 of the Code.

30) *Section 2031.*—Definition of Gross Estate.—Actuarial factors for valuing interests in the prospective gross estate of a living person.

31) *Section 2512.*—Valuation of Gifts.—Actuarial factors for valuing prospective or hypothetical gifts of a donor.

32) *Section 7701.*—Definitions.—Whether a foreign arrangement that is a participant in a domestic arrangement classified as a partnership for U.S. tax purposes will itself be classified as a partnership.

33) *Section 7701.*—Definitions.—Whether a foreign limited liability company will be classified as a partnership if the taxpayer requests classification as a partnership and (1) the taxpayer is a corporation and less than 20 percent of the interests in the limited liability company are held by independent parties or (2) the taxpayer is not a corporation and independent parties hold only a nominal interest in the company.

34) *Section 7701.*—Definitions.—The classification of arrangements formed as partnerships under local law where the members of such partnerships are professional corporations.

## .02 General Areas

1) The results of transactions that lack bona fide business purpose or have as their principal purpose the reduction of federal taxes.

2) A matter upon which a court decision adverse to the government has been handed down and the question of following the decision or litigating further has not yet been resolved.

3) A matter involving the prospective application of the estate tax to the property or the estate of a living person.

4) A matter involving alternate plans of proposed transactions or involving hypothetical situations.

5) A matter involving the federal tax consequences of any proposed federal, state, local, or municipal legislation. The Service may provide general information in response to an inquiry.

6) Whether reasonable cause exists under Subtitle F (Procedure and Administration) of the Code.

7) Whether a proposed transaction would subject the taxpayer to a criminal penalty.

8) A request that does not comply with the provisions of Rev. Proc. 80-20.

The following are areas in which rulings will not ordinarily be issued:

*.01 Specific questions and problems*

1) *Sections 61 and 163.*—Gross Income Defined; Interest.—Determinations as to who is the true owner of property or the true borrower of money in cases in which the formal ownership of the property or liability for the indebtedness is in another party.

2) *Section 167.*—Depreciation.

   (A) Useful lives of assets.
   (B) Depreciation rates.
   (C) Salvage value of assets.

3) *Section 170(c).*—Charitable, etc., Contributions and Gifts.—Whether a taxpayer who transfers property to a charitable organization and thereafter leases back all or a portion of the transferred property, may deduct the fair market value of the property transferred and leased back as a charitable contribution.

4) *Section 302.*—Redemption of Stock.—The tax effect of the redemption of stock for notes, when the payments on the notes are to be made over a period in excess of fifteen years from the date of issuance of such notes.

5) *Sections 304 and 357.*—Redemption Through Use of Related Corporation; Assumption of Liability.—A transaction similar to that described in Rev. Rul. 80-240, 1980-36 1. R. B. 8, holding that sections 304(a)(1) and 357(a) of the Code are inapplicable because there was no assumption of liability, unless the taxpayer can satisfy the Internal Revenue Service that the liability was incurred by the taxpayer as a mere intermediary agent for the newly created corporate transferee. To establish this, the taxpayer

must submit to the Internal Revenue Service documented evidence, composed at the time the liability was incurred, which indicates that the unrelated lender had agreed to release the transferor-borrower from any and all obligation on the liability in favor of the corporate transferee. Further, the taxpayer must show, or represent to, the Internal Revenue Service that the transfer and assumption actually occurred, or will actually occur within twelve months of the date the debt was incurred.

6) *Section 306.*—Disposition of Certain Stock.—Whether the distribution or disposition or redemption of "section 306 stock" in a closely held corporation is in pursuance of a plan having as one of its principal purposes the avoidance of federal income taxes within the meaning of section 306(b)(4) of the Code.

7) *Section 331.*—Gain or Loss to Shareholders in Corporate Liquidations.— The tax effect of the liquidation of a corporation by a series of distributions, when the distributions in liquidation are to be made over a period in excess of three years from the adoption of the plan of liquidation.

8) *Section 341.*—Collapsible Corporations.—Whether a corporation will be considered to be a "collapsible corporation", that is, whether it was "formed or availed of" with the view of certain tax consequences. However, ruling requests will be considered on this matter when the enterprise (1) has been in existence for at least twenty years, (2) has had substantially the same owners during that period, and (3) has conducted substantially the same trade or business during that period.

9) *Section 351.*—Transfers to Controlled Corporation.—The tax effect of the transfer when part of the consideration received by the transferors consists of bonds, debentures, or any other evidence of indebtedness of the transferee and the term of "indebtedness" is either less than ten years or a determination as to whether the "indebtedness" is properly classified as debt or equity is required in order to establish that the requirements of section 351 are met.

10) *Section 871.*—Classification of alien individuals as resident or nonresident.—The determination as to whether an alien individual is either a resident or nonresident of the United States will not be made with respect to situations in which the determination is dependent on factual representations that cannot be confirmed until the close of the alien individual's affected taxable year(s), that is, representations concerning an alien individual's projected stay and activities in the United States.

11) *Section 992.*—Requirements of a Domestic International Sales Corporation.—The tax effects of the Domestic International Sales Corporation's

stock being held by individuals who are also shareholders in a related supplier corporation.

12) *Section 7701.*—Definitions.—Whether what is generally known as a foreign corporation will be classified as a partnersip for U. S. tax purposes if the taxpayer requests classification as a partnership.

13) *Section 7701.*—Definitions.—Whether a foreign partnership will be classified as an association for U. S. tax purposes if the taxpayer requests classification as an association.

*.02 General areas*

1) Any matter in which the determination requested is primarily one of fact, e.g., market value of property, or whether an interest in a corporation is to be treated as stock or indebtedness.

2) The tax effect of any transaction to be consummated at some indefinite future time.

3) Any matter dealing with the question of whether property is held primarily for sale to customers in the ordinary course of trade or business.

The following are areas under extensive study in which rulings will not be issued until the Service resolves the issue through publication of a Revenue Ruling, Revenue Procedure, Regulations or otherwise:

*.01 Section 79.*—Group Term Life Insurance Purchased for Employees.—Whether life insurance provided for employees under a "retired lives reserve" plan will be considered group term insurance (also sections 61, 72, 83, 101, 162, 264, and 641).

*.02 Section 820.*—Optional treatment of Policies Reinsured Under Modified Coinsurance Contracts.—The tax consequences of modified coinsurance contracts to which section 820 of the Code may apply, including whether taxpayers who have entered into a modified coinsurance contract may allocate between the reinsured and reinsurer certain items to which section 820(c) applies.

*.03 Section 1001.*—Determination of Amount of and Recognition of Gain or Loss.—Determination of amount of, and recognition of, gain or loss in divorce property settlements.

*.04 Section 1372.*—Election by Small Business Corporation.—Whether trailer or mobile home parks or aircraft rental business qualify as electing small business corporations.

*.05 Section 7701.*—Definitions.—Whether a trust which is beneficially owned by the shareholders of the settlor corporation is a trust for federal income tax purposes if the corporation remains in existence after the transfer in trust, and if the corporation retains working interests in oil, gas, or mineral properties, the royalty interests of which properties are transferred to the trust.

The following are areas in which the Service is prohibited by statute from issuing rulings:

*.01 Section 61.*—Gross Income Defined.—Employee fringe benefits. Pub. L. 96-167, 1980-5 I. R. B. 12.

*.02 Section 162.*—Trade or Business Expenses.—Expenses of commuting. Pub. L. 96-167.

*.03 Section 170.*—Charitable, etc., Contributions and Gifts.—Application of revenue ruling (Rev. Rul. 79-99, 1979-1 C.B. 108) to deny a charitable contribution deduction. Pub. L. 96-74, 1979-2 C. B. 473.

## Requirements for obtaining a ruling

Generally, the national office issues rulings on prospective transactions and on completed transactions before the return is filed for them. It will not ordinarily issue a ruling if at the time the ruling is requested, the identical issue is involved in the taxpayer's return for an earlier period, and

1) that issue is being examined by a district director or is being considered by an appeals office,

2) that issue has been examined by a district director or considered by an appeals office and the statutory period of limitation on assessment or refund of tax has not expired, or

3) a closing agreement covering the issue or liability has not been entered into by a district director or by an appeals office.

A ruling will also not be issued on alternative plans of proposed transactions or on hypothetical situations.

## How to request a ruling
## (reference numbers refer to accompanying
## sample letter)

1) A request for a ruling by the national office should be sent to the Internal Revenue Service, Assistant Commissioner (Technical), Attention T:FP:T, 1111 Constitution Avenue, NW, Washington, D.C. 20224

2) Each request for a ruling must contain a complete statement of all of the facts relating to the transaction. Such facts include: names, addresses, and taxpayer identification numbers of all interested parties; the location of the district office that has or will have jurisdiction over the return; a full and precise statement of the business reasons for the transaction; and a carefully detailed description of the transaction.

3) If the taxpayer asserts a particular determination, an explanation of the grounds for the assertion must be furnished, together with a statement of relevant authorities in support of the taxpayer's views. Even though the taxpayer is urging no particular determination of a proposed or prospective transaction, the taxpayer's views must be furnished. In addition, the taxpayer is encouraged to inform the Service of, and discuss the implications of, any legislation, or tax treaties, court decisions, regulations, revenue rulings or revenue procedures that the taxpayer determines to be contrary to the position advanced. If the taxpayer determines that there are no contrary authorities, a statement to this effect would be helpful in the ruling request. Identification and discussion of contrary authorities will generally enable Service personnel to arrive more quickly at a full understanding of the issue and the relevant authorities. There is a further advantage to the taxpayer. When Service personnel receive the request, they will have before them the taxpayer's thinking on the effect and applicability of contrary authorities. Such information should, therefore, make research easier and lead to earlier action by the Service. Conversely, failure to disclose and distinguish significant contrary authorities may result in requests for additional information memoranda which will delay action on the ruling request.

4) True copies of all contracts, deeds, agreements and other documents must be submitted with the request.

5) A taxpayer who wants to have a conference on the issue or issues involved should indicate this in writing when, or soon after, filing the request.

6) The request must contain a statement of whether, to the best of the knowledge of the taxpayer and the taxpayer's representative(s), if any, the identical issue is in a return of the taxpayer (or of a related taxpayer within the meaning of section 267 of the Code, or a member of an affiliated group of which the taxpayer is also a member within the meaning of section 1504) and, if so, whether the issue (A) is being examined by a district director, (B) has been examined and the statutory period of limitation on assessment or refund of tax has not expired, (C) is being considered by an appeals office in connection with the taxpayer's return for an earlier period, or that issue has been considered by an appeals office and the statutory period of limitation on assessment or refund of tax has not expired, or (D) is pending in litigation in a case involving the taxpayer.

7) The request must contain a statement whether, to the best of the knowledge of the taxpayer and the taxpayer's representative(s), the identical or similar issue

has been ruled on by the Service to the taxpayer or to the taxpayer's predecessor and, if so, when and with what results.

8) To assist the national office in making the deletions, required by section 6110(c) of the Code, from the text of rulings, to be made open to public inspection under 6110(a), a deletions statement must accompany requests. The statement must either state that no information other than names, addresses, and identifying numbers be deleted, or if more information is proposed to be deleted, the statement must indicate the deletions proposed by the person requesting the ruling. If the latter alternative is chosen, the statement must be made in a separate document, and it must be accompanied by a copy of the request for a ruling and supporting documents, on which must be shown, by the use of brackets, the material that the person making the request believes should be deleted pursuant to section 6110(c). The statement of proposed deletions must indicate the statutory basis, under section 6110(c), for each proposed deletion. The statement of proposed deletions must not appear or be referred to anywhere in the request for a ruling. If the person making the request decides to ask for additional deletions before the ruling is issued, additional statements may be submitted.

9) A request by or for a taxpayer must be signed by the taxpayer or the taxpayer's authorized representative.

10) A request for a ruling and any factual information submitted at a later time must be accompanied by a declaration in the following form. "Under penalties of perjury, I declare that I have examined this request, including accompanying documents, and to the best of my knowledge and belief, the facts presented in support of the requested ruling are true, correct, and complete." The declaration may not be made by the taxpayer's representative. It must be signed by the person or persons on whose behalf the request is made. The person who must sign for a corporate taxpayer must be an officer of the corporate taxpayer who has personal knowledge of the facts. The officer must be one whose duties are not limited to obtaining a ruling from the Service. The person signing for a trust or a partnership must be a trustee or partner who has personal knowledge of the facts.

### Form request for a ruling

[Date]

Internal Revenue Service
Assistant Commissioner (Technical)
1 1111 Constitution Avenue, NW
Washington, D.C. 20224

Attention T:FP:T

Re: Ajax, Inc.
13-6579087

Dear Sir:

A ruling is requested on behalf of the above captioned taxpayer, with respect to [set forth a brief summary of the proposed transaction].

2   Ajax, Inc. was incorporated in the state of New York on November 1, 1973, maintains its principal place of business at 747 Third Avenue, New York, N.Y. 10017, and files its tax return with the district director for Manhattan.

## PROPOSED TRANSACTION

2   [Set forth a full and precise statement of the business reasons for the transaction and a carefully detailed description of the transaction.]

## FACTS

[Set forth the relevant facts.]

## LAW

3   [Set forth relevant authorities, implications of any legislation, revenue rulings, etc., both pro and con.]

## RULING[S] REQUESTED

It is requested that the following ruling[s] be issued: [Set forth, in the affirmative, the ruling(s) sought.]

## OTHER INFORMATION

4   Copies of all documents referred to in this letter are annexed hereto with the relevant portions underlined.

5   The taxpayer requests a conference on the issue[s] involved if any action inconsistent with this request is contemplated.

## STATEMENTS

6   To the best of my knowledge the ruling[s] requested herein is not in a return of the taxpayer.

7   To the best of my knowledge the identical or similiar issue has not been ruled on by the Service to the taxpayer or the taxpayer's predecessor.

8   No information other than the names, addresses and identifying numbers need be deleted.

A Power of Attorney executed by the taxpayer is enclosed.

Sincerely,

9

Allen Scott, Esq.

10 Under penalties of perjury, I declare that I have examined this request, including accompanying documents, and to the best of my knowledge and belief, the facts presented in support of the requested ruling are true, correct, and complete.

Ajax, Inc.

by _____
John Smith, President

## Other information on requesting a ruling

1) The taxpayer should submit a request for a ruling in duplicate only if more than one issue is presented in the request, or if a closing agreement is requested on the issue presented.

2) If, after the request is filed but before a ruling is issued, the taxpayer knows that an examination of the issue by a district director has been started, the taxpayer must notify the national office of such action. If a return is filed before a ruling is received from the national office concerning the return, a copy of the request must be attached to the return. This alerts the district office and avoids premature district action on the issue.

3) A taxpayer who receives a ruling letter before filing a return about any transaction that has been consummated and that is relevant to the return being filed should attach a copy of the ruling to the return when it is filed.

4) Within fifteen workdays after a ruling request has been received, a representative of the branch will contact the taxpayer to discuss the procedural and substantive issues in the ruling requests. As to each issue coming within the jurisdiction of the branch, the branch representative will tell the taxpayer:

   A) whether the branch representative will recommend the Service rule as the taxpayer requested, rule adversely on the matter, or not rule

   B) whether the taxpayer should submit additional information or representations to enable the Service to rule on the matter

    C) whether because of the nature of the transaction, or the issue present-
    ed, a tentative conclusion on the issue cannot be reached

5) A taxpayer may request a conference only in connection with a ruling
request. Normally, a conference is scheduled only when the national office
considers it to be helpful in deciding the case or when an adverse decision
is indicated. If a conference has been requested, the taxpayer will be notified by telephone, if possible, of the time and place of the conference.
The conference must be held within twenty-one calendar days after such
contact has been made. An extension of the twenty-one-day period may be
requested.

6) A request for a ruling may be withdrawn at any time before the signing of
the letter of reply. If a request is withdrawn, the national office may give
its views on the subject matter of the request to the district director whose
office has examination jurisdiction over the taxpayer's return, for consideration in any later examination of the return. Even though a request is
withdrawn, all correspondence and exhibits will be kept by the Service and
will not be returned to the taxpayer. In appropriate cases, the Service may
publish its findings in a revenue ruling or revenue procedure.

## Closing agreements

### What are they?

Pursuant to Internal Revenue Code section 7121 and the regulations thereunder, the IRS may enter into a closing agreement in any case in which there appears to be an advantage in having a case permanently and conclusively closed.

Although closing agreements have some attributes of contracts they are not controlled by the law of contracts. For example, legal consideration is not required
and the agreement is final—as provided for by statute. The agreement may not
be reopened except where there was fraud, malfeasance or a misrepresentation of a
material fact.

### When would you enter into a closing agreement?

The following are instances when it may be appropriate to enter into a closing
agreement:

1) The taxpayer wishes to establish definitely his tax liability in order that a
transaction may be facilitated, such as the sale of its stock.

2) The fiduciary of an estate desires a closing agreement so he can be discharged by the court.

3) A corporation in the process of liquidation or dissolution desires a closing agreement in order to wind up its affairs.

4) A taxpayer wishes to fulfill creditors' demands for authentic evidence of the status of its tax liability.

5) To determine cost, fair market value, or adjusted basis as at a given past date.

6) To determine the amount of a net operating loss.

7) To determine gross income, the amount of income from a transaction, the amounts of deductions for losses, depreciation, depletion, etc., or the year of includability or deductibility.

### Requesting a closing agreement

A request for a closing agreement may accompany a request for a private ruling. Alternatively, a request for a closing agreement can be directed to the revenue agent examining your client's tax return.

# Appendices

# IRS Organization Charts

1. IRS Organization Chart: National and Field Offices
2. District Office Organization
3. Examination Division Organization
4. Collection Division Organization
5. IRS Regions, Districts & Service Centers
6. Organization of the IRS Service Center
7. Establishing your own IRS Directory

# IRS Organization Chart

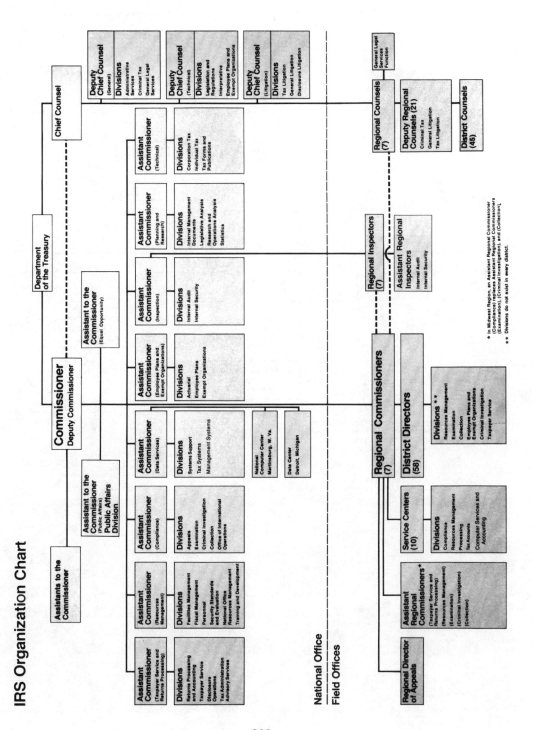

**Department of the Treasury**

**Commissioner**
Deputy Commissioner

Assistants to the Commissioner

Assistant to the Commissioner
(Public Affairs)
**Public Affairs Division**

Assistant to the Commissioner
(Equal Opportunity)

**Chief Counsel**

**Deputy Chief Counsel**
(General)
**Divisions**
Administrative Services
Criminal Tax
General Legal Services

**Deputy Chief Counsel**
(Technical)
**Divisions**
Legislation and Regulations
Interpretative
Employee Plans and Exempt Organizations

**Deputy Chief Counsel**
(Litigation)
**Divisions**
Tax Litigation
General Litigation
Disclosure Litigation

**Assistant Commissioner**
(Taxpayer Service and Returns Processing)
**Divisions**
Returns Processing and Accounting
Taxpayer Service
Disclosure Operations
Tax Administration Advisory Services

**Assistant Commissioner**
(Resources Management)
**Divisions**
Facilities Management
Fiscal Management
Personnel
Security Standards and Evaluation
National Office Resources Management
Training and Development

**Assistant Commissioner**
(Compliance)
**Divisions**
Appeals
Examination
Criminal Investigation
Collection
Office of International Operations

**Assistant Commissioner**
(Data Services)
**Divisions**
Systems Support
Tax Systems
Management Systems

National Computer Center
Martinsburg, W. Va.

Data Center
Detroit, Michigan

**Assistant Commissioner**
(Employee Plans and Exempt Organizations)
**Divisions**
Actuarial
Employee Plans
Exempt Organizations

**Assistant Commissioner**
(Inspection)
**Divisions**
Internal Audit
Internal Security

**Assistant Commissioner**
(Planning and Research)
**Divisions**
Internal Management Documents
Legislative Analysis
Research and Operations Analysis
Statistics

**Assistant Commissioner**
(Technical)
**Divisions**
Corporation Tax
Individual Tax
Tax Forms and Publications

**Regional Commissioners**
(7)

**Regional Inspectors**
(7)

Assistant Regional Inspectors
Internal Audit
Internal Security

**Regional Counsels**
(7)

**Deputy Regional Counsels (21)**
Criminal Tax
General Litigation
Tax Litigation

General Legal Services Function

**District Counsels**
(45)

**Regional Director of Appeals**

**Assistant Regional Commissioners***
(Taxpayer Service and Returns Processing)
(Resources Management)
(Examination)
(Criminal Investigation)
(Collection)

**District Directors**
(58)
**Divisions ** **
Resources Management
Examination
Collection
Employee Plans and Exempt Organizations
Criminal Investigation
Taxpayer Service

**Service Centers**
(10)
**Divisions**
Compliance
Resources Management
Processing
Tax Accounts
Computer Services and Accounting

National Office
Field Offices

\* In Midwest Region, an Assistant Regional Commissioner (Compliance) replaces Assistant Regional Commissioners (Examination), (Criminal Investigation), and (Collection).
\*\* Divisions do not exist in every district.

303

# District Office Organization

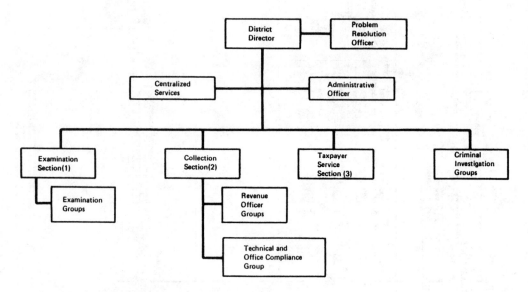

(1) Established in Districts with 4 or more Groups
(2) Established in Districts with 3 or more Groups and
    a Technical and Office Compliance Group
(3) May include Disclosure and Public Affairs functions

# Examination Division Organization

**Examination Division**

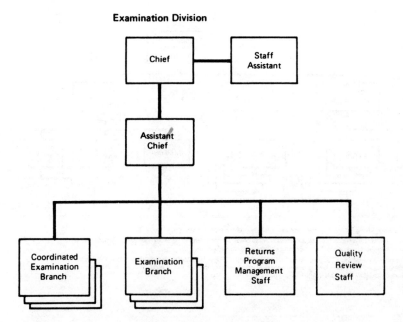

Staff Assistant position subject to approval of the Deputy Commissioner. Incumbency limited to 36 months.

Incumbency of Returns Program Manager position limited to 36 months.

Examination Branches are authorized in multiples of 13 Examination Groups (e.g., two for 14-26 groups, three for 27-39 groups, etc.) Separate Examination Branch may be authorized, primarily for office examinations in districts having 375 or more authorized technical Examination positions, but are subject to the guides concerning integrated Examination Branches.

Coordinated Examination Branch is authorized in districts having more than six large case groups. Districts with four to six groups may also qualify for a Coordinated Examination Branch by assigning the requisite number of specialty or revenue agent groups to bring the total number of groups to seven.

# Collection Division Organization

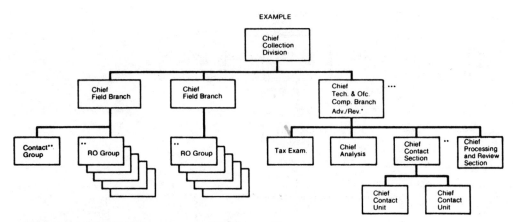

EXAMPLE

*Districts currently having an Advisor/Reviewer Section may retain a separate section.

**Management may place revenue representatives and office collection representatives in revenue officer groups, separate contact groups (or both), or, in the Technical and Office Compliance Branch.

***Streamlined districts will form a Technical and Office Compliance Group. Nonstreamlined districts may also form a Technical and Office Compliance Group when management determines the number of employees is insufficient to warrant a branch. (See IRM 133T.(8)(d)).

# Internal Revenue Service Regions, Districts and Service Centers

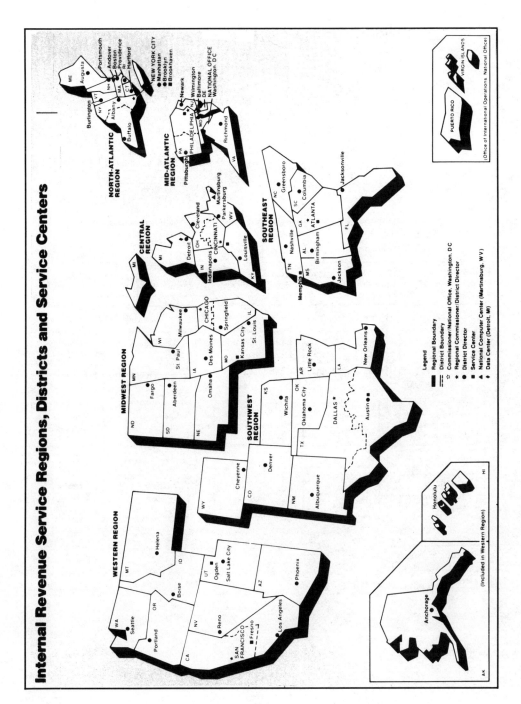

**WESTERN REGION**
WA ● Seattle, OR ● Portland, CA, NV ● Reno, ● Fresno, ★ SAN FRANCISCO, ● Los Angeles, AZ ● Phoenix, Salt Lake City, Ogden ● UT, ID ● Boise, ● Helena MT

**SOUTHWEST REGION**
ND, SD, NE ● Omaha, MN ● Fargo, ● Aberdeen, WY ● Cheyenne, CO ● Denver, NM ● Albuquerque, KS ● Wichita, OK ● Oklahoma City, TX, DALLAS ★, Austin ●

**MIDWEST REGION**
WI ● Milwaukee, ● St Paul, IA ● Des Moines, IL ● Springfield, ★ CHICAGO, MO ● Kansas City, ● St Louis

**CENTRAL REGION**
MI ● Detroit, OH ● Cleveland, Cincinnati, ★ CINCINNATI, IN ● Indianapolis, Martinsburg ▲, Parkersburg ●, WV, KY ● Louisville

**SOUTHEAST REGION**
TN ● Nashville, Memphis ■, MS ● Jackson, AL ● Birmingham, GA ● ATLANTA ☆, NC ● Greensboro, SC ● Columbia, FL ● Jacksonville

**NORTH-ATLANTIC REGION**
ME ● Augusta, Portsmouth, ● Andover, Boston, Providence, Hartford, NH, VT, MA, CT, RI, NY ● Albany, ● Buffalo, Burlington, ● NEW YORK CITY ● Manhattan ● Brooklyn ● Brookhaven

**MID-ATLANTIC REGION**
● Newark, NJ, ● Wilmington, DE, ● Baltimore, NATIONAL OFFICE ★, Washington DC ■, MD, PA ● PHILADELPHIA ■, ● Pittsburgh, VA ● Richmond

**Legend**
- Regional Boundary
- District Boundary
- ★ Commissioner/National Office, Washington, DC
- ☆ Regional Commissioner/District Director
- ■ District Director
- ■ Service Center
- ▲ National Computer Center (Martinsburg, W V)
- ◆ Data Center (Detroit, MI)

PUERTO RICO, VIRGIN ISLANDS (Office of International Operations, National Office)

● New Orleans, LA, AR ● Little Rock

Honolulu ● HI (Included in Western Region)

Anchorage ● AK

# Organization of the Internal Revenue Service Center

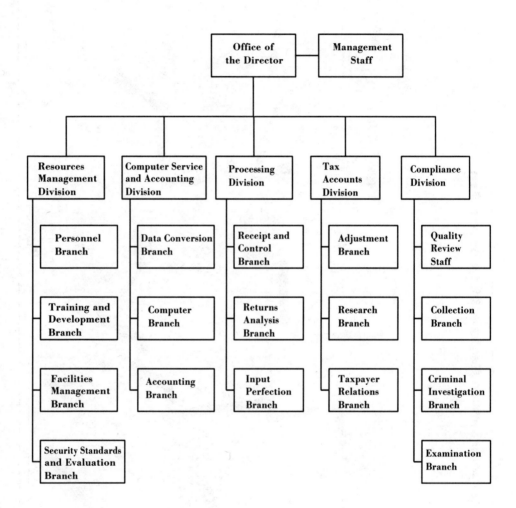

# Service Center Organization (information taken from the Manual)

## General

1) The principal organizational components of the typical Service Center are the immediate office of the Service Center Director, Management Staff, Compliance Division, Resources Management Division, Computer Services and Accounting Division, Processing Division, and Accounts Division.

2) The organizational structure depicted in the accompanying chart is intended to prescribe the Service Center organization through the branch level. Regional Commissioners are authorized to establish the Service Center organization below branch level as they see fit.

## Office of the Director

Within the structure of the Internal Revenue Service, the Internal Revenue Service Center has organizational status comparable to that of the District Offices. It operates under the line supervision of the Service Center Director, who is responsible to the Regional Commissioner in the same manner as a District Director. The Director plans, directs, and administers functions of the Internal Revenue Service Center which provides services for the region(s). Its functions are to process tax returns and related documents through the use of automatic and manual data processing systems and high-speed processing devices and to maintain accountability records for internal revenue taxes collected within the region. Typical programs include the processing, analysis, and accounting control of income tax returns, estimated tax returns, wages and excise tax returns, corporation tax returns, income information documents, and mailing of income tax forms to individual taxpayers. The Director also plans, directs, and administers assigned Examination, Criminal Investigation, Problem Resolution, and Collection functions. Responsible for public affairs and the budget, fiscal and personnel operations of the Service Center. In addition, the Philadelphia Service Center assists the Assistant Commissioner (Compliance) in the exchange of authorized routine information with foreign countries having tax treaties with the United States.

## Management Staff

Provides staff assistance to the Director and line officials in the general management of Service Center operations. Assists by coordinating the preparation of work plans, work schedules, staffing and accession schedules. Monitors the Work Planning and Control System and maintains the daily production control system. As requested, provides assistance in analyzing day-to-day problems concerning systems and procedures. Monitors and coordinates various projects, particularly those in the implementation stage such as IDRS, RMF, and Returns Preparer Program. Coordinates the consolidation and referral of problems to the Regional or National Office. Monitors the Statistics of income sampling and the Quality Review Program. Develops and coordinates public information plans, techniques, guidelines, and informational materials. Establishes and maintains good relations with mass media in the vicinity of the Service Center, determines information needed, gathers and analyzes statistical and other data generated, and prepares information material for distribution to media outlets; and coordinates visits of media representatives, and others, from the entire region.

### Resources Management Division

Directs and coordinates the personnel, facilities management, training, fiscal management, security standards and evaluation, and resources management improvement programs. Serves as the principal administrative adviser to the Director, Assistant Director, and operating division chiefs. Provides functional leadership for the numerous and varied administrative programs designed to support and increase the effectiveness of Service Center operations. Executes the resources management analysis program and coordinates the management improvement program for the Service Center. Conducts management studies and provides staff assistance to Resources Management branch chiefs and operating officials as required. Prepares budget and financial plans estimates, maintains fiscal control, and recommends appropriate financial management actions.

### Facilities Management Branch

Advises, informs, and assists Service Center management on operations relating to facilities management programs such as: space, property, communications, paperwork (including microfilm), records retention and disposal, distribution, emergency planning and safety; may perform a variety of machine operations such as labeling, folding and inserting. Plans, develops, determines requirements, and evaluates these programs; provides additional, improved, or modified programs as required. Furnishes procurement, transportation, storage, supply, and messenger services; provides general building maintenance and maintenance of office, electronic, processing, and materials-handling equipment.

## Personnel Branch

Develops, executes and evaluates the Service Center personnel program and standards relating to recruitment, examination, and selection of employees, employee relations, union-management relationships, performance evaluation, promotions, in-Service placements, incentive awards, records, reports, and other aspects of a complete personnel program within the framework of policies, programs, and procedures established by the National and Regional Offices. Conducts the position classification program within delegated authority. Provides staff assistance to operating officials in all personnel areas.

## Training and Development Branch

Provides leadership and coordination to the various Service Center training programs, promotes employee development programs and evaluates and reports on all such programs. Conducts studies and analyzes operating data to determine training needs; studies trends and developments in the employee development field and appraises new principles, concepts, methods, training devices, and material, for use in Service Center training programs. Develops or assists in the development of local and Service-wide course materials, audio-visual aids and training devices. Assists Service Center management in developing a job environment which will enable trainees to maintain and improve their skills. At the request of the National or Regional Offices, provides data processing training for other than Service Center personnel. Prepares training program estimates for developing the Operating Financial Plan; prepares obligating documents for charges to the training portion of the Operating Financial Plan.

## Security Standards and Evaluation Branch

The Security Branch is responsible for planning and coordinating all aspects of the security program within the service center. Provides advice and assistance on policy, techniques and procedures on matters relating to the protection of the service center building, property, equipment, personnel, data in all forms, and information systems under the jurisdiction of the Director. Provides advice to the Regional Office on security matters relating to data systems. Develops local guidelines as necessary to implement National and regional office programs and procedures and to achieve service center objectives. Monitors compliance with all security controls, procedures and practices through review of reports and printouts, consultation with the line managers, investigation of security violations in the

Center. Assists regional office in onsite visitations as requested. Analyzes problems encountered and recommends corrective action to appropriate management officials. In coordination with Facilities Management, prepares budget estimates for all requirements related to security and recommends the most effective use of available funding. Coordinates with Facilities Management concerning equipment selection and space layout and design as it relates to security. Develops requirements for guard service and monitors guard contractors performance. Administers Service Center ID media program. Maintains master record of all control numbers and all data base users. Controls and issues IDRS security passwords and manuals. Reviews and approves employee and terminal profiles. Processes security clearances. Conducts local security awareness and orientation programs. Provides technical assistance in development and conduct of Regionwide Security Training program.

## Offices of the Chief, All Operating Divisions

Receives, analyzes, and evaluates all new programs and procedures, prepares supplemental or clarifying instructions as necessary; and ensures full implementation. Determines resources needed in the Division through the preparation of work plans and schedules, personnel staffing and accession schedules, space requirements, formulation of training needs, and other logistical processes. Participates with other Division Chiefs and the Director in the final allocation of resources to accomplish the total Service Center work program. Coordinates with other Division Chiefs on interdivisional matters as appropriate. Continuously reviews, analyzes, and evaluates the status of work programs with the aim of keeping the Director informed of operational problems on an exception basis. When appropriate, requests assistance from the Management Staff, or from the Office of the Assistant Regional Commissioner having functional responsibility.

## Compliance Division

Directs and coordinates the Collection, Criminal Investigation and Examination programs and activities assigned to the Service Center. Provides support to districts in processing, and issuance and disposition of cases and accounts. Serves as the principal advisor to the Director, Assistant Director, and Assistant Regional Commissioners on the operational capabilities and status of programs performed by the Service Center Compliance Division. Ensures full program implementation by the Compliance branches, recommends necessary changes, improvements in practices or procedures or improved use of resources. Coordinates with other Divisions on inter-divisional matters and as appropriate, obtains assistance from the Management Staff, or from the Office of the Assistant Regional Commissioner having functional responsibility.

## Quality Review Staff

Reviews work performed by the Compliance Division. Performs quality review of technical, procedural, and clerical operations. Assumes primary responsibility within the Compliance Division for maintaining quality standards and technical accuracy of all matters subject to review. Provides feedback to Compliance managers. Provides technical assistance as requested.

## Collection Branch

Plans, directs, and coordinates Collection operations in service centers, as covered by appropriate procedures. Analyzes, researches, evaluates, processes, and inputs work related to Collection activity. Initiates contacts with taxpayers to resolve accounts before district office action is required and replies to taxpayers' inquiries on Collection matters. Furnishes assistance and advice on Collection matters to other service center components. Also, as appropriate, provides Collection information and other data to district offices, regions, and National Office. Ensures that Collection and other service center personnel are aware of Collection objectives. Coordinates service center–district office actions on Collection-related problems.

## Criminal Investigation Branch

Manages the Centralized Evaluation and Processing of Information Items System (CEPIIS), which includes: verifying and controlling informants communications; evaluating information items for fraud potential; transmitting items with potential to the field for evaulation; and inputting district case openings and closures into CEPIIS. Interviews informants who appear at or contact the service center. Directs the Questionable Refund Program in the service center and coordinates identification of possible fraudulent schemes with district Criminal Investigation management. Serves as coordination point for Case Management and Time Reporting System (CM & TRS) table production; answers field inquiries regarding terminal input procedures; and transfers collateral investigative time between service centers. Provides liaison between District and Regional Criminal Investigation Personnel with the service center and supports district criminal investigative efforts as follows: Expedites requests for returns and transcripts; locates addresses of taxpayers and witnesses from service center files when district file searches are unsuccessful; establishes and maintains master file controls on subjects of criminal investigations; processes district requests for queries of the Treasury Enforcement Communications System (TECS) data base; and provides advice and direct support in the use of ADP facilities in ongoing cases and projects. Provides necessary training for service center pipeline processing personnel to recognize potentially fraudulent returns; develops appropriate Criminal Investigation referral criteria; and screens returns identified in normal Service Center return processing as having fraud potential.

## Examination Branch

Administers the Compliance examination and verification activities centralized within service centers. These include: correspondence examination; verification of information document income; classification of returns and related on-line review of selected returns; claims and related documents; processing Examination/Appeals adjustments; and issuing claims disallowance notices, preliminary letters and statutory notices. Performs the classification function and maintains central storage files for streamlined districts. Furnishes assistance and technical information to other service center Compliance components.

## Tax Accounts Division

Provides services to the taxpaying public by answering inquiries received by telephone, or through the mail. Controls, monitors, and takes necessary action on complaints and special cases requiring expedite action. Controls and makes adjustments to taxpayers' accounts on all files (IMF, BMF, RMF, NMF, etc.). Controls and processes statutory case adjustments. Performs microfilm research requested by all functional activities. Establishes, maintains and controls permanent and temporary returns files. Retires returns and documents in accordance with prescribed procedures. Performs output review and necessary correction. Performs payment tracing functions. Is responsible for planning, coordinating, executing and evaluating Freedom of Information, Privacy Act, and other disclosure matters of the Service Center. Processing of all Exempt Organization returns was centralized in the Philadelphia Service Center through processing year 1975. Because of the scope and size of this function, the Philadelphia Service Center was authorized an Exempt Organization Returns Branch which is responsible for processing, except for deposit and transcription operations, all Exempt Organization tax returns and related documents. Starting in 1976, the processing of Exempt Organization workloads began to be decentralized to the other Service Centers (except for Memphis) according to a phase-in timetable. As this work is phased out of the Philadelphia Service Center, this Branch will gradually be reduced in size and finally disbanded. The scope and size of the EO workloads which will remain at the Philadelphia Service Center after the decentralization is completed will not warrant the existence of a special Branch.

### Adjustment Branch

Receives taxpayer inquiries initiated by correspondence. Receives and controls requests for adjustments and determines appropriate action to be taken including adjustment to tax, penalty, and interest, and to the entity section of taxpayer accounts. Prepares written replies to taxpayer on contacts by telephone. Processes IMF and BMF Restricted Interest cases, combination overassessment and deficiency cases, Joint Committee cases, Appeals Overassessment and Deficiency Cases, Justice Department cases, cases containing second agreements and partial agreements. Processes applications for Tentative Carryback Adjustments. Performs payment tracing functions.

### Research Branch

Performs research through microfilm, source documents, and other sources for entity and account information requested by all functional activities. Establishes, maintains, and controls permanent and temporary returns files. Retires returns and documents in accordance with prescribed procedures. Performs delinquency checks for Non-Master File returns. Reviews computer output, except that pertaining to taxpayer delinquent accounts and returns, for quality and accuracy and for validity of refunds; corrects any processing errors discovered.

### Taxpayer Relations Branch

Performs taxpayer service functions in connection with telephone inquiries and written inquiries. When necessary, prepares replies to taxpayer inquiries which accompany returns and which indicate that complex issues need to be resolved before the return can be processed. Takes necessary action to process special or unusual cases and complaints. Maintains close liaison with Social Security Administration on unusual problems. Prepares and types replies to taxpayer correspondence and requests for correspondence from other activities which generally require individually tailored letters. Serves as the Problem Resolution office in the service center.

## Computer Services and Accounting Division

Converts data from source documents to a form processable by computers. Operates computer and peripheral equipment used to verify tax liability and service the accounts of all taxpayers within the Districts assigned to the Center and to convert input data to magnetic tape. Maintains tape files of rejected documents for reinput to Service Center Processing. Prepares computer printouts relating to outputs received from the National Computer Center for mailing to taxpayers, for internal reports and statistics, and for tax information authorized for external use. Programs projects as assigned from the National Office and provides the necessary liaison and programming for maintenance of National Office computer programs. Maintains an accounting system to provide subsidiary records and general ledger accounts that reflect the Director's accountability for the Master File and Non-Master File tax revenue collected within Districts assigned to the Center. Records assessments, collections, receivables, refunds, overassessments, and other elements of revenue accounting affecting accountability. Responsible for maintaining an accounting and control system for Federal tax deposits and serves as focal point for the entire FTD system. Receives, verifies, balances and processes accounting outputs from the National Computer Center; and prepares special and periodic accounting reports. Determines the validity of taxpayer delinquent accounts and returns notices. Prepares various reports for the Service Center, Region, and National Office.

## Data Conversion Branch

Transcribes, verifies and corrects pertinent information of all tax returns, information documents and related documents associated with other miscellaneous programs. Processes documents related to all files (IMF, BMF, RMF, NMF, etc.), subsequent activity programs, and documents which have been previously transcribed for which error conditions have been detected in subsequent processing. Responsible for resolving error conditions identified by the Computer Branch. Enters corrections for each error condition into machine-generated listings. Responsible for resolving and re-entering blocks out of balance or rejected blocks received from transcription control clerks.

## Computer Branch

Operates all computer systems used in processing, verifying, computing the tax liabilities, and servicing the accounts of all Master Files (IMF, BMF, RMF, NMF, etc.) taxpayers within Districts assigned to the Center, maintains tape library, processes tax information and documents for mailing to taxpayers and for internal use by the Service; generates computer reports; statistical information and other information for use by the National, Regional, District and Service Center offices, other program areas of the Service, and by various States. Processes other programs assigned by the National Office. Provides programming services as required for the maintenance of the system, as directed by the National Office. Performs quality review on computer generated output. Operates an EAM System for preconversion perfection of input data and processing of other Service Center card-oriented projects. Receives and processes applications from wage and information return filers to file magnetic media returns; maintains case history file and control of paper returns (i.e., 941, W2, 1099 and 1087) prior to approval of magnetic media filing request.

## Accounting Branch

Maintains general ledger accounts and subsidiary records covering revenue transactions for the recording of assessments, collections, receivables, refunds, over-assessments and other transactions affecting taxpayer's accounts. Controls accounting documents for entry to tax accounts. Establishes and maintains individual accounts for non-ADP (NMF) and pre-ADP tax returns and documents. Liaison for the FTD system. Reconciles, verifies, balances and corrects FTD records received from the banking industry. Receives Master File accounting summaries for posted account transactions and accomplishes required journalization and general ledger postings. Initiates or processes account transfers, account adjustments, debit and credit transfers related to tax accounts. Reconciles National Computer Center accounting control records and refund appropriation accounts of Regional Disbursing Centers with general ledger balances. Prepares all accounting and ledger reports as required. Prepares various reports for the Service Center, Region, and National Office.

## Processing Division

Receives, blocks, sorts, and controls documents, both Master File and Non-Master File, received from taxpayers and District Offices, processes all remittance returns and documents via Remittance Processing devices or encoding equipment; deposits and initiates accounting control of remittances. Ships processed documents to District Offices; and prepares a variety of forms, and other material for mailing to taxpayers, tax practitioners, District Offices, and other Government agencies. Examines, perfects, and codes returns and documents for all files (IMF, BMF, NMF, etc.) for subsequent processing; examines, edits, and codes returns for the Statistics of Income Program; prepares form and pattern paragraph letters to taxpayers requesting additional or clarifying information incidental to the initial processing of returns. Performs research, perfects and resolves processing errors detected during work cycles within the service center. Receives, processes and maintains control over applications for Employer Identification Numbers and Social Security Numbers.

### Receipt and Control Branch

Receives and categorically classifies all incoming returns, documents, remittances, and taxpayer correspondence. Sorts and establishes batch control prior to release of returns and documents into the initial work process, in accordance with work schedules. In coordination with the Management Staff, makes necessary adjustments in work schedules as dictated by actual work receipt patterns to maintain a steady balanced work flow. Numbers and blocks all non-remittance returns and documents. Examines and sorts documents and related remittances. Via the Remittance Processing System, processes remittance documents, numbers documents and remittances, prepares appropriate registers and Deposit Tickets prior to transmitting monies to local depository. May perform a variety of machine operations such as labeling, folding, and inserting; if these operations are performed in this branch within a service center, they may not also be reported in the Facilities Management Branch. Ships processed documents to District Offices and prepares forms and other material for mailing to taxpayers, tax practitioners, District Offices and other Government Agencies.

### Returns Analysis Branch

Examines, edits, perfects and codes tax documents for all files (IMF, BMF, RMF, NMF, etc.) for transcription and other purposes; prepares form and pattern paragraph letter correspondence to District Offices and taxpayers to obtain missing or clarifying information necessary for the perfection of the return; and edits, codes, and extracts information from returns for audit and statistical programs.

### Input Perfection Branch

Perfects and resolves processing and taxpayers errors detected during work cycles within the Service Center. Prepares correspondence action sheets to obtain additional information from taxpayers and District Offices in order to make returns acceptable for processing. Responsible for control, examination, perfection and final disposition of all RMF rejected tax returns and documents. Perfects and resolves unpostable returns and documents. Resolves unpostable conditions arising from the attempt to input all documents and returns relating to the IMF, BMF, RMF, etc., and prepares necessary input documents. Receives and processes applications for Employer Identification and Social Security Numbers. Maintains control over the assignment of Employer Identification Numbers. Performs all necessary actions concerning the control and maintenance of account numbers.

## Establishing your own IRS directory

One of the most time saving tools the practitioner can possess is his or her own IRS directory. Every time you have the occasion to meet with or call an IRS employee, record his or her name, division and telephone number. You will find that the next time an IRS problem comes up you will have somebody to call. Surprisingly, you will find that the person you have called will be happy to tell you how to solve your problem.

**Typical directory**

| Name | Office/Position | Phone | Client |
|------|-----------------|-------|--------|
| Jim Stone | REVENUE AGENT | 264-8769 | Ajax, Inc. |
| Ms. West | 90 Day Section | 264-7543 | Brown |
| Mr. Day | REVENUE OFFICER | 264-5425 | A & D, Inc. |

*Technical Research:* Stumped on a problem? Call someone you know at the IRS first to get their views.

# APPENDIX II

# Information the IRS Suggests
# You Bring to an Audit

## Medical and dental expenses

1) Canceled checks, receipts, etc., for all medical and dental expenses. Identify the person for whom each expense was incurred.

2) Itemized receipts for drugs and medicine. Canceled checks alone are not acceptable because they may include payment for drugstore items that are not deductible. Identify the person for whom the drugs and medicine were purchased.

3) Record of any expense reimbursed or paid directly by insurance.

4) Insurance policies on which you deducted the cost of premiums paid. Include canceled checks or other receipts for payment of these premiums.

## Taxes

For real estate and personal property taxes:

1) Canceled checks or receipts for taxes paid.

2) If you sold or purchased real property, a copy of the settlement statement.

3) Identification of any special assessments deducted as taxes, and an explanation of their purpose.

For sales tax:

1) Receipts for sales taxes paid on a car, truck, boat, airplane, mobile or prefabricated home, or building materials you bought to build a new home.

2) If you paid more sales tax on items not listed above than the amount shown for your income in the Optional State Sales Tax Tables (See Form 1040 instructions), verification of purchases on which sales tax was paid.

**For gas tax:**

Verification of nonbusiness miles driven *or* of your gas purchases, with figures to show how you computed the gas tax.

**For state and local income taxes:**

1) Copies of state and local income tax returns.
2) Canceled checks or receipts showing taxes paid. (Amounts of state and local income tax refunds you received or that were credited to you may be taxable to you in the year received or credited. This is generally the case if you claimed the tax as an itemized deduction in a previous year.)

## Interest expenses

1) Receipts, canceled checks, or statements from creditors showing amounts of interest paid and names of payees. If the checks cover principal and interest payments, be able to show the amount representing interest.
2) Payment books on installment purchases or contract on purchase, and evidence of payments made on the contract.
3) Land contract for land contract interest or mortgage receipts.

## Contributions

1) Canceled checks or receipts for church contributions.
2) Canceled checks or receipts for contributions to charitable organizations.
3) If the contribution was other than money, show:
    A) Name and address of the recipient organization.
    B) What was contributed.
    C) The fair market value of each item on the date of contribution.
4) If you reported expenses for attending a church convention or similar activity, furnish evidence that you were an official representative of your church.

## Child or dependent care

1) If you are a divorced or separated parent, furnish—
    A) Date of divorce or separation.

     B)  Dates you had custody of the qualifying individual.

     C)  Dates the other parent had custody of the qualifying individual.

2)  A)  Amounts you paid for household services for the entire year.

     B)  Amounts you (or, if married, you and your spouse) paid for the care of a qualifying individual during any period of the year.

3)  A)  Names and addresses of persons or organizations you paid for child care.

     B)  Copies of canceled checks or receipts to verify child care costs.

4)  If you paid for care of a disabled dependent, furnish information showing that:

     A)  The dependent was physically or mentally unable to care for self.

     B)  The dependent or spouse was cared for in your household.

## Rental income and expenses

1)  Evidence to verify:

     A)  Ownership of property.

     B)  Date property acquired.

     C)  Cost or other basis showing amount allocated to land and to buildings.

     D)  If property was converted from a personal residence to rental property:

         i)  Date converted.

         ii)  Fair market value when converted.

     E)  Cost of improvements and additions to property.

2)  Type of construction of buildings and explanation of estimated useful life used for computing depreciation.

3)  If any units were occupied rent-free or below rental value during the year, explain why.

4)  Canceled checks or receipts to verify all expenses claimed.

5)  Any records you have showing total amount of rent you received.

## Capital gains and losses

### Stock sales

1)  Brokerage vouchers establishing the purchase price and sales price of stock sold.

2) If you sold securities on which you had a return of capital during the holding period of the stock, provide records showing adjusted basis of stock.

3) If you claim worthless securities, provide verification of dissolution of the corporation.

4) For stock held in a liquidated or defunct corporation, provide verification of liquidation and liquidation distribution.

### Other property

1) Closing statements on purchase of property.

2) Verification of capital improvements to property.

3) If you reported gain or loss from sale of property, furnish:
   A) Records which show terms of sale and expense of sale.
   B) Copy of closing statement or settlement sheet.

4) If you sold your principal residence and you have purchased a new residence, furnish purchase agreement documents for the new residence.

5) If sale involved rental or other business property, furnish copies of your income tax returns for the two years before the year of sale.

6) If you reported gain or loss from repossession, furnish:
   A) Copy of your income tax return for the year of the original sale.
   B) All contracts or legal documents involved.
   C) Verification of repossession costs.

## Scholarship or fellowship grant

1) A statement indicating:
   A) Funds from which grant was paid.
   B) Amount of the grant and the period covered.
   C) Requirements of the grant including any present, past, or future obligations or services. (Are all candidates for the degree you're working toward required to perform these services?)
   D) Benefits derived by the recipient.
   E) Benefits derived by the grantor.
   F) Selection criteria for recipients.
   G) Number of credits you obtained toward the degree for the period of the grant.

2) Current transcript of credits for degree.
3) University bulletin outlining degree requirements.

## Casualty losses

1) Insured property:
   A) Date and nature of loss or damages claimed.
   B) Amount of damages claimed on insurance.
   C) Amount of coverage carried.
   D) Date and amount of claim paid by insurance.
2) Uninsured property: Any fire or police department reports on fire losses, theft losses, or losses from accidents. If you are unable to obtain a copy of the fire or police department report, furnish the name or number of the precinct or police station where the accident or theft was reported.
3) If available, photographs showing extent of loss.
4) Fair market value of property before and after the casualty, or estimate of damage from qualified estimator or adjuster.
5) Cost or other basis of property and date you acquired the property.

## Uniforms, equipment and tools

1) Explanation of how the expense claimed relates to your employment.
2) A statement from your employer if your employment required this expense.
3) Cancelled checks or receipts to verify the expense claimed.

## Alimony payments

1) Copy of divorce decree, separate maintenance decree, or other written document which specifies the basis for alimony payments.
2) Current name and address of divorced or separated spouse.
3) Canceled checks or receipts to verify payments you made. If you do not make alimony payments directly, please furnish documents showing the source of the payments. Examples of such documents are insurance policies, endowments, and annuity contracts.

## Education expenses

1) Document showing period of enrollment in educational institution or participation in educational activity, and number of hours of instruction each week.

2) Document showing principal subjects studied, or description of educational activity.

3) Canceled checks or receipts to verify amounts you spent for:
   A) Tuition and books.
   B) Meals and lodging while away from home overnight.
   C) Travel and transportation.
   D) Other educational expenses.

4) Statement from your employer explaining:
   A) Whether the education was necessary for you to keep your employment, salary, or status.
   B) How the education helped maintain or improve skills needed in your employment.
   C) How much educational expense reimbursement you received. (Show this by types of expense.)

5) Brief description of the nature of your employment during the year.

6) Complete information about any scholarship or fellowship grant you or your dependent received during the year.

7) Teachers Only: a statement showing:
   A) Type of teacher's certificate under which you taught.
   B) Date certificate was issued.
   C) List of subjects taught.

## Sick pay exclusions

1) Dates of each period of absence due to illness or disability.

2) If hospitalized, a statement from hospital showing dates admitted and discharged.

3) Amount of normal weekly wages.

4) Amount of wages received for periods of absence.

5) Amount of sick and accident benefits received for periods of absence.

6) If your sick pay plan is financed partly by you and partly by your employer, show percentage of sick and accident benefits your employer contributed to the plan. (If unknown to you, consult employer.)

## Employee travel and entertainment expenses

1) Statement from your employer showing:

   A) Employer's reimbursement policy.

   B) Amount and kind of expense reimbursed, charged, or provided.

   C) Specific expenses not covered by reimbursement policy.

   D) Territory assigned to you and a brief outline of your duties.

2) Explanatory statement from your employer if you are required to provide an office in your home or elsewhere or to use your home telephone in connection with your employment. Furnish receipts or canceled checks to verify these expenses.

3) Copies of expense vouchers submitted to your employer for reimbursement.

4) Receipts and records of expenses for business purposes:

   A) Lodging and meals while away from home.

   B) Gifts.

   C) Promotional items.

   D) Entertainment.

5) Verification of automobile expenses for business purposes:

   A) Invoice of purchase or lease of vehicles.

   B) Receipts for oil, gas, repairs, etc.

   C) Records of business mileage and total mileage.

## Moving expenses

1) Canceled checks or receipts to verify amounts of moving expenses you paid.

2) Names and relationship to you of members of your household who moved with you.

3) Computations showing number of miles by direct route from your old residence to:

   A) Your new place of employment.

   B) Your old place of employment.

4) Name and address of each employer since moving to new place of employment and period of time employed by each.

5) Statement from your employer of the allowance or reimbursement paid you for moving expenses. Show amounts by types of expense, such as transportation fares, meals and lodging, automobile expense, transportation of household and personal property.

## Exemptions for your children

1) If you were divorced or legally separated from the dependent's other parent, a copy of the applicable documents:
   A) Your divorce decree.
   B) Your separate maintenance decree.
   C) The written agreement showing which parent will claim the dependency exemption.

2) If the dependent did not live with you:
   A) Copies of canceled checks and receipts to verify amounts you spent for the dependent's support. Also, if you were not divorced or legally separated, a record of the funds spent for the dependent's support from all other sources.
   B) The name, address, and social security number, if known, of each person the dependent lived with during the tax year.
   C) If you were not divorced or legally separated, a signed statement from each person the dependent lived with, confirming that such person did not claim an exemption for this dependent and that you furnished more than half of the dependent's total support.

3) If the dependent lived with you:
   A) A record of income or other funds received by or for the dependent. (Show how these funds were used if not for the dependent's support.)
   B) A record of the amounts contributed to household expenses by each person living in the household with the dependent.
   C) If you were not divorced or legally separated, a record of the funds spent for the dependent's support from all sources.

# APPENDIX III

## Form Letters Used in Office Audit

| Current Form Letter Number | Old Form Letter Number | Purpose |
|---|---|---|
| Letter 555(C/SC/DO/IO) | L-275 | To transmit a supplemental report or to inform taxpayer that change in prior determination is not justified (statutory notice cases) |
| Letter 565(SC/DO/IO) | L-135 | To secure additional information from a taxpayer |
| Letter 566(SC/DO/IO) | L-134 | To set up correspondence examination and ask taxpayer to mail us certain information |
| Letter 569(C/SC/DO/IO) | L-93 | To inform taxpayer that claim is disallowed in full or in part |
| Letter 570(C/SC/DO/IO) | L-267 | To inform taxpayer of allowance of claim in full and amount of overassessment |
| Letter 645(C/SC/DO/IO) | L-275A | To inform taxpayer his/her return is accepted as filed (statutory notice cases) |
| Letter 686(C/SC/DO) | L-265 | To grant a taxpayer's request for additional time to send information requested, come in for an interview, send a written protest, or arrange for a district conference |
| Letter 691(C/SC/DO) | L-312 | To answer taxpayer's inquiry about the method of payment |
| Letter 692(SC/DO/IO) | L-315 | To inform taxpayer of our findings upon consideration of additional information submitted after issuance of an examination report |
| Letter 693(SC/DO/IO) | L-340 | To reply to taxpayer who has requested re- |

| | | |
|---|---|---|
| | | consideration of a previously closed examination, when request is not considered a claim for refund |
| Letter 694(SC/DO) | L-354 | To solicit a taxpayer's agreement to proposed adjustments when he/she has indicated his/her agreement by letter but has not signed an appropriate agreement form |
| Letter 889(DO) | L-14<br>L-14B | To set initial appointment of an office interview examination (nonbusiness and business returns) |
| Letter 890(DO) | L-14A | To ask taxpayers to call us to set up initial appointment of an office interview examination |
| Letter 904(DO) | L-57 | To set initial appointment of a field examination |
| Letter 915(DO)(IO) | L-87 | To transmit report of individual income tax audit changes |
| Letter 994(C/DO)<br>Letter 990(DO) | L-264<br>L-273 | To schedule or change an appointment for an interview when requested by the taxpayer or to arrange an appointment to complete an audit when the examiner feels an interview is needed except if a statutory notice of deficiency has been issued |
| Letter 1003(DO) | L-290 | To inform taxpayer that it is not practical to arrange an interview until some future date |
| Letter 1008(DO) | L-300 | To set an appointment after issuance of a statutory notice |
| Letter 1020(DO)(IO) | L-341 | To transmit records, or to inform taxpayer on other matters |
| Letter 1025(DO) | L-360 | To advise a taxpayer that his/her consent signed under protest cannot be accepted. Letter 1033(DO) (formerly L-369) also serves as transmittal for another consent form |
| Letter 1031(C/DO) | L-367 | To contact a third party concerning alimony received from a taxpayer whose return is under examination |

Letter 1041(C/DO)    L-380    To clarify the filing status of an individual income tax return or when examination of a husband's separate return discloses that the wife has unreported income

# INDEX